Mexico Between Hitler and Roosevelt

Mexico Between Hitler and Roosevelt

Mexican Foreign Relations in the Age of Lázaro Cárdenas, 1934–1940

Friedrich E. Schuler

UNIVERSITY OF NEW MEXICO PRESS / ALBUQUERQUE

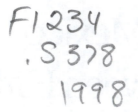

Library of Congress Cataloging-in-Publication Data

Schuler, Friedrich Engelbert, 1960–
Mexico between Hitler and Roosevelt : Mexican foreign relations in the
age of Lázaro Cárdenas, 1934–1940 / Frederich E. Schuler. — 1st ed.
        p.   cm.
Includes bibliographical references and index.
ISBN 0-8263-1851-7 (cloth)   0-8263-2160-7 (paper)
    1. Mexico—Foreign relations—1910–1946.
        2. Mexico—Economic conditions.
        3. Cárdenas, Lázaro, 1895–1970.
            I. Title.
        F1234.S378   1998
    327.72´009´043—dc21
        97-37255
            CIP

Cover designed by Matt Cohen

To Julia Mary Schuler,
my favorite daughter

Contents

Acknowledgments

THIS IS THE PLACE TO SAY THANK YOU TO INDIVIDUALS AND INSTITUTIONS without whose support, advice, and ideas I could not have written this book. Professor Dr. Knud Krakau at the John F. Kennedy Institute of the Freie Universität Berlin offered me professorial support and encouragement for the study of Latin American foreign relations. I am extremely grateful for his repeated, but futile efforts to gain funding for my research from German institutions. I hope that, eventually, German funding agencies recognize the value of supporting young generations of scholars before they are forced to leave German academia to pursue their research interests abroad. Professor Robert Konrad, while on a sabbatical at the Freie Universität Berlin's Lateinamerika Institut, introduced me to the opportunities that U.S. universities offer in Latin American Studies. Professor Engelke introduced me to the Fulbright Scholarship and the Fulbright Commission of Germany paid for my first trip to the academic heavens of America.

At the University of Texas at Austin, Professor Stanley Ross quickly taught me much about American English and the art of editing. Professor Nettie Lee Benson encouraged me to study the history of Germans in Latin America. Additional thanks go to Professors Lawrence Graham, W. W. Rostow, William Glade, and John Brown. Professor Arturo Valenzuela offered me a first opportunity to study the history of Germans in Latin America through the Duke University—Chile exchange program.

At the University of Chicago Professor Friedrich Katz became a most gracious, inspirational, and always supportive mentor for my work during the last ten years of this project. Before coming to America, I grew interested in Mexican history, reading Katz's outstanding scholarship in German while riding Berlin's subway to the university. I did not dream then that I would have the privilege to work with him on my Ph.D. He is one of the greatest European professors of Mexican history. Professor John Coatsworth became another invaluable mentor at the University of Chicago, with his brilliance and sharp questions providing much insight and focus. Professor Michael Geyer opened new theoretical horizons for me. My thesis would have been very different without his input. These three advisers, the unwavering support of the Department of History, and Linnea Cameron's guidance gave me some of the happiest times of my academic life.

In Portland, Oregon, Professor Frederick M. Nunn became my next mentor and provided invaluable support and guidance that allowed me to turn my Ph.D. into a book. I am extremely fortunate to have him as a mentor, friend, and colleague. From Texas and Arizona, Professor William Beezley and Professor Michael Meyer provided additional, very important encouragement and advice in times of doubt. Their words and deeds mean much to me.

Many library staffs made the research part of this work delightful. Special thanks go to Sandy Applegate at the University of Chicago Regenstein Library for organizing any source I needed. In Mexico, the small but dedicated teams of the Archivo Historico de la Secretaria de las Relaciones Exteriores, the Archivo de la Nación in Mexico City and at the Centro Lázaro Cárdenas in Jiquilpan, Michoacán, made a big difference. A special thank you goes to the Roosevelt Presidential Library in Hyde Park, New York, and the Ibero-Amerikanisches Institut in Berlin.

In the United States Professors Peter Guardino, Rich Warren, Susan Crane, David LaFrance, John Hart, Roderic Ai Camp, William French, and Adrian Bantjes read part of this manuscript and offered excellent feedback. In Mexico, Professors Alicia Hernandez, Brígida von Mentz, Paolo Riguzzi, Enrique Cárdenas, Ricardo Perez Montfort, and Carmen Nava y Nava shared their opinions with me during various stages of this work. Their advice made this a much better book. Its mistakes, however, are solely my own.

A very special thanks goes to the University of Chicago, which believed in me and financed my graduate work. Also, the Fulbright Commission, the Social Science Research Council, the National Endowment for the Humanities, and the Portland State Foundation offered critical financial help that made this study possible.

Additionally, special thanks go to Professor Nick Kreofsky, Dr. Gale, and the overseer, all of whom know so much in other important historiographical areas. Brian Koelling and Molly Brown-Koelling mixed infinite cappuccinos at Cafe Electra, inspiring my work with distant echoes of a European café. Jorge Espinoza provided the cigars. Diane Gould's editing skills are very much appreciated.

Ruth Dettman supported me during the entire research period of this work. Nancy Finn encouraged me to transform the research into a book. Julia Mary Schuler motivates me to carry on. Thank you to all of you.

1
Introduction

THIS BOOK EXAMINES HOW THE MEXICAN GOVERNMENT PURSUED ITS NATIONAL interests within an international environment that drifted toward a large-scale international war later called World War II. It is a study of the interrelationship between Mexico's politics, economy, culture, and defense and changes in the international environment between 1934 and 1940.

The book analyzes a complex picture of domestic–international interaction that defies simple clichés of dependency. Mexico was not simply a Third World stage for great power conflicts. Mexican policy makers and diplomats did not act like individuals who had resigned themselves to suffer as neighbors to the United States. Quite the contrary, for Mexicans were better skilled in international negotiations, more realistic in the evaluation of historical contexts, and more creative in situations of crisis than their European and U.S. counterparts. With few exceptions, Mexican skills easily countered the alleged, intrinsic power advantages that are supposed to come with open hegemony and indirect imperialism. Mexican leaders made shrewd and calculated policy choices that benefited the Mexican postrevolutionary state and its nomenclature.

In contrast, the Great Powers in this book are often small in vision when it comes to Mexican affairs, plagued by indifferent bureaucracies and, with the exception of U.S. Ambassador Daniels, burdened by second-class diplomats. U.S., European, and Asian diplomats were guided either by short-term gains or traditional Western stereotypes about Latin America. None of them recognized, and thus failed to communicate to their superiors, that Mexican foreign relations diversified in response to the Great Depression. They also missed the rise to power of the Mexican state's bureaucracy, which developed a distinctly technocratic-professional idea about the purpose of Mexican foreign relations. Foreign diplomats stationed in Mexico City between 1934 and 1940 missed the deeper meaning of Mexican foreign relations.

The Mexicans exploited these weaknesses of the Great Powers without hesitation. If possible, Mexican diplomats told foreigners what they wanted to hear. At the same time, they stayed focused on their long-term objectives and used opportunities, when they arose, to their own advantage. Their reward was an expansion of Mexico's economic and political sovereignty in the midst of the all- consuming conflict between the fascist, communist, and liberal political orders of the 1930s.

This interplay between Mexican domestic developments and foreign misperceptions can be followed in several ways in this book. First, it can be read as a traditional, almost chronological examination of Mexico's foreign relations. The book's chapters deal, step by step, with the key issues as they pertain to Mexican diplomacy, trade, petroleum, state finances, silver policy, domestic economy, propaganda, military, rebellions, and cultural policies. Thus, the reader gains a deeper understanding of the dynamic between Cardenismo and changes in the international economic system in the 1930s.

Second, this book is also the account of a dramatic transformation of the postrevolutionary Mexican state before World War II. During the 1930s, Mexican federal bureaucrats emerged as influential policy planners and actors, whose institutional power bases and technical expertise began to rival the powers of Mexican presidents. In other words, Mexico's foreign relations are described as a struggle between the Mexican president and Mexican bureaucratic professionals over the meaning and nature of Mexico's links abroad.

From that perspective, this book is an attempt to add the study of political elites in Mexican politics to that of popular forces, social groups, and genders. It examines the actions of a relatively small number of Mexican politicians and technocrats whose power over the Mexican state, nevertheless, had far- reaching implications for the entire Mexican population. This focus on elites is not a veiled attempt to revive Eurocentric, predemocratic historical paradigms of kings, queens, or great men. It is merely a recognition of the disturbing fact that in the Mexico of the 1930s a small group of individuals influenced the course of the lives of millions of people, directly, immediately, and with far-reaching consequences. In what way these elites redistributed the fruits of their significant gains to the Mexican population is a different issue. Obviously, Mexican policy elites failed to use this period to provide more meaningful political participation, social justice, and individual liberties.

Finally, this is also a study of the interrelationship between Mexican national economic development and changes in the international economy. The motivation behind most Mexican economic foreign relations before and during World War II was the creation of a more integrated national economic market and a more industrialized Mexico.

From a theoretical perspective this book addresses five historiographical traditions that, so far, have dominated the research about Mexican foreign relations. The first tradition is the view of Mexican foreign relations as separate, bilateral linkages. Part of this approach proceeds from the assumption that after the Mexican Revolution only Mexican–U.S. relations are of importance because the United States becomes Mexico's most important economic partner. Such an approach overlooks the fact that Mexican policy makers themselves never subscribed to such a limited perspective, although they did not hesitate to nourish this illusion in the minds of many North American observers. Also, it served Mexican politicians in domestic political matters when nationalism declared the neighbor of the North as the source of all past and future evils.

But Mexican elites distinguished between cliché and reality. While the U.S.–Mexican link mattered economically more than those with Great Britain and Germany during the 1930s it continued to compete with Mexican social and cultural links with Spain and France. Systematically, Mexicans continued to seek alternatives to the Mexican–U.S. linkage in relations with Europe, Latin America, and even in Asia. More importantly, Mexican policy makers never looked at one relationship only, but always perceived foreign relations as a system of several interdependent relationships. In other words, a multilateral research approach is more advantageous in revealing the intricacies of Mexican foreign relations.

A second tradition is the compartmentalization of foreign- relations research and its isolation from domestic issues. Mexican-history research is still relatively young compared to research in European or U.S. history. Researchers often prefer a single-issue approach in identifying the core building blocks of Mexican history. But the reality in Mexico in the 1930s was different. Mexican foreign policy makers never adhered to a strict separation between domestic and foreign affairs. For them, whatever happened in domestic politics was significant for foreign relations and vice versa. In short, an integrational, horizontal research that connects foreign relations with domestic economic, social, political, cultural, and systemic aspects of Mexico's history is able to re-create the dynamics of the examined era more accurately.

A third tradition involves the trend toward explaining Cardenismo almost exclusively as a domestic political or cultural story. Consequently, domestic factors have become exclusive explanation patterns for Mexican history of the 1930s. And yet it is obvious that below all the rich political rhetoric of Cardenismo domestic and international economic realities unfolded that any Mexican president had to pay attention to. Despite its unique leftist political rhetoric before 1938, the Cárdenas state was a capitalist state whose technocrats chose to work within the foreign-developed parameters of Western economic structures and theories. This also includes technical parameters—such as exchange rates, inflation, and devaluations. They too were important factors that influenced Mexican history of the 1930s, as important as domestic political events, regardless of the noise of public discourses that suggest the opposite. Mexican bureaucratic professionals respected this reality and operated consciously and comfortably in domestic as well as external parameters. The key players of the Cárdenas administration never separated politics, culture, and economics.

A fourth tradition is the ongoing and very entertaining love affair with foreign conspiracies and subversion during the 1930s. Dramatic warnings and rumors about Axis activities in Mexico were a successful tool to use in mobilizing the public in the Western Hemisphere against international fascism in the 1930s. Nobody knew the international plans of fascism, nor was one certain of its defeat. U.S. and British governments built on this fear a necessary propaganda campaign that mobilized citizens against the Axis powers in North and South America. What was necessary and constructive then is now a hindrance for the understanding of Cardenismo. Propaganda and counterintelligence activities have created a huge paper trail and injected innumerable documents with rumors, half-truths, and deliberate misinformation. Today, this fact still misleads researchers by overemphasizing conspiracy theories and entertaining fantasies such as blond, blue-eyed German Nazis hiding in the jungle of Yucatán. While one must not diminish the potential threat of fascist subversion to the Western Hemisphere in the 1930s, it needs to be set in the wider context of other forces that did shape ordinary Mexican lives more strongly. Mexican lives in the 1930s were affected more by economic factors than by fascist plots. Mexico must no longer be reduced to just another exotic backdrop for the worldwide struggle against fascism. Otherwise, Mexicans would remain mere objects of Western manipulations, rather than the skilled and sophisticated shapers of their own history.

The fifth research perspective to be challenged is the preference of explaining Mexican history of the 1930s through the person of President Cárdenas himself. This is partly attributable to Cárdenas's exemplary moral convictions and political accountability compared to later Mexican presidents. However, by 1934 the Mexican state was far too large and complex for Cárdenas to control its entire operation. Cárdenas was one player among several when it came to foreign relations, although a powerful one. But his involvement was selective, and by far the majority of Mexican exchanges with foreign countries were conceived of and executed by Mexican bureaucrats and technocratic professionals, without his involvement. Cardenismo was less *presidencialismo* and much more *bureaucratismo* than the existing historical portrayal suggests.

The book is organized into seven chapters. Following the introduction, chapter 2 examines the bureaucratic reinstitutionalization of Mexican foreign relations between 1920 and 1940. The driving forces behind this process were the Mexican Secretariat of Foreign Relations and the Mexican Ministry of Hacienda (Treasury). These ministries instrumentalized Mexico's economic and diplomatic foreign relations as tools for Mexico's national economic development. At the same time, Mexican presidents pursued their own foreign-relations initiatives, particularly in regard to Central America and toward the United States. Members of the Foreign Ministry tried to expand their influence through activities in the Pan-American Conference system and, eventually, in the League of Nations.

The reinstitutionalization of Mexican foreign relations changed course in response to the external impulse of the Great Depression and an emerging domestic economic consensus to modernize Mexico's agricultural sector and to accelerate industrialization. The increased need for state intervention in national economic development opened the door for financial technocrats of the Mexican Treasury to regain importance in Mexican foreign relations. The Mexican Foreign Ministry reacted to these changes by recasting itself as an effective foreign economic and political intelligence service in the early 1930s. More importantly, other government agencies joined the rise of Mexican bureaucracies as important foreign-relations players as they sought foreign markets for Mexico's agricultural and petroleum products. The Mexican oil expropriation of 1938 and the next great international war—World War II—reinforced these trends. By the end of Cárdenas's presidency, the structure of Mexican foreign relations had become diverse and its focus market-oriented, ready to exploit the expected opportunities of international war. The Mexican president was no longer the alpha and omega of Mexican foreign relations. The technical and economic expertise needed to run a state in the middle of the twentieth century had elevated technocrats and bureaucrats as influential players in foreign relations.

Chapter 3 provides an overview of Mexican foreign relations as they developed between 1920 and 1936, within the structural changes described in chapter 2. Mexico's key economic relationships with the United States, Great Britain, Germany, and France are contrasted with its important political and cultural links with Spain. Also covered are relations with Latin America, the Soviet Union, Japan, and Italy.

Chapter 4 examines Mexico's economic crisis of 1937 as a watershed for Mexico's domestic and foreign relations. Bad luck in domestic agricultural policy, the economic harassment by foreign petroleum companies, pressures by domestic labor groups and the strengthening of the domestic political right pushed the Cárdenas administration into an unprecedented economic and, subsequently, political crisis that moved the Mexican state toward bankruptcy. This chapter reconstructs the growing crisis and how the Cárdenas administration desperately tried to reverse its course, first with domestic measures and then with foreign support. The collapse of Mexico's domestic economy also meant the collapse of Mexico's developmental strategy from previous years. But when all measures failed and Cárdenismo had lost legitimacy and power among most Mexican social sectors, the Mexican administration decided to resolve the crisis with a most dramatic measure: the nationalization of Mexico's foreign-owned petroleum sector.

Chapter 5 analyzes the oil expropriation as a dramatic and ultimately successful step toward the rebuilding of the economic foundations of the Mexican state, which translated into the political survival of the Cárdenas administration. The sale of the petroleum of the nationalized petroleum sector at home and abroad was the critical aspect in this effort. This chapter examines the complex meaning of the international boycott that followed the expropriation by analyzing Mexico's foreign economic relations with independent U.S. oil dealer Davis, as well as Germany, Italy, Japan, and France until summer 1940.

Chapter 6 examines Mexico's self-defense in the diplomatic and cultural realm during the same period. It explores the diplomatic elimination of Great Britain from Mexico, Cárdenas's increasingly successful efforts to exploit U.S. President Roosevelt's domestic vulnerabilities so that he was forced to intervene in the oil conflict on behalf of Mexico against the foreign oil companies. These successful efforts by the Cárdenas administration occurred against the background of Franco's victory in the Spanish Civil War, which reverberated deeply into Mexican politics. Increasingly, domestic and foreign pro-fascist forces agitated inside Mexico, trying to exploit the continuing social and political tensions within the Mexican state. This chapter ends with an examination of how the Hitler-Stalin pact paralyzed the rising tensions between Mexico's political right and left for the benefit of the Cárdenas administration and the Mexican presidential elections of 1940.

Chapter 7 focuses on the interrelationship between the modernization of Mexico's military, between 1935 and 1940, and changes in the international weapons market. On the one hand, the rise of state violence in Asia and Europe provided the Mexican armed forces with a much-needed external mission that, hopefully, would translate into renewed importance for the Mexican armed forces as part of the Mexican state. On the other hand, the very same developments hindered the Mexican military from purchasing modern weaponry abroad, thus keeping it from developing an effective military deterrent against foreigners. By the time of the stunning German victories in 1939 and 1940, Mexico's inability to translate its idea of modernization through foreign military technology into reality redefines the U.S.–Mexican border as a national security liability for the outgoing Cárdenas administration. Even worse, it convinces U.S. military planners to make Mexico's military readiness a matter of U.S. national-security concerns. This chapter examines how Mexico's political leadership and military bureaucracy develop separate answers to this dangerous problem. Whereas a small group around President Cárdenas sought to gain time and avoid a close U.S.–Mexican military cooperation by building a Latin American defense force, Mexican military planners sought a closer bilateral military link. Their hope was that the fascist threat to Latin America would convince U.S. government and arms manufacturers to sell them weapons that they had desired for years, and finally bring about the repeatedly postponed modernization of the Mexican armed forces. Finally, the Second World War not only promised the Mexican military an opportunity to make their foreign mission credible, but also to create a Mexican military that, after World War II, could deter a possible revival of U.S. interventionism into Mexican affairs.

Chapter 8 examines the transition from President Lázaro Cárdenas to President Ávila Camacho. It began in the immediate aftermath of the 1938 oil expropriation, when a new developmental course focused on the expected external stimulus of the Second World War as the force that would bring about the industrialization of Mexico. With this technocratic solution to national development, the foundation for the social and political conservatism of the Ávila Camacho years was laid. But Mexico could only profit from the war when the postrevolutionary state remained stable, and the transition of power to Ávila Camacho would be realized against the considerable rightist opposition that gathered around the candidacy of Andreu Almazán. This chapter examines how the Mexican and U.S. administration prevented the Almazán challenge from turning into a more serious, violent Almazán rebellion. In spite of considerable foreign fascist interest in this opportunity, U.S.–Mexican government cooperation assured the desired peaceful transition of power.

Since the publication of the first edition of this book I discovered one new, key document in Spain's national archive at Alcalá de Henares. It is a confidential summary of a meeting between exiled ex-President Plutarco Elias

Calles and an emissary of the Spanish Franco government. On September 8, 1940, Calles presented the Spaniard with a detailed plan for a full scale military uprising against Lázaro Cárdenas and President-Elect Ávila Camacho in Mexico's north. Thus my allegations in chapter eight of a possible personal link between ex-President Calles, the Almazán opposition group, and Franco have been proven. Of course, this find further underlines the seriousness of the Almazán challenge and its potential danger to the Mexican state. It also elevates the accomplishment of U.S. and Mexican security forces who prevented Franco from gaining a foothold in Mexico during this time of instability. Scholars interested in the memorandum can find it in Alcalá de Henares at collection Presidencia SGM, Vol. I, No. 5, Doc. 2.

For the Mexican postrevolutionary state, the suppression of this domestic struggle between the political right and left over the implications of Mexican development offered the longed-for economic opportunity of World War II. For the United States, it brought about stability south of the border and historically unprecedented U.S.–Mexican economic and military cooperation.

The book's conclusion is an attempt to move toward a new theory of Mexican foreign relations during the 1930s. Mexican foreign relations during this period are reinterpreted as a critical tool and resource for the Mexican administration to gain leverage in domestic political contests as well as in international events. The result is a distinct, complex understanding of Mexican foreign relations, looking from the Mexican capital into the world, rather than from the diplomatic schools of Europe or the United States toward Mexico.

2

The Reinstitutionalization of Postrevolutionary Mexican Foreign Relations (1920–1940)

CARDENISMO'S FOREIGN RELATIONS WERE PART OF LARGER CYCLES OF Mexican history. The desire of Mexican politicians to develop economically their geographical region reaches back to the Bourbon reforms and continues with nineteenth-century economic liberalism. Cardenismo's pursuit of different political initiatives toward the United States and Europe echoed Porfirian moves to play off Europe against the United States in an effort to further Mexico's industrialization. Not surprisingly, Cárdenas's ambassador to the League of Nations learned his trade as a confidant of President Venustiano Carranza. This great tactician of Mexican foreign relations during the Mexican Revolution handed the Sonoran dynasty a state that, once again, could be developed into a pivotal agent of national development during the following decades. And yet the foreign relations of Cardenismo are unique in postrevolutionary Mexican history.

What distinguishes the foreign relations of the Cárdenas years is the central role that technocrats played in foreign-policy development and execution. During Cárdenas's presidency, members of the Mexican cabinet and heads of federal bureaucracies fostered their own relations with foreign companies and foreign governments, often without the involvement of the Mexican president. For the first time, institutional players mattered as much as, and occasionally more, than the Mexican president in the conduct of Mexican foreign relations. The often- idealistic revolutionary and *político* Lázaro Cárdenas acted as president within an increasingly institutionalized state that came to be dominated by bureaucrats.

As will be shown in the following chapters, the several federal ministries and the technocrats that worked in them had become surprisingly independent from the presidential palace, and only a few months after the end of the Maximato. More importantly, bureaucratic planners proved powerful enough to initiate the move toward more conservative economic developmental plans as early as three years after Cárdenas came to power. A permanent institutionalized tug of war over development emerged between technocratic, bureaucratic policy makers, other more traditional political elites, and changes in the international economic system.

This chapter will reconstruct the reinstitutionalization process of Mexican postrevolutionary foreign relations. It began with Obregón's rise to the presidency. By the time Lázaro Cárdenas was president bureaucratic players had become autonomous enough to change the course of Mexican history. This reinstitutionalization process represents a critical structural underpinning of Cardenismo. The story of the 1938 oil expropriation, Mexican silver policy, postrevolutionary military reform, and agrarian reform in the Laguna district and Chiapas, as well as antifascist diplomacy in the Geneva League of Nations, were not only presidential politics but also bureaucratic politics.

President Venustiano Carranza had developed Mexico's foreign policy by himself and conducted it out of the Presidential Palace. A few trusted aides, among them Ambassador Isidro Fabela, executed his strategic designs as personal emissaries to Europe and Latin America. In 1920, after Carranza's assassination, President Obregón changed this practice. He reserved for himself control over the most important part of contemporary Mexican foreign affairs—all aspects of the U.S.–Mexican relationship—and ordered his aide Alberto Pani to rebuild the *Secretaria de las Relaciones Exteriores,* the Mexican Foreign Ministry.[1] During the next four years, Pani re-created a professional Mexican diplomatic corps and consular service.

Whereas previously diplomatic posts and consulships had been given to individuals as a way to pay back a political debt or to isolate a political opponent, service in the SRE again became a professional career. In his memoirs, Pani admitted that he could not eliminate favoritism entirely, but at least he was able to hire a professional diplomatic staff that provided continuity in day-to-day operations of Mexican embassies and consulates, regardless of the skills of political high-level diplomatic appointments.[2]

Pani defined professional standards, published rules for civil-service members, and spelled out responsibilities of lower-rank diplomatic personnel. He provided the SRE with a secure share of the government's annual budget and attracted Mexico's emerging diplomats with a generous pension. Next, in 1921, he purchased buildings in Washington, Hamburg, Berlin, and Geneva so that Mexican diplomats could represent their country in a building of their own, rather than an office of a larger building. Mexican embassy buildings in London and Paris were added in 1926.

Mexican foreign relations during the Obregón administration focused on the U.S.–Mexican relationship. Linda Hall has examined the intricacies of Mexican diplomacy toward the United States during that period as it related to oil, foreign debt, recognition, and military affairs.[3] To this work on the executive level, we need to add the activities of Mexican consuls in Europe, the United States, and Latin America who reestablished a permanent Mexican presence, at least as it related to commercial issues. Once the U.S. administration recognized the Obregón government, Mexican diplomacy widened its attention from the United States to the entire Western Hemisphere.

President Plutarco Ellias Calles kept the Mexican relationship with the United States as his personal domain. He added to it an aggressive anti-U.S. policy in Central America that actively opposed U.S. gun-boat diplomacy and U.S. military intervention. Thus, Mexican diplomatic intervention in Nicaragua and Guatemala in 1926 occurred in accordance with orders from the *Jefe Máximo*. Nevertheless, it was Pani's new generation of professional diplomats who executed Mexico's needling anti-U.S. propaganda campaigns in Central America. At the same time, they helped the Sandino rebellion in Nicaragua and tried to counter anti-Mexico sentiments inside the United States. Professional diplomats were gaining a new arena in which to develop a distinct, professional identity by articulating Mexico's insistence on national self-determination and territorial sovereignty.

More importantly, the Inter-American Conference system became a central stage for SRE professionals to act more independently from the micromanagement of President Calles. For example, in 1924, at the Fifth Inter-American Conference in Santiago, Chile, Mexico's ambassador to Chile worked feverishly behind the scenes to squash a Uruguayan initiative that could have created an American League of Nations under the domination of the United States.[4] In 1928, at the Sixth Inter-American Conference in Havana, Mexico once again blocked a move toward greater regional political clout for the Inter-American Conference system.[5] One year later, in early 1929, Mexican diplomat Fernando González Roa became a leading figure at a Washington conference where Mexico joined seven other Latin American countries and the United States in signing a Convention on Conciliation and a Treaty of Arbitration.[6] Finally, in 1930, Mexico's distinct regional policy became an internationally recognized corollary. Mexican Minister of Foreign Relations Gerardo Estrada proclaimed the so-called Estrada Doctrine. It granted diplomatic recognition to a government in principle, regardless of whether it had come to power by the ballot or the bullet. No longer should the United States and conservative Latin American governments have the power to determine which revolutionary Latin American government was legitimate and which one was not. Between 1924 and 1930 the Inter-American Conference system had become a place for professional diplomats to articulate a distinctly Mexican regional diplomacy.

During the same period all Mexican administrations declined repeated invitations to join the worldwide forum of the League of Nations in Geneva. Mexican diplomats saw no use in joining an organization that could not protect their rights against the United States, since the League accepted the validity of the U.S. Monroe Doctrine and, consequently, abstained from intervening in Latin American affairs.[7] Thus, Mexico's diplomatic activity in Europe had remained marginal during most of the 1920s. One notable exception was President-elect Calles's visit to the European continent during a health-related trip to Germany in 1924.

The world depression became the most important stimulus for the further growth and expansion of Mexico's foreign ministry during the 1930s. First, it caused a reorientation of U.S. policy toward Latin America. Under President Hoover the cornerstone for the Good Neighbor policy was laid and direct interventionism began to fade. Second, the economic contraction of U.S. markets forced the Mexicans, more than ever, to find alternative markets in Europe and Asia. Third, it provided the revolutionary state with a new mandate to act as economic financier, developer, and marketing agent. These tasks required professionals who sat inside the federal Mexican bureaucracy.

The waning of U.S. interventionism suggested to Mexican diplomats that the time might have come to use the League of Nations to set the politics of postrevolutionary Mexico apart from the conservative militaristic paths of other Latin American countries. By 1929, Mexico began direct transactions with the League and participated in its technical assemblies. One year later, Foreign Minister Estrada sent diplomat Castro Leal to Geneva to explore possible Mexican participation in the League's Institute of Intellectual Cooperation and the International Conferences of Labor.[8] The Mexican public learned about Mexico's entry into the world arena in September 1931. During the president's message to Congress, a perplexed Mexican public learned that Mexico's attitude toward the League of Nations had "undergone an almost radical change and that by an exchange of good-will and effective collaboration we have reached a point which promises a brilliant future."[9] After ten years of concentration on the Western Hemisphere, Mexican diplomats were about to became active in issues that pertained to Europe, Africa, and Asia. And yet Mexico's first action in Geneva challenged the legitimacy of the League's Covenant Article 21, which recognized the Monroe Doctrine.

Mexico's changed attitude toward the League of Nations was not only motivated by political considerations; economics also played an important role. One year earlier, Mexican Foreign Minister Estrada had approached the British Minister in Mexico and hinted to the United States' rival in Latin America to "cease looking on Mexico through the eyes of Washington." Instead, he urged Great Britain to launch a trade offensive toward Mexico and sponsor a new invitation to Mexico to join the League.[10] In turn, Estrada promised to open a backdoor for Great Britain in the Pan-American Conference system by renewing a campaign to admit Canada as full permanent member to the Pan-American meetings. The British foreign office had enough sense to realize that it could not openly challenge the United States in Mexico. Nevertheless, Mexico received its desired invitation to join the League, only now it was sponsored jointly by Great Britain, Germany, Spain, France, Italy, and Japan.

Initially, the entry into the League provided the SRE with an opportunity to expand its share of the government's budget. Foreign Minister Estrada reorganized the SRE diplomatic department into three sections: Pan-American Affairs, League of Nations Affairs and the Protection of Mexicans Abroad.[11] However, by 1932 the rival Mexican Treasury, the Ministry of Hacienda, decided to cut the SRE back to its previous size. In response to the ongoing depression, the funds for the Mexican embassy in Geneva were canceled. The Mexican delegate to the League moved to the Mexican Embassy in Paris and commuted to Switzerland. Next, the ministry cut the salary for Mexico's representative at the League and forced the SRE to give the League the minimum notice of two years. Mexico would withdraw from the League after 1934.[12] At the same time, Mexican Foreign Minister Estrada left his position.[13] Suddenly, it seemed as if Mexico's excursion into diplomatic internationalism was doomed to be very short-lived.

Not surprisingly, Estrada's successor, Puig Casauranc, inherited a ministry in crisis. Budget cuts and the fight over participation in the League of Nations had tossed the SRE into an identity crisis. With U.S. pressure on Latin America decreasing and the political benefit of membership in the League of Nations being questioned, what was to be the role of the SRE within the Mexican government? First, Foreign Minister Puig Casauranc commissioned an internal administrative review. It revealed a ministry that lacked professionalism. The review stated that although Mexico had established firm principles of its foreign policy in the previous years, its "outlines are so general and almost abstract in their nature, that, in concrete cases, they do not ordinarily assist in achieving fully the ends sought."[14] Despite Foreign Minister Pani's efforts before 1924, the SRE still lacked continuity in methods and personnel policy. It seemed to be "static and a place of routine and files," which often were lost or not organized in a way that was helpful to Mexico's interests.

Also, the performance of Mexican diplomats abroad had remained poor and suffered from a lack of consistency. Diplomatic reports were not sent according to a regular schedule and most diplomats showed little interest in interpreting world events in light of their consequences for Mexico. Instead, they focused on events and individuals without considering social, political, and economic contexts. Still, in 1932 it had been necessary to order Mexican consuls who were leaving their posts to write a summary about their previous activities for their successor "in order to avoid an interruption of the gathering of information, investigation and propaganda."[15] It was generally assumed that their analyses were of little importance for other parts of the Mexican government.[16] As one Mexican diplomat remembered: "our diplomats used to orient themselves more according to their personal intuition than by the expressed instructions of their superiors."[17]

Foreign Minister Puig Casauranc reacted by starting a major organizational shakeup that would improve the SRE and make it responsible to the needs of a state trying to come to terms with the consequences of the world depression. He demanded from his diplomats a

> frank and full study of the practical measures which might lead to the closest moral and economic cooperation between Mexico and each of the other countries. That means, we need to consider each country,—and particularly those of special interest to Mexico—, socially, culturally or economically as a unit, whose integral study might become of immediate importance in view of Mexico's moral and material interests.

In the future, it was

> expected that the studies be carried out by heads of missions and consular agents. The ministry of foreign relations, jointly with the department of national economy, will furnish *concrete*, not general, outlines for an international policy for Mexico, a policy which shall endure as a result of impersonal action.

This professionalization was expected to lead "to the better comprehension of Mexico and to the perfect development of her commercial and economic possibilities."[18]

It was a watershed in the ministry's history. Whereas previously it had worked in a classic Western diplomatic style, Puig Casauranc turned it into a modern economic intelligence service. From that point on, Mexican diplomats were directed to collect data and information about foreign events and to interpret them in relationship to Mexican needs. Their task would be to observe and register developments in Asia, Europe, Latin America, and the United States and to report them before their consequences damaged Mexico. Mexico's professional diplomats and consuls were becoming the eyes and ears of the Mexican government abroad.

In December 1934, newly appointed Foreign Minister Portes Gil focused on improving the report-writing skills of Mexican diplomats abroad. He wrote private evaluations to individual ambassadors and suggested specific research projects.[19] After Gil's short tenure, Foreign Minister José Cenisceros initiated a new round of internal reorganization that was completed by his successor, Eduardo Hay. During the first years of Cardenismo, Mexican foreign ministers expanded the SRE's diplomatic department from three to six sections: Diplomatic Personnel, Treaties and Conferences, League of Nations, Pan-American Affairs, Borders and International Waters, and a Ceremonial Section.

The SRE gained more influence when newly elected President Cárdenas reevaluated the League of Nations policy of previous administrations and reinstated Mexico's membership in the League of Nations.

U.S. President Roosevelt's recognition of the doctrine of nonintervention in the Western Hemisphere had increased the utility of the League as a place for Mexican negotiations and diplomatic initiatives. In order to demonstrate to other Latin American administrations that the League could be an effective tool for the resolution of inter-American disputes, the Mexican representative involved himself deeply in the successful mediation of the Chaco conflict. Moreover, after the U.S. pledge of nonintervention, the most serious threat to national sovereignty and self-determination arose from European fascist movements, as evidenced by the Italian invasion of Ethiopia. Most other Latin American governments at this time were pursuing conservative politics with the increasing involvement of the military, which changed the atmosphere in the Inter-American Conference system. In contrast, the League of Nations would serve as Mexico's display case for a distinctly leftist Latin American nationalism that opposed fascist tendencies before they reached Latin American shores.[20] This became a second important task for the professionals of the SRE during Cárdenas's presidency.

The oil expropriation in March of 1938 brought the next push for administrative reform. Now, more than ever, Mexican diplomats had to identify markets for Mexican oil and *ejido* agricultural products. In addition, the Mexican diplomatic service became the frontline of the Mexican state's defense against the boycott by international oil companies and their industrial affiliates. A special section in the SRE's diplomatic department was created that did nothing but interpret reports from abroad. This was a remarkable change compared to 1935, when only one individual, the Undersecretary of Foreign Relations, had the task of interpreting reports and making policy suggestions. Now, a group of people had become the collective brain of the ministry.[21]

Finally, in 1939, Foreign Minister Hay reorganized the SRE's diplomatic archive. For the first time, diplomatic professionals gained instant access to important documents and reports.[22] Also, a new key for confidential reports was introduced that prevented their study by unauthorized individuals or, even worse, their loss within the distribution channels of the ministry.[23]

An analysis of SRE diplomatic reports for the period between 1934 and 1940 proves that these administrative reforms brought about significant improvements in the SRE's service. By the time Lázaro Cárdenas had broken with Calles, Mexican legations and embassies sent reports to Mexico on a regular schedule.[24] Those legations that mailed their reports late were reprimanded. When reports were unsatisfactory, SRE feedback was harsh. For example, in 1938, the head of the ministry's diplomatic department evaluated a report by the Mexican legation in England with the words: "Your information was not appreciated at all . . . its style is a disgrace to the Mexican Foreign Ministry."[25]

By 1938, a regular report from Germany or England consisted of four separate segments that covered not only political and commercial, but also social and cultural developments. All reports included a segment that explained the implications for Mexico. In addition to the regular reporting, the SRE asked its diplomats for special reports about foreign developments in the military, the economy, and industry,[26] according to precise instructions.[27] Ironically, the task of report writing became so demanding for diplomats that the SRE had to relax its regulations and allow more time for preparation.[28] Diplomatic reports were read and forwarded by the SRE's director of the diplomatic department to the level of the Undersecretary of Foreign Relations.[29] When information was of broader interest, it was forwarded to the undersecretary level of other ministries that were concerned with its content.[30]

In sum, this professionalization of the Mexican Foreign Ministry between 1920 and 1940 created an effective diplomatic organization that generated critical information and an understanding of international relations with great speed. It is important to realize that many dangerous Mexican political maneuvers, like the oil expropriation in 1938 or Mexico's wartime cooperation from 1939 on, was based on information that Mexican diplomatic professionals sent to Mexico from Berlin, London, Paris, and Washington. Their insightful and timely reports allowed Mexican administrations to turn difficult political dilemmas into calculated risks. During these twenty years the SRE had become an effective and valuable information-gathering tool that provided Mexican administrations with eyes and ears in the political and economic centers of the world.

The SRE, however, was not the only bureaucratic state institution that acquired an important role in the conduct of Mexican foreign relations during this period. The newly founded Ministry of National Economy, the Ministry of War, and the Ministry of Public Communication and Infrastructure became involved in direct exchanges with foreign companies and governments that were not closely controlled by the Mexican president. But none of them amassed as much real power as the Mexican Treasury, the Ministry of Hacienda and its head Eduardo Suárez.

Between 1920 and 1940, the Mexican Ministry of Hacienda (Treasury) gained the most power of all Mexican ministries over Mexican foreign relations because it gained control over the administration's budget and influenced exchange-rate and money-supply policies. After 1935, particularly, these indirect measures shaped foreign relations as much as presidential policy preferences and political principles.

Under President Obregón, the *político* Adolfo de la Huerta had been in charge of Mexico's foreign financial relations. As Linda Hall showed, it proved a great tragedy for the postrevolutionary state to entrust critical financial negotiations to somebody who lacked the technical background to understand its true implications.[31]

Once President Calles came to power, the organization and management of the state's finances were put into the hands of bureaucratic professionals. Alberto Pani was asked to move from the SRE to the Ministry of Hacienda and to spearhead an administrative reorganization. It was the launch of a "revolution in the Ministry of Hacienda," which initiated the ministry's growth toward becoming the key financial institution of the postrevolutionary state.[32] In the following years, Mexican financial experts revised the country's tax structure and created a national banking system with a central bank. For the first time in its history, the Mexican state gained control over vital economic aggregates, such as exchange rates, currency circulation, and federal budgets. This achievement allowed subsequent Mexican presidents to use the state as developmental agent. At the same time, the mathematical laws of international capitalism predetermined the economic direction that presidents could pursue. The logic of national capitalistic development was different from that of the Mexican Revolution.

This new generation of Mexican economists oriented itself along the expanding science of international economics, not the political ideas of Sonoran political leaders. Manuel Gómez Morin, Eduardo Pani, Montes de Oca, Jesús Silva Herzog, and Eduardo Suárez had studied and traveled in Europe. They saw themselves as participants in a worldwide bureaucratic quest to organize large masses of people into industrial systems for the benefit of the nation-state. At the same time, they tried to avoid the potentially dangerous social and political repercussions of free, uncontrolled capitalist development. Thus they observed and studied economic experiments in the United States, the Soviet Union, Great Britain, and Italy,[33] hoping to learn from the mistakes abroad and apply positive lessons at home within the unique context of postrevolutionary Mexico.

Eduardo Suárez is the best example of this generation of economic professionals. He had begun his career as a lawyer in the Mexican Foreign Ministry during the Obregón presidency, and there he gained Pani's attention. Under President Calles, he followed Pani to the Ministry of Hacienda. After the Geneva Conference of 1925, he studied closely British experiments with monetary stability and Mussolini's monetary experiments. The financial collapse of 1929 turned Suárez into an ardent advocate of Keynesian economic policies. For President Portes Gil, Suárez worked as legal counselor to the International Commission of Waters and Boundaries. He also represented Mexico at the International Conference on Silver in London. In addition, he served briefly as Mexican representative to the League of Nations and participated in the Sixth Pan-American Conference at Montevideo. Finally, he played a key role in the Mexican Commission on Tariffs and Coinage.[34]

Roosevelt's New Deal economic policies after 1933 gained Suárez's admiration. The U.S. administration devalued the dollar, injected large amounts of money into the national economy with the help of a liberal federal reserve policy, employed gigantic public works programs, and subsidized the unemployed. All of this was financed with a deficit-spending economic program never seen before in U.S. history.[35] Suárez saw it as a model application of Keynesian ideas in the depression era.

In 1934, newly installed President Lázaro Cárdenas chose Eduardo Suárez as head of the Ministry of Hacienda, upon the recommendation of ex-president Portes Gil. He placed two Cardenistas at Suárez's side. The rest of the ministry, however, was staffed according to professional merit. Right away, Suárez exerted his influence beyond the ministry. He became instrumental in firing the head of the Bank of Mexico because of incompetence and replaced him with Calles's former Minister of Hacienda, Montes de Oca. More importantly, he made sure that Montes de Oca could not outmaneuver him politically with Cárdenas. Suárez demanded and received from Cárdenas the promise that he would be present at every meeting that the Mexican president would hold with the new head of the Bank of Mexico. In other words, most presidential orders for Montes de Oca came from Suárez's desk since Cárdenas had little technical knowledge.[36] Later, when Montes de Oca resigned his post to join the presidential campaign of Almazán, Suárez moved his Undersecretary of Hacienda, Eduardo Villaseñor, another financial technocrat and student of British monetary-policy theory, to the important chair of the Bank of Mexico. Villaseñor remained in his position until the end of the Avila Camacho administration, just as Suárez continued to serve as Avila Camacho's Minister of Hacienda. In other words, the economic structure of the Mexican state between 1934 and 1945 was controlled by a very small group of highly influential individuals. These financial specialists shaped Mexico's foreign economic relations more than Mexico's *políticos* would have liked to admit.

Since Mexican presidents of the 1930s came out of military careers, they depended on the skill and vision of specialists to generate the financial base for their policies. Often it was the Minister of Hacienda, not the Mexican president, who determined whether a federal project received funding. Suárez granted us a glimpse at his real power behind the presidential chair in a few sentences hidden in the hundreds of pages of his memoirs. He wrote:

> The interior difficulties in the administration preoccupied me most. Often, I had to object to a project which the president was sympathizing with. I had to resign myself to endure the discontent of the president, when the Ministry of Hacienda objected to a project to which the president had given some hope of realization, mostly because of the financial impossibility to bring the project forward.[37]

Another documented example of Suárez's clout is the conflict over the Sabalo oil-exploration contracts in 1937. Minister of Economy Sánchez Tapia and ex-president Ortiz Rubio, head of the semiprivate Petro-Mex company, had arranged a contract concerning wells in the Poza Rica region with the foreign-owned Sabalo company. In reality, the Sabalo served as a front for El Águila. It was attempting to monopolize the remaining drilling areas of the potentially lucrative Poza Rica region for British interests. If the deal had materialized, it would have been financially rewarding for the two Mexican officials, but highly disadvantageous for Mexico's national interest.[38] Sánchez Tapia tried to assure presidential approval for the deal by bypassing the Ministry of Hacienda. Unfortunately for him, Suárez learned

about these efforts, intervened, and successfully squashed the ongoing negotiations with a single phone call to the president. In the aftermath of the
scandal, Ortiz Rubio was forced to resign from the Petro-Mex directorship
and was replaced by another technocrat, the geologist Licenciado Santillan.
Also, Minister of National Economy Sánchez Tapia was replaced by Eduardo
Suárez's Undersecretary of Hacienda, Efraín Buenrostro.[39]

After the 1938 oil expropriation, Suárez became even more influential.
The old semiprivate Petro-Mex company was dissolved and a state-owned
General Council for the Petroleum Administration took over the manage-
ment of the production and marketing of Mexico's oil exports. Suárez and
Buenrostro appointed themselves as two of four governmental board mem-
bers of the new organization.[40]

By 1938 the Ministry of Hacienda had established complete veto-power
over all international contracts and purchases of the Mexican state. In addition, the increasing Mexican barter trade with European countries involved
the Ministry of Hacienda as pivotal administrator of state-owned barter
currency accounts. The ministry controlled how Mexican barter credits would
be spent in Europe.

In sum, by 1938 the Ministry of Hacienda had become a "super ministry." Indirectly, it controlled Mexico's international trade and the Mexican
state's financial linkages abroad. Suárez and his professionals conducted all
foreign financial negotiations and functioned increasingly as the economic
command center of the Cárdenas administration. Whatever radical vision
Cardenismo evoked, it was financed by the professionals in the Mexican
Ministry of Hacienda and its head, Eduardo Suárez.

This reinstitutionalization of Mexican economic foreign relations is critical for the understanding of Mexican history between 1920 and 1940. It
suggests that Mexican presidents of this era were not, as Brandenburg stated,
the alpha and omega of Mexican foreign relations.[41] Calles, Portes Gil, Ortiz
Rubio, Rodríguez, and Cárdenas did not have the international experience
nor the professional knowledge to design and conduct foreign economic
relations by themselves. By the 1930s most questions of international trade,
business, and finance had become highly technical and were decided by the
heads of Mexican ministries. Thus, Mexico's foreign relations of that era
evolved out of an interplay between presidential preferences and limitations
put upon them by the recommendations of bureaucratic professionals. Bureaucratic understanding of changes in the international arena mattered as
much as personal presidential-policy ideas. It would be a mistake to interpret Mexico's international linkages purely from the vantage point of the
national palace.

These technocrats were committed to Mexico and the Mexican state, but not necessarily to one individual Mexican president. Suárez explained in his memoirs that he and the members of his ministry "considered themselves in their positions as technicians and they were difficult to substitute with political friends at the change of the administration."[42] The ministry's professionals followed, first of all, the laws of economy, finance, and exchange rates. In sum, leftist as well as conservative policies of Mexican presidents between 1920 and 1945 rested on a traditional fiscal structure of capitalist financing and budgeting.

Bureaucratic Visions for the Quest of National Development

With the expanding role of bureaucracies also came demands to find solutions to Mexico's problems. Thus the political ideals of presidents were joined by developmental blueprints of professionals.

In the 1920s bureaucratic ideas about the role of the state in Mexican development had been vague. The historical situation had forced the Sonoran presidents to focus first on reestablishing central control over the nation. By 1928, when the worldwide depression hit Mexico, the creation of a new federal fiscal structure had barely been accomplished and the reinstitutionalization of national popular political participation was still in its infancy.

State involvement in Mexican industrialization had been expanding during the 1920s.[43] After 1929, private investment in Mexican industrialization stagnated at less than half a million U.S. dollars per year.[44] The state had to take over the task of industrializing the country. The question was how.

Mexican planners saw only experimentation abroad. Italy was pursuing the formation of a socialist, nationalistic state that drifted toward fascism. In Germany they observed the collapse of the young democratic state under the burden of economic crisis. In the Soviet Marxist-Leninist state, the government experimented with extremes ranging from the elimination of private economy to the New Economic Policy under party control. Finally, in the United States too, the depression was challenging the existing political structure. Mexican planners realized that there existed no easy answers. It would be difficult to propose specific long-term recommendations. In the years to come the Mexican economy would operate in a period of international social and economic transformation.

In 1933, after the election of President Roosevelt in the United States, there existed great hope that the world economic conference in London would bring about a revival of the world economy. But the conference was a great disappointment. Mexican representatives experienced a confused U.S. delegation and European planners who focused on assigning blame to the lack of leadership that came from the United States.[45] Mexican planners had to find a solution to economic crisis at home. In the years to come Mexico's growing corporate institutions—the bureaucracy and the *Partido Nacional Revolucionario* (PNR)–became the think tanks that produced solutions.

The PNR's six-year plan had given a relatively vague prescription for Mexico's future developmental path. Still, in 1933 Lázaro Cárdenas, as PNR president, had stated that the Mexican state should act

> as regulator of the important economic phenomena of our regimen:
> of wealth production and wealth distribution. The Mexican Revolu-
> tion progresses toward socialism, a movement that draws away
> equally from the superannuated tenet of classical liberalism and
> from the norms of the communist experiment being made in Soviet
> Russia.[46]

After his election to the presidency in 1934, he appointed his close personal friend and political adviser Francisco Múgica as the head of the recently founded Ministry of National Economy. Cárdenas charged Múgica with the development of a more coherent plan for a Mexican state-directed economy.

A 1935 memorandum provides us with an impression of how Mexico's bureaucrats envisioned a unique development strategy that was based on "Mexican reality".[47]

Múgica's ministry proposed a dualistic developmental course. First, a "socialist education" would be used to integrate and raise the consciousness of the culturally diverse Mexican population. Second, a policy should be found "that would allow the necessary economic and legal transformations centered around the reorganization of national production." In other words, socialist education and land distribution would be part of a national economic plan, not just a political tool or the realization of a promise of the Mexican Revolution.

The government would generate money for this plan through the modernization of agriculture and the expansion of the national industrial base. A more productive agriculture would be achieved through the application of the latest agricultural science and modern technology. In other words, the objective was not the distribution of land alone, but to give farmers land ready to be immediately exploited and to organize them conveniently so that their work may be fully productive, ever increasing and never diminishing the country's agricultural output.[48]

Here the revolutionary slogan of *tierra y libertad*—which had centered around ownership—was being redefined into *desarollo y producción,* a focus on the exploitation of natural resources. One planner explained:

Once the distribution of lands has been effected, the best manner of obtaining an increase in agricultural production through the convenient organization of all *ejido* commoners should be sought, through the introduction of the most adequate crops, through what crop rotations and agricultural science may advise, through the industrialization of farm products, through the employment in as wide a scope as possible of machinery for increasing yields or for dispatching chores more speedily, through the use of fertilizers and through the thorough commercial and industrial use of all the products and by-products of the land.[49]

The Mexican state would

wage an intensive campaign to raise the economic and technological standards of our agricultural development, combating until its disappearance the rutted methods of husbanding the land which tradition has maintained in the countryside . . .[50]

From the perspective of economic planners, Cárdenas's *ejido* program was part of an effort to transform Mexican agriculture into communal agribusiness. The process would transform peasants into wage earners whose purchasing power would become the financial base of the second phase of the 1935 development plan: the expansion of Mexico's growing national industry.

A PNR planner explained

that industry, as a source of production, is one of the factors that most powerfully contributes to the general economy of the country, and therefore, it [the PNR] shall support and promote every industrial activity until this important branch attains the development and perfectibility for an economically self-sufficient national existence.[51]

Bureaucratic statements of this period impress with their positivistic outlook on industrialization. One writer stated:

Industrial development, properly directed through painstaking and accurate planning and through trustworthy statistics, in the case of both large and small industries can powerfully contribute to the economic aggrandizement of Mexico.[52]

Another writer postulated:

> We think that we should attempt to industrialize Mexico consciously, intelligently avoiding the avoidable evils of industrialism, such as urbanism, exploitation of man by man, production for sale instead of production for the satisfaction of human needs, economic insecurity, waste shabby goods and the mechanization of the workmen . . . We are convinced that the evils of capitalism are not to be found in the application of machinery to the productive process, but rather are due to a merely legal question: who is the owner of the machinery? . . . In these communities machinery made goods may still be beautiful for they will be made by the same people whose artistic sense is now expressed by the works of their hands, and there is no reason to believe that the changing tools will per se make them different. What mechanizes men is not the use of machinery, it is the pressure brought to bear upon them to produce at the highest speed the largest amount possible.[53]

But it was not enough for the state to transform agriculture and industrialize. The state also had to act as marketing agent. Federal bureaucrats had to find markets at home and abroad for the products of Mexico's *ejidos* and state- sponsored industry. Only then would economic growth take place and the Mexican state receive the income to maintain the flow of investment and sustain the cycle of national development. President Cárdenas himself explained this challenge to the German economic attaché Burandt in early 1936:

> No country of the world, with the exception of Germany, would have any interest that the world production in raw materials and agricultural goods would be increased, in other words, that in all areas a new (Mexican) rival would arise. Thus, Mexico would have to expect that the exportation of its products would be hindered by all sides with the help of economic and political pressure, especially from the economically powerful states Great Britain and the U.S. Thus, the economic development of Mexico must be complemented by securing a market for its products.[54]

This developmental outline was translated into reality by various bureaucracies beginning in 1935. The Mexican Ministry of Hacienda created the seed money to finance agrarian reform, industrialization, and the growing state bureaucracy. In the first year of the Cárdenas presidency, Eduardo Suárez applied his special knowledge in accounting methods, acquired in courses at George Washington University in Washington, D.C., to challenge tax payments of foreign companies operating in Mexico. In 1934 alone, negotiations generated a thirty-million-peso tax surplus.[55] The money went to the Ministry of Communication and Public Works to fund the systematic improvement of Mexico's infrastructure, which would further integrate Mexico's regional markets into a national one. An ever-growing number of infrastructure projects like highways, railroads, irrigation, electrification projects, and hydroelectric and petroleum facilities generated work for Mexicans and helped to push the Mexican economy toward the creation of a domestic market that would be strong enough to sustain future national economic development.

At that time Cardenismo's radical rhetoric was perceived as a problem by some Mexican bureaucrats. The diplomats of the Mexican Ministry of Foreign Relations became more and more convinced that radical Mexican political and social policies were incompatible with the desired trade expansion, since most European and American countries looked at Mexican leftist economic nationalism with growing concern. Thus, when possible, the SRE blocked domestic political initiatives it deemed counterproductive to Mexico's foreign-trade efforts. For example, in 1935, Jewish and Mexican leftist organizations tried to organize a nationwide boycott of German goods and merchants in Mexico to protest National Socialist policies in Germany. But the members of the SRE recommended that Cárdenas withhold endorsement of the boycott.[56] From the SRE's point of view, the small political gain that was possible did not justify the damage to future trade relations with Germany. The SRE also made sure that the German legation in Mexico learned that they adamantly opposed this "irresponsible attitude" of the leftist political camp.[57]

The SRE's dedication in finding and keeping markets abroad also fostered the appointment of diplomats who put trade above politics. A good example is the case of the Mexican minister to Germany in the early Cárdenas administration. During 1933, Mexico had been represented in Germany by Sánchez Mejorada, an outspoken critic of Hitler and German National Socialism.[58] In 1934, however, Mejorada was replaced by Leopoldo Ortiz, who had served in Germany before. Ortiz's interest in Germany was economic, not political. Upon his arrival in Germany, the new minister publicly declared that both Germany and Mexico had many things in common, among them a dependency on the course of economic developments in the United States.[59] Ortiz joined the most adamant Mexican advocate of trade over politics in Europe, the Mexican Consul General in Hamburg, Alfonso Guerra.[60] In the years to come these diplomats would urge Mexico City to consider long-term trade advantages, rather than short-term political gains. They advocated the marketing of Mexican products in any country, regardless of its political stance. Mexico should deal with any country as long as it was willing to import products from *ejidos* and could supply Mexico with know-how and technology for industrialization.

This strategy worked well in 1935 and 1936. State-sponsored infrastructure projects had a positive stimulating effect on the Mexican economy. They provided many contracts for underemployed contractors and offered hundred of thousands of new jobs to unemployed workers. Their income stimulated local and regional economies. By the end of the third year of Cardenismo, economic reports from Mexico painted an increasingly rosier picture. However, the creation of sources for future state funding remained a central problem for the Cárdenas administration. Suárez and his planners had decided to expand the state's role in the exploration, production, and processing of Mexico's oil and mining reserves. Mexican planners sought out German and Japanese joint ventures to explore oil deposits in the Tehuantepec region. It was hoped that German technical know-how would bring about an independent small mining sector in the Mexican North. Barter trade with Germany also seemed to offer industrial plants that produced fertilizers and high-octane gasoline for a national Mexican aviation industry. Thus, foreign technology and joint ventures were to bring into production previously unused national resources. Within two years, these productions would generate new and expanding income for the Mexican state, enough to sustain the state-financed development process. In the meantime, Mexican planners expected to finance development with increasing deficit spending and revenues from the expanding domestic economy. The developmental game plan from 1935 was progressing.

In December 1936, the creation of the *ejidos* in the Laguna district began the formation of modern cooperative agribusiness in Mexico. In reality, at that point in time the Mexican state had no extra funds available to finance this step of the development plan. Yet Minister Suárez borrowed from the Bank of Mexico and used the expected harvest as collateral. This was very risky financing, but the political coordinates of the time left little other choice if Cárdenas's political work was to be realized by the end of his *sexeño*.

In the summer of 1937, a combination of events resulted in a rapid collapse of the established economic plan nine months later. As subsequent chapters will show, during the next six months the combination of bad weather, labor unrest, pressure by the foreign oil companies, price increases, inflation, Mexican consumer behavior, and rapidly strengthening domestic political opposition caused the Mexican economy to contract. These events converged, robbing the Mexican state of its prior ability to fund national development.

Between November 1937 and January 1938, Suárez tried desperately to save his economic plan by entering into unprecedented and publicly unpopular joint ventures with English oil companies, as well as financial arrangements with U.S. private banks. When even the secret support of the U.S. Treasury failed to revive the Mexican economy, the Mexican government had to act to stop a vicious cycle in which economic, social, and political crises reinforced the growing suspicion that the Cárdenas government was nearing its end. Mexico's economy continued to slide and the Cárdenas administration faced bankruptcy and subsequent political collapse.

The March 1938 oil expropriation was the lifesaver of the Mexican state. The instant takeover of the already developed and producing oil sector promised immediate access to reliable revenue that was desperately needed to provide the state with the necessary revenue for state-sponsored development. A successful expropriation promised unprecedented petroleum collateral for the Mexican state. By then the domestic political and economic situation had become so desperate that Cardenismo had nothing further to lose. The administration proceeded with the dangerous expropriation, which was seen as a calculated risk, almost an opportunity.

The economic boycott by the foreign oil companies and their affiliated companies immediately endangered this strategy. Any pursuit of a step-by-step plan of national development was suspended. Until the pace of the domestic economy revived and the peso exchange rate stabilized, only one economic credo remained: survival. The reorganization of the national economy around a crippled nationalized oil sector dominated bureaucratic efforts during the rest of 1938.

By 1939 this goal had been achieved. But by then the international political setting was dramatically different than that of 1935. Fascist aggressions in Asia and Europe were spreading fast and the United States, Great Britain and France seemed unable to confront them directly. Germany and Japan's military might was growing daily, and when the allies finally decided to counter Hitler by force, a long battle would start that, once again, could redefine the strategy of Mexican development. When the debate over national economic development resumed inside the Mexican ministries, Mexico's planners charted a new course.

A critical aspect in this reorientation was the changing relationship between Mexican workers, the Mexican state, and national labor organizations. The state was no longer the mediator between Mexican labor and foreign companies, but the proprietor of the oil fields and the employer of the oil workers. Now that the oil industry was the key economic asset for their policy objectives, representatives of the Mexican government quickly abandoned their previous sympathy for labor demands. A new bureaucratic conservatism emerged that demanded from Mexicans identification with the nation, not the previous sectoral identifications of workers or agrarians of early Cardenismo. For example, already in May of 1938, Cárdenas's adviser, Francisco Múgica, now head of the Mexican Ministry of Communication and Public Works, suggested to the Mexican president that the most serious problems of the petroleum sector were the export situation, the administration of the industry, and the leadership of the syndicates. Suddenly, the previously radical Múgica complained that the worker's leaders, handicapped by corruption and alcohol,

> were used to preaching the religion of their rights, but now they do not know how to preach the religion of duty, which would be appropriate . . . There is no doubt that one needs to take steps to centralize and discipline . . .

A memorandum of the presidential study commission, written immediately after the expropriation, also suggested the abandonment of sectoral interpretations of the contemporary situation. It wrote that the oil expropriation

> is a national problem, not only of political, but essentially of economic nature. It effects every Mexican and the unity of nationality, demonstrated clearly by the united expression of interests and solidarity of all Mexican sectors . . . The same leftist and rightists, Catholics, Protestants and atheists, capitalists as well as employees, all have one common interest in the economic independence of Mexico and in the development of the exploitation of its natural riches, because this will be to the benefit of everybody, improving the general living standard and releasing the consumptive capacity of every Mexican.[61]

In June 1938, Cárdenas's presidential study commission also demanded "discipline and responsibility" from Mexicans. Even socialist education was redefined as a tool to increase "the will to work"![62]

In this emerging technocratic, statist discourse, the social label of the Mexican individual was being redefined. Whereas during earlier years official documents were filled with sectoral classifications for Mexicans, such as peasant and worker, now bureaucrats invented an opaque Mexican *homo economicus*, a creature of the economy that rested above social sectors. This Mexican no longer defined itself by its relation to land, factory, or the historical past, but purely by living standard and consumptive power.

In other words, by late 1938 the idea of national development was detaching itself from particular social groups. National development, as an abstract goal in and of itself, was becoming paramount to the earlier heralded goal of developing Mexico's agrarian and labor groups. In early Cardenismo, social and economic changes in labor and agrarian sectors were to bring about national economic independence. Now, national economic independence was to bring about improvement in the labor and agricultural sectors.

The outbreak of fighting in Poland in the fall of 1939 and the subsequent creation of the British economic blockade in the Atlantic Ocean caused the collapse of Mexico's European markets. Critical markets for *ejido* products and nationalized oil disappeared overnight. This meant that the developmental strategy of 1935 could not be revived.

Mexico discovered an alternative path. By December 1939 a new report from the presidential study commission advised Cárdenas

> that the opportunity to initiate the industrialization of the nation
> has not passed, quite the opposite. . . . The world war actually
> brings us great economic damage, but in return it gives us the possi-
> bility to industrialize, let us use it.[63]

In May of 1940, presidential candidate Sánchez Tapia urged Cárdenas to see the war as an economic cure for Mexico's problems. He argued that the unavoidable cooperation with the United States would provide Mexico with the desired stimuli for development in the areas of steel, mining, and livestock. It would guarantee the repair of railroads and streets of military importance and bring about the improvement and fortification of Mexican ports and airports. Most importantly, all of this would be realized with the "financial support of our allies and the investment of large capital."[64]

Other voices warned Cárdenas not to miss this unique opportunity. If Mexico refused to exploit the circumstances of the war, others would not. The Mexican consul in Hamburg pointed to efforts by Peru, Colombia, Venezuela, Argentina, and Uruguay when he wrote that Mexico should be

> remembering that all the countries are assisting the war without
> realizing it, and especially the neutral, great producers of primary
> materials act as belligerents in the economic sector which the totali-
> tarian war is creating.[65]

By the summer of 1940 Minister Suárez had become the champion of the new course as it was debated inside the Mexican cabinet.[66] During a cabinet meeting, Suárez declared that the wartime cooperation with the United States was unavoidable. However, he emphasized, Mexico's cooperation could be sold to the United States as expensively as possible. Also, Minister of Gobernación García Téllez believed that the United States was in a bind because it actually needed Mexican raw material to fight a war in Europe or Asia. This, he emphasized, was a unique chance for Mexico. For once, the United States would have to cooperate with Mexico and reciprocate on the economic level, which would provide Mexico with the needed external stimulus for industrialization. Once the war ended, Suárez warned, the benevolent economic cooperation with the United States would vanish and the northern neighbor would again be a competitor for an industrializing Mexico. Mexico's expanding domestic agribusiness was no longer the engine that pulled Mexico's industrialization; it was now the widening international war. The aftermath of the oil expropriation at home and the international war abroad had dramatically changed the institutional vision of Mexicans. A conservative, technocratic approach had replaced the more socially and politically motivated proposals of the early 1930s.

President Cárdenas subscribed to the new vision. His new sense of realism is documented in his response to the second six-year plan. In the fall of 1939, Cárdenas rejected bitterly the vagueness of the first draft of the second six-year plan that had been drawn up by PNR políticos. Instead, he demanded a detailed plan that specified projects and their financing within the national budget. In a counterproposal, he specified the completion of remote railroads, half-finished highways, flood-control projects, electricity plants, telegraph systems, and special roads that would connect the coast and the interior of the country. In addition, he demanded the creation of a merchant and fishing fleet, the enlargement of ports, and the expansion of the Coast Guard.[67] This was the new technocratic developmentalism without the previous social and political discourse. The socially inspired Cárdenas of earlier years had become a statist micromanager of state-sponsored economic projects. One year later, during negotiations with the unions that ran the nationalized railroad system, Cárdenas went so far as to redefine their request for wage increases as anti-patriotic behavior. Like Múgica two years before, Cárdenas accused the railroad union of lacking discipline and of sabotaging goods that the state had entrusted to them.[68] He claimed that the union lacked patriotism and suggested that it was committing treason. His Minister of Hacienda, Suárez, went even further. Although he understood macroeconomic processes well, he attributed the inflation of 1940 to the behavior of the railroad unions. It occurred, he argued, simply because of the "falling productivity of the workers,—if productivity increases, then also wages will increase." He repeated Cárdenas's claim that the key issue was not the terrible state of the railroad system or the declining wages of workers, but merely "responsibility and patriotism."[69]

Part of this process was that Mexican planners preferred to see the war as a structural economic challenge, not a social one. For example, the Mexican Ministry of Agriculture and Development suggested to the national palace that the central problem of the war was to "reestablish an equilibrium between production, consumption and exportation of Mexican products for which foreign demand decreases." Another key issue would be the "internal rationalization of the centers of production with the goal that the goods reach the market cheaper." The ministry recommended that the administration give "financial support and investment preferably to groups that make or establish production centers which serve and strengthen the general economy of the country." The authors included a mild caveat, suggesting "necessary modifications for those groups that make big profit from the war trade."[70] This was technocratic language that could have come from any Western bureaucracy at that time.

Possibly drastic social consequences for Mexico as a result of the war were only indirectly considered in macroeconomic terms. Planners warned about "price increases for imported goods," or the "increased emigration of valuable Mexican labor force to the U.S."

The political and social tensions that would result from the industrialization process under war conditions were simply referred back to the local level. There, producers and consumers were supposed to create local associations that negotiated production, demand, and prices between themselves. While these organizations were to watch over "problems of distribution and prices," special emphasis was given to the fact that they should show "owners, directors and administrators how to promote the rationalization of centers of productions, save material and be careful with the enumeration of workers." The varied social reality of a still relatively rural Mexico with a diverse subsistence population had disappeared from state records.

In December 1940, the outgoing president, Cárdenas, heard his successor, Ávila Camacho, proclaim during his inauguration that the social emphasis of early Cardenismo was a thing of the past. He explained that

> everybody will reach the conclusion that the Mexican Revolution has been a social movement guided by justice alone, which is now historical. It has achieved for a people the essentials of living.[71]

In other words, Mexican workers and peasants had to postpone their struggle for social and economic improvement once again for the greater good of the nation. The increasingly important role of federal bureaucracies

in developmental policy making, the events surrounding the oil expropriation, and the arrival of the Second World War had redirected the path of
Mexican national development toward technocratic bureaucratic visions that
were full of conservative political assumptions.

3

An Overview

Mexico's Key Foreign Relations (1920–1936)

THE EXPANSION OF MEXICO'S INSTITUTIONAL STRUCTURES AND BUREAUCRATIC-policy ideas created multifaceted connections between Mexico and the world. Between 1920 and 1936, Mexico's foreign-relations professionals anchored the postrevolutionary state within a network of international connections that influenced the Mexican state economically, politically, and culturally. For an understanding of the dramatic changes that took place in Mexican foreign relations after 1936, we need to examine first how Mexico was linked to international affairs between 1920 and 1936.

Mexico City was not a diplomatic post of distinction within the diplomatic profession. Thirty-four nations had diplomatic relations with the Mexican government in 1935, but only eight of them considered Mexico important enough to give their representation the rank of embassy. Seven belonged to American nations: Argentina, Brazil, Chile, Cuba, Guatemala, Peru, and the United States. Only the eighth belonged to a European country: the government of Republican Spain.

From the distance of Europe, a tenure in Mexico City promised stereo-typical exoticism, archeological mysteries, and a society where people "with Indian blood" played a growing role in national and foreign policies. But after a few months in Mexico City, European diplomats learned fast to distinguish between European romanticism and Mexican reality. Most diplomats and their families dreaded the effects of Mexico City's altitude on their health and yearned for the weekend to come, when they could escape to the other side of the mountain range into Cuernavaca or, even better, put in their name for an assignment in the more comfortable European climate. For Latin American diplomats, who were only too familiar with Latin American reality, Mexico provided the still rare and, therefore, threatening challenge of dealing with a "leftist revolutionary regime." For any U.S. ambassador to Mexico, a tenure south of the border was a personal and professional challenge, given the legacy of the U.S.–Mexican war and the U.S. intervention in Veracruz in 1914. For an Asian diplomat, Mexico represented the backyard of the United States, a pawn in big power relations. African diplomats were not represented in Mexico. In short, for foreign diplomatic professionals Mexico City lacked the prestige and glamour of Paris, London, or Berlin, locations considered to be the most prestigious diplomatic assignments. A tour in Mexico City was a mid-level appointment, a training ground for aspiring younger diplomats, a career peak for second-ranking diplomats or a pasture for candidates awaiting retirement. In other words, when foreign diplomats met with highly sophisticated Mexican foreign-policy professionals it was not a meeting between equals.

Latin American countries shared with Mexico geographic proximity and a colonial past. Ever since the 1920s, Mexican diplomatic relations with Latin American countries had been strained.

In spite of a shared geography and a common colonial past, revolutionary Mexico and the mostly conservative Latin American countries had little in common. First, Mexican trade with Latin American countries remained minimal.[1] Mexico's small industry produced few goods that were in demand in its sister countries. More importantly, Mexico's primary economic function in the international economic system remained that of an exporter of raw materials to Europe and the United States. Mexico's lack of a national merchant marine assured the flow of Mexican raw materials carried on European and U.S. ships to European and U.S. manufacturers. Throughout the 1930s this situation did not change. Still, in 1937 an internal Mexican governmental report admitted that besides foreign-owned petroleum products, Mexico had no other products to export south.[2]

Second, the Mexican government continued to advertise its revolutionary path to Latin Americans as a viable alternative to the U.S. economic hegemony, Spanish cultural domination, the disregard of conservative dictators, and the manipulations of rightist nationalism. Mexican administrations underlined their commitment to Latin American revolutionary movements in Latin America by providing exile for political refugees from Central America, Peru, Chile, and Venezuela. In particular, President Plutarco Ellias Calles had personally orchestrated a strong foreign policy that was accommodating and compromising with U.S. interests inside Mexico, while at the same time being confrontational in Central America and the Pan-American Conference system.[3] Later, the young Cárdenas administration went so far as to actively support and train guerrillas inside Mexico for Latin American insurrection movements.[4]

Thirdly, when it came to the presentation of Latin American issues vis-à-vis the United States in the Pan-American arena, the Mexican administration had the annoying habit of acting as a self-appointed spokesperson for other Latin America governments. For example, in July 1934, Mexican Foreign Minister Puig Casauranc published a memorandum in collaboration with the Peruvian and Ecuadorian ministers in Mexico that attacked the unilateral U.S. Monroe Doctrine, this "vague tradition, full of complexities, implications and reserves," and demanded its conversion into a multilateral pact to which all Latin American countries could adhere. Later in the year, Mexico demanded that the United States accept as "a juridical principle the renunciation of armed force and all pressure and economic reprisals for the collection of foreign debts."[5] Next, when Cuba and the United States signed an annulment of the Platt Amendment, the Cárdenas administration stepped forward unsolicited and officially expressed its satisfaction with "this striking and concrete illustration of the new regime in inter-American politics." It claimed that the Cuban–U.S. agreement was reached in large measure because of Mexico's insistence on equal treatment of all Latin American nations. In Washington, the Mexican ambassador and his entire staff paid a formal visit to the Cuban ambassador and to the U.S. Secretary of State to convey in person the congratulations of the Mexican government.[6]

Yet until 1935 Mexico's persistent challenge of U.S. hegemony had not translated into deeper Mexican friendship with other Latin American countries. Only Colombia recognized, to a limited degree, a special Mexican role as evidenced by an eleven-day state visit of the Colombian president-elect, Sr. Alfonso Lopez, on July 19, 1935. The Cárdenas administration used the occasion to turn the event into a spectacle that, hopefully, reenforced its message in the Americas. One year later, in 1936, the inimicable proceedings of the Pan-American Congress meeting at Buenos Aires proved once again to Mexican politicians that the deep ideological cleavage between Mexico and its Latin American siblings was persisting. The overwhelmingly conservative political elites of South and Central American countries continued to resent the Mexican claim to leadership in the region, and rejected Mexico's call for leftist nationalism and greater social justice.[7]

One might expect that diplomats from South America's largest countries played a prominent role in Mexican diplomatic circles. Quite to the contrary, their influence was marginal.[8] In 1935, the dean of Mexico's diplomatic corps was Brazilian Ambassador Abelardo Rocas, who had come to Mexico in 1932. He failed, however, to turn this ceremonial position into political clout. From the beginning of his tenure, Mexico City's society paid more attention to his flamboyant Chilean wife than to his diplomatic initiatives. She had left her previous husband for him and it seemed that, with a little encouragement, she was willing to leave him for someone else.[9] Consequently, Rocas spend most of his time dealing with marital issues, although with little detriment to Brazilian–Mexican relations. Argentina had sent Roberto Levillier to Mexico in April 1935. He had previously served in Poland, Portugal, and the League of Nations. Then, at the end of July 1935, just when he was beginning to gain influence, he was recalled. The Chilean government also had sent an experienced diplomat to Mexico City. Manuel Bianchi Gundian could look back to a long career, serving in Berlin, Rio, Panama, and Cuba as well as in the Pan-American Conference system. Yet, since his wife was afraid of big cities, he lived in a small villa outside of Mexico City, far from the repetitious but obligatory diplomatic social life. If one adds to the personal difficulties of these individuals the political tensions between their conservative governments and the increasingly leftist Cárdenas administration, it is no surprise that the representatives of the ABC countries played a very limited role in Mexico.

Their isolation offered diplomats from smaller Latin American countries the chance of formulating a distinct Latin American position among their U.S., European, and Asian colleagues in Mexico. The Cubans, traditionally close to Mexico, had just sent a new diplomat to Mexico due to the fall of President Grau San Martín. General García Vélez, an elderly man with international diplomatic experience, had so far impressed fellow diplomats only with his fatalistic comment that he had spent most of his life in practical exile, representing his country in the world. The Colombian minister was gaining in popularity with the Mexicans since his liberal López government was the only Latin American government that publicly showed sympathy for Mexico's political path. But it was the Guatemalan ambassador, Sr. Echeverria y Vidaurre, well liked among his colleagues and the bureaucrats of the SRE, who appointed himself dean of the corps of Central and South American diplomats in Mexico. In public, he carried himself like an elderly Frenchman of the old school, proudly displaying a personal style and taste that he had refined during an extended tour in France. But even his social and communication skills could do little to ease the ongoing tensions between Mexico and the other Latin American governments. Mexico remained isolated among her hemispheric siblings.

The United States was Mexico's most important trading partner. In 1934, 61 percent of Mexico's imports and 52 percent of Mexico's exports were exchanged with the United States. Great Britain was a distant second, with 10.5 percent of Mexican imports and 20 percent of Mexican exports, followed by Germany, which provided 10 percent of Mexican imports and received 6.5 percent of Mexican exports. France was a distant fourth.[10] Unlike

Mexican–Latin American relations, it seemed that Mexico's relations with the United States were steadily improving. Both the Roosevelt and the Cárdenas administrations were able to build on the goodwill that had been created by years of informal arrangements between ex-president Plutarco Elias Calles and U.S. Ambassador Dwight Morrow during the Hoover administration and the earlier part of the Maximato.

From the Mexican perspective, Roosevelt's expansion of Hoover's policy idea of the Good Neighbor—at its center the pledge of nonintervention, as well as respect for national self-determination and territorial sovereignty— was finally giving Mexico the customary respect that international law required and increasingly replacing confrontation with dialogue.

This Mexican–U.S. rapprochement between the two countries was evidenced by the resolution of an increasing number of bilateral disputes. For example, already on December 26, 1934, the Mexican–U.S. claims convention of April 1934 was ratified and, more importantly, Mexico made its first payment on time on January 2, 1935. In March 1935, the Cárdenas administration agreed to appoint a three-member team whose task it would be to study with the U.S. government the question of equitable water distribution of the three international rivers, the Bravo, the Colorado, and the Tijuana. Then, in June 1935, Mexico and the United States signed a salvage treaty to facilitate help for ships in danger and for shipwrecked or damaged vessels in coastal waters of either country. Since Mexico had no merchant fleet to speak of, this was a Mexican concession to U.S. lines. The Mexican government even considered publicly negotiations about a trade treaty with the United States, although it did nothing to start trade talks. U.S. tourists were flocking to Mexico in ever- growing numbers. Both administrations were looking forward to the approaching completion of the first highway to link Mexico City with Nuevo Laredo at the U.S. border.[11] In the industrial sector, U.S. mining companies in Mexico were enjoying a recovery of metal prices, stimulated by U.S. monetary policy, although they were not yet putting any new foreign investment into the Mexican mining facilities. Even foreign oil companies registered a moderate optimism in the Mexican oil business. Thus, it mattered less that the U.S. State Department continued to be frustrated when it pushed for amicable settlements for U.S. agrarian claims, or that a bomb exploded inside the U.S. embassy compound in June 1935. A major public uproar in the United States over Mexican religious policy—the central issue of U.S.–Mexican diplomacy in 1935—did not succeed in convincing Roosevelt to abandon the Good Neighbor approach and to revert to the big-stick policy of previous Republican U.S. administrations, still the preferred policy for Mexico among many regional and national U.S. politicians.

Yet, behind closed doors, most Mexican government officials remained weary about future U.S. policy. Two years into the New Deal, the economic situation in the United States was not improving and it seemed possible that a future Republican U.S. administration might reverse Roosevelt's soft approach. Still, in 1935 the Mexican military attaché to Washington, Juan F. Azcárate, warned Mexico City that the policy of the Good Neighbor was just a new disguise for old-fashioned U.S. imperialism. He urged continued alertness and preparation against a future U.S. military intervention.[12] Also, Cárdenas's advisers, Ramón B. Beteta and Francisco Múgica, remained afraid of the United States and urged the Mexican president to develop alternative relations with European and Asian countries in order to counterbalance, as they saw it, certain future U.S. pressures. Mexico's continued engagement in the European-based League of Nations after 1935 was such an attempt to present Mexican policy outside the "Yankee Forum" of the Pan-American conferences.[13]

In particular, the domestic political process in the United States and how it related to the formulation and conduct of U.S. foreign policy toward Mexico was creating continued anxiety, confusion, and fear among Mexican professionals. From Mexico City, U.S. foreign policy appeared volatile and too much influenced by a U.S. public completely ignorant of the reality inside Mexico.

This notion was certainly justified. A growing number of interests were fighting over U.S. policy toward Mexico. First, there were the agencies of the U.S. government in Washington, among whom the career diplomats of the U.S. Secretary of State were the most influential players when it came to Mexican affairs. However, the agency did not pursue one unified policy course. Rather, it was divided into two camps. One group, led by Undersecretary of State Sumner Welles, consisted of Assistant Secretary for Political Affairs Laurence Duggan, Chief of the Division of American Republic Affairs Philipp Bonsal, and the Special Assistant to the Undersecretary Emilio Callado. These men, who, in the words of Randall Bennett Woods, had been "Harvard educated and reform oriented . . . ardent New Dealers, regarded Latin America as their area of expertise and their private policy-making domain."[14] They were "intensely parochial and thus tended to view the entire panorama of international affairs from the perspective of the hemispheric community."[15] The group pursued one central goal:

> the U.S. should develop a long-term nonpartisan policy toward Latin America . . . to eradicate the anti-Americanism created by years of U.S. intervention and, after 1936, to establish an inter-American

consultative system that could act to protect the hemisphere in the event of an external threat.[16]

Against this group worked a second group of career diplomats, who gathered behind Secretary of State Cordell Hull and Assistant Secretary Breckinridge Long. Both men were old Wilsonians, who believed "that the U.S. ought to be the supreme moral factor in the World's progress." From that belief followed the corollary that American political institutions were superior to all others. Thus, Hull and his supporters "tended to view U.S. relations with Latin America as part of a much larger whole," and therefore, for them the Good Neighbor policy was

> only a means to a larger end. In return for Washington's renunciation of intervention and for its virtual abandonment of U.S. business interests south of the Rio Grande, the internationalists anticipated that the other American states would trust Washington to determine hemispheric policy toward the rest of the world.[17]

Then, slowly but steadily, additional U.S. agencies entered Mexican affairs. Traditionally, the U.S. Navy was observing the course of Mexican politics from a strategic point of view. The U.S. Secretary of the Treasury became a major player in Mexican affairs after 1936. Secretary of the Treasury Henry Morgenthau used silver policy as a critical tool to keep the influence of Axis powers in Mexico low. He remained influential throughout all following Roosevelt administrations. In 1938, Adolf Berle, an academic and close Roosevelt friend, joined the State Department as Assistant Secretary of State for Latin American Affairs and worked on Mexican issues. Secretary of Agriculture Henry Wallace had a personal interest in Mexico's agricultural development and was attracted to the leftist rhetoric of the Mexican Revolution. In 1939, J. Edgar Hoover and the FBI established themselves permanently in Mexico and tried to gain Roosevelt's attention with reports about Axis activity south of the border. In 1940, the U.S. army began to push its own ideas about the U.S.–Mexican relationship.

Then there was the U.S. White House. President Roosevelt was personally interested in U.S.–Mexican affairs from the beginning of 1933 on. However, until the oil expropriation in 1938 he left its conduct to Undersecretary of State Sumner Welles and his ambassador to Mexico City, Josephus Daniels. From 1938 on, however, events in Mexico became a permanent item on the White House agenda. Increasingly, Roosevelt micromanaged U.S.–Mexican policy.

Also, U.S. Congress created policy that affected Mexican–U.S. issues. Most senators and congressmen were not familiar with events in Mexico. Nevertheless, when it came to Mexican affairs they were highly receptive to pressure from their religious or business constituencies. One of the most influential figures was Senator Pittman, who represented the powerful silver-mining interests of the state of Nevada.

Then there was the U.S. press, which fed its readers only too often the familiar stereotypes about the land south of the border. Independent, intelligent foreign correspondents, like Betty Kirk from the *Christian Science Monitor,* were the exception. More representative was Mr. Kluckhohn from the *New York Times,* who reported from Mexico with his own agenda in mind; eventually, the Cárdenas administration expelled him from the country. In particular, the Hearst newspapers specialized in sensationalism in Mexican affairs. After the oil expropriation in 1938, the U.S. oil companies organized a full-fledged anti-Mexican campaign in the U.S. press, with the goal of forever discrediting the Cárdenas administration among the ignorant U.S. public.

Finally, between these conflicting U.S. voices stood the U.S. ambassador to Mexico, who had the impossible task of representing their often competing interests as one policy to the Mexican government. Wood described this procedural nightmare correctly as unceasing bureaucratic warfare, not only inside the State Department, where

> bureaucratic coalitions presented policy alternatives to the president
> in ways designed to gain his approval and to discredit each other.
> One organization triumphed over the other because of its special
> relationship to the White House, exclusive access to certain intelli-
> gence data, and control over the actual implementation of policy.[18]

Yet the U.S. ambassador to Mexico, Josephus Daniels, nevertheless succeeded in diverting the destructive energy of this institutionalized, ongoing bureaucratic mumbo jumbo in Washington. Soon he emphasized those policies he considered beneficial to the national interest.

Josephus Daniels, as editor and owner of the North Carolina newspaper *Raleigh News and Observer,* had taken a deep interest in policy early on. During World War I he had served as U.S. Secretary of the Navy to President Wilson and, in that capacity, organized the U.S. invasion of Veracruz. At the department, he had formed a close friendship with his assistant secretary, Franklin D. Roosevelt. In 1933, Roosevelt, now newly elected president of the United States, was looking for an individual he could trust personally to represent his Good Neighbor policy in Mexico City. Daniels accepted with the understanding that first of all he would serve his friend Franklin Roosevelt and his political vision for the United States, and only then would he consider the objectives of his official employer, the U.S. State

Department. Daniels was also determined to put the national interest above U.S. corporate interests in Mexico. To everybody's surprise, Daniels soon managed to establish himself in Mexico City and put a personable face on Roosevelt's still largely theoretical policy ideals. In hindsight, it is no exaggeration to state that Daniels represented the proverbial good neighbor in Mexico more than any other U.S. ambassador to Latin America during all of Roosevelt's administrations.[19]

Daniels had arrived in Mexico City in 1933, during the presidency of Abelardo Rodríguez. Initially Daniels was welcomed with great reservations, not only by the Mexican government, which remembered his role in the Veracruz invasion, but also by the U.S. community and the staff of the U.S. embassy. Overwhelmingly, embassy employees had voted for the Republican ticket and were hesitant to work for this new "liberal" ambassador. This sentiment was shared by the leadership of the U.S. community in Mexico. Unlike his predecessor, Morrow, Daniels was not part of the East Coast establishment and had no experience in big business. Even worse, as a southern Methodist he and his wife were teetotalers, which made many compatriots feel guilty of their alcoholic excesses in the land of tequila. Longtime U.S. residents in Mexico were simply amazed about Daniels's unceremonial, yet warm and folksy personal style. He did not hesitate to dress up in national Mexican costumes, which was beneath the dignity of sophisticated U.S. citizens, but very endearing to the Mexican public. Unlike his European and Latin American colleagues, Daniels was a free spirit whose creativity and personality had not yet been broken by the grind of career diplomacy.

Daniels more than made up for the support that he lacked in Mexico City by his privilege of total access to President Roosevelt. From the outset of his tenure, Daniels, a prolific letter writer, provided his friend in the White House with weekly updates from the Mexican capital. In contrast to the frightened pro-business attitude of State Department officials, Daniels sent to Roosevelt positive, sympathetic Mexican images. And as we will see in the following chapters, Roosevelt listened to the voice of his Mexican ambassador more than to those of the State Department or U.S. business.

When Mexican President Rodríguez was replaced by Lázaro Cárdenas in 1934, Daniels went to great length to build a personal relationship with this new Mexican president. Daniels liked Cárdenas, who, like him, was a nonintellectual politician and, like Roosevelt, cared deeply and sincerely about the plight of his people. Moreover, Daniels loved Cárdenas's sincerity and passion for his convictions. Roosevelt soon gained the impression from Daniels's letters that Cárdenas was just another "New Dealer" who was trying to do in Mexico what the U.S. president was working toward in the United States.

In contrast, Daniels made no particular effort to establish a close relationship with Mexico's political strongman and ex-president Plutarco Elias Calles, who, until 1935, was still the central political figure behind the Mexican political system. Daniels had met Calles for the first time after his arrival in Mexico in 1933. During their first meeting, Calles expressed a lukewarm welcome to Roosevelt's New Deal, telling Daniels that "Mexico and the U.S. were working along somewhat similar lines."[20] No record exists of another meeting between the two men until November 1934, when Daniels and Calles met to discuss the Mexican religious question.[21] After that, Daniels did not deal with Calles again until the break between Calles and Cárdenas in the summer of 1935. For Daniels, Calles never became a New Dealer. He always remained the "*Jefe Máximo*, a term that, for Daniels, was uncomfortably close to *dictator* and seemed to belong more to the past.

This became apparent during the final confrontation between Calles and Cárdenas in the summer of 1935. During the confrontation, Daniels was vacationing in the United States. He returned to Mexico City, just when Cárdenas was demanding the resignation of his first cabinet in order to break the hold of the Callistas on his administration.[22] Calles was too astute to approach Daniels directly and ask him for help. Instead, he send his confidant, American businessman Smithers, to the U.S. ambassador with the following message: "General Calles wishes you to know that things in Mexico look black," and that "the U.S. could not be quiet while its interests were endangered by a country so near to it."[23] Calles did not suggest any specific action to Daniels, but the U.S. ambassador nevertheless gained the impression that he was solicited to help in the destruction of Cárdenas. Daniels simply ignored the request.[24] Equally important was how he interpreted the events in Mexico in the letters to Roosevelt. He discounted the alarmist analysis from the State Department, which claimed that the tug of war between the two men could be a threat to U.S. interests in Mexico. Instead, he categorized the Cárdenas–Calles conflict as a test of will by a young, committed president who was liberating himself from the long-standing and overbearing political tutelage of an aging, narrow-minded political boss— something that was very much to Daniels's liking and felt familiar to Roosevelt, who was trying desperately at that time to renovate the political system inside Washington. Thus, Daniels reassured Roosevelt that the United States had nothing to worry about. To the contrary, Daniels emphasized, the Mexican people were relieved that the political turnover seemed not to lead to rebellion or to civil war. "Mexico," he wrote, "was quiet with no indications of the revolution which has so frequently occurred here when there was a break between strong leaders."[25] The event had demonstrated, Daniels pointed out, that the Mexican political system had matured and was capable of dealing with this disturbance. The event was "indicative of the progress in the arts of peaceful government in Mexico. Ten years ago these differences would have resulted in the employment of force, if not in revolution."[26] In short, Daniels portrayed the Calles–Cárdenas confrontation as a move toward peace and stability south of the border. Consequently, there seemed to be no need for the White House to contemplate direct or indirect intervention.

Cooperation in silver policy was another, very important link between the two countries. In 1934, the U.S. Congress had enacted the Silver Purchase Act to counter worldwide inflationary trends as well as to boost foreign purchasing power. This policy, it was hoped, would eventually translate into increased U.S. exports. China and Hong Kong became the largest silver supplier to the United States, with Mexico taking third place. In the next three years, annual U.S. silver purchases from Mexico grew from 74.1 million to 85.7 million ounces.[27]

For the Cárdenas administration, this U.S. policy brought significant windfall profits. First, U.S. mining companies in Mexico increased production in order to sell more to the U.S. government, thus increasing Mexican employment in the mining sector. More importantly, the Cárdenas administration earned increased tax revenue from the growing mining production. Finally, the United States bought Mexican silver at an artificially high rate that earned the Bank of Mexico 36 cents profit on each ounce of silver. By 1935, Mexican Minister of Hacienda Suárez admitted that the Mexican state had increasingly become dependent "for a large share of its revenue on taxes collected on high priced silver."[28]

In January 1936, the U.S.–Mexican silver purchase agreement was up for renegotiation. Since U.S. silver policy continued and the Mexican government continued to benefit from the bilateral arrangement, the deal was renewed without problems.[29] In addition, the Roosevelt administration gave the Mexican administration access to the U.S. stabilization fund to balance its foreign currency holdings and to keep the peso exchange rate stable but tied to the U.S. dollar.[30] At the end of 1936, the financial cooperation on the executive level between the United States and Mexico had reached an unprecedented degree. Mexico's cooperation allowed the Roosevelt administration to bring about the stabilization of world silver prices, as envisaged in 1934. It had also created a powerful counterweight against the British-dominated open silver market. In fact, Suárez was to approach Canada and ask whether its administration would like to join a North American Central Data Institution, which would gather data about American silver production and sales, further increasing U.S. control over world silver.

The Mexican government was delighted about this development. Minister Súarez told U.S. Secretary of Treasury Morgenthau that the Cárdenas administration appreciated "all that we have done for them and asked that this be passed on to the President."[31] In the future, too, U.S. silver purchases would bring a stable source of income to Mexico's treasury. U.S.–Mexican financial relations had reached a state of interdependence.

Great Britain was still Mexico's second most important trading partner in 1935, but it was steadily losing ground to the Germans. The opening words of the 1934 annual diplomatic report, written by recently arrived British Minister Monson, describe the British economic decline in Mexico with devastating poignancy:

> The golden era of British enterprise in Mexico, when the vast
> Pearson interests and other important British concerns, such as the
> Shell Oil Company, the Light and Power Company and the Mexican
> railway enjoyed a privileged position and were able to return hand-
> some dividends, has gone for ever.[32]

In 1934 the last of the British and Canadian banks in Mexico had closed its doors. After twenty-four years of business in Mexico City, the manager of the Bank of Montreal told the British minister that "lately, a banker had to devote more of his time to defending himself against the government than attending to his business."

In London, the British decline in Mexico received little attention. The Labour cabinet of MacDonald focused on the serious domestic economic crisis. Its Conservative successor, the Baldwin administration, did not pay any more attention to Mexico. British foreign policy, at that time, concentrated on the rise of fascism in Europe.

The decline of British influence in Mexico was administered by the British Foreign Office. As head of the American desk, John Balfour single-handedly designed most of British policy toward Mexico. As a career diplomat, he was still looking back to the time when the empire was strong and competed successfully with the United States in Latin America. His opinions and his arguments on the sheets of the diplomatic reports give the impression of a man who lacked flexibility and prided himself in defending diplomatic principles that the former British lion could no longer enforce successfully. Balfour lacked any clear understanding of the political and social forces of Latin America. For him, a country like Mexico belonged to the increasing number of non-European people who created nagging, persistent complications by asserting their political and economic sovereignty. Since Mexico, as a sphere of direct political and economic influence, had been conceded to the United States after the Mexican Revolution, Mexican nationalism was feared by the Foreign Office first and foremost as a dangerous trendsetter for other countries in Latin America and the Near East, where British stakes were still larger and stronger. Therefore, the official British stance toward the remaining interests in Mexican agricultural property, railroads, foreign bonds, and petroleum should be understood as a signal to countries like Venezuela, Argentina, or Iran to discourage the use of economic nationalism.[33]

The interests of the Shell subsidiary El Águila were represented to the Mexican government directly by its local president, Anderson, who listened first to the orders from his board in London, second to his U.S. colleague from Standard Oil, and only thirdly to the British diplomatic representative in Mexico City.[34] In other words, the British diplomatic minister in Mexico was relatively isolated and often remained a highly educated observer of processes that he could not influence.

The growing British isolation in Mexico was particularly painful, because of what the British perceived as Josephus Daniels's unnecessary refusal to form a common front with his Anglo-Saxon cousins. Daniels's persistent refusal "to pull any British chestnuts out of the Mexican fire if there is the slightest risk of burning his fingers in the process" brought British diplomats close to a state of desperation. For example, in January and February 1935, British and U.S. oil representatives approached Daniels and the U.S. State Department to use a health-related stay of Calles in the United States to arrange an informal meeting at the bedside of the *jefe máximo*. The oil companies hoped to enlist Calles's authority in reestablishing the strength of foreign oil companies in Mexico, which had eroded under the increasing radicalization of labor under President Cárdenas. Daniels, and therefore Washington, ignored the request. Soon, Calles returned to Mexico and the opportunity had passed. Next, the British thought that the break between Cárdenas and Calles could be used as "an opportune psychological moment to settle their differences with the Mexican government." Against the advice of Mexican Shell President Anderson, the Shell board in London hired Mr. Reuben Clark, the former legal adviser to U.S. Ambassador to Mexico Morrow, and sent him to Mexico to exert pressure on the reorganizing Cárdenas government. Clark himself was convinced that Calles would soon experience a political comeback, and Clark would be willing to help orchestrate Calles's return to power. However, after a talk with U.S. Ambassador Daniels in Mexico City, Clark reported to the British with great frustration that Daniels had not the slightest interest in supporting the plan. He told the British minister "that nothing short of categorical instructions from the State Department would induce Mr. Daniels to intervene with the Mexican government on behalf of the oil interests.[35]" In 1935, this was nothing but wishful thinking. While Secretary of State Hull was still willing to help U.S. companies abroad, President Roosevelt himself was busy fighting the petroleum companies in the United States. The British minister to Mexico correctly described the simple, but crippling, effect of the U.S. Good Neighbor policy on traditional British imperialistic pressure tactics in Mexico. He complained:

> The Mexican government, largely as a result of President Roosevelt's declaration of a new deal as regards U.S. relations with all other countries in the American continent, are convinced that they have now no reason to fear intervention or even serious diplomatic pressure from the outside: they realize that they have little to hope for as regards a foreign loan or foreign financial assistance in view of the extent to which they have already practically repudiated their existing foreign obligations; and they feel, consequently, perfectly safe in carrying out their socialistic, anti-foreign and, to a certain extent, confiscatory policy at the expense of foreign companies.[36]

In the Mexican Secretary of Foreign Relations and the Mexican Presidential Palace, the British decline and its increasingly helpless position in Mexico did not remain unnoticed. Already in 1933, SRE officials had studied how the British government reacted when the Shah nationalized British petroleum concessions in Persia.[37] From London, Mexican diplomats sent reports that painted pictures of a weak and confused former world power. Mexican ministers assured Mexican policy makers that the British cabinet was not paying attention to Mexico. Rather, Great Britain was entirely absorbed with domestic affairs, and the only item related to foreign affairs that the cabinet cared about was the rise of fascism in Europe. A 1937 statement by Mexican Minister to London Primo Villa Michel summed it up best. He declared that the British "empire is sick with a weak soul."[38]

To make matters worse, the Cárdenas administration let the British feel their weakening position in Mexico. While Mexico celebrated one accord after the other with the United States, in 1934 and 1935 British initiatives were ignored or politely rejected. The British were not really surprised that during much of 1934 and 1935 efforts to get the Cárdenas administration to deal with issues that concerned the Shell company went nowhere. But also other, minor problems remained unresolved. British representations to obtain agrarian bonds for expropriated property became increasingly futile. Next, a British request to ease cumbersome formalities for British sailors who went ashore in Mexico was ignored for half a year and then denied because "these formalities were expressly required under the regulations of the existing law of migration."[39] A British request to ease modifications for the importation of patent medicines was refused because the Cárdenas administration "was unable to depart from the strict application of the regulations of their sanitary code." Attempts to move toward a Mexican–British trade treaty failed for even more banal reasons: the treaty commission of the SRE declined to prepare a treaty draft. Finally, a British initiative to form a chicle cartel between British Honduras, Mexico, and Guatemala and against the United States remained unanswered. The only positive Mexican–British diplomatic cooperation occurred when both countries reached an agreement to prohibit for ten years the pursuit or capture of the sea cow off British Honduras; and this proposal had been initiated by the Mexicans themselves.[40] When British Minister Morton was replaced by Minister Murray, the new minister sent another warning to London: "the shelter which the [Monroe] Doctrine provides against squalls from across the Atlantic makes the feelings of European governments a matter of relative indifference to the Mexican government.[41]" But in London, few individuals heeded the warning. The fascist threat from Germany was growing every day and was much more immediate than the problems of nationalist Mexico.

In the years that followed, the British decline continued, particularly in trade. By 1937, the British, whose trade with Great Britain had slowed down to a "spasmodic and casual"[42] level, had been replaced by the Germans as Mexico's second most important trading partner. The German introduction of artificial currencies and barter trade, as well as better marketing networks inside Mexico, had pushed Great Britain into third place.[43]

Germany had never gained control over any Mexican territory or raw materials. Germany had never violated Mexico's territorial sovereignty, unlike the United States, Great Britain, France, and Spain. True, the Zimmermann-Depesche incident of 1917 had proven that German diplomats and military planners might also have "Mexican designs," but even then Mexico had mattered to Germany primarily as a neighbor of the United States. Consequently, before Hitler's rise to power, when Mexican politicians thought about economic cooperation with European powers, Germany caused them the least amount of anxiety. To the contrary, cooperation with Germany promised access to German technological achievements as well as a huge market that needed Mexican raw materials and agricultural products.

German influence in Mexico rose with the influx of German immigrants into Mexico. Since the late nineteenth century, they and their descendants had specialized as merchant traders in the import of European retail goods and played a minor role in early Mexican industrialization.[44] Others were prominent in Mexican retail business. On German ships, German hardware, manufactured products, toys, chemicals, and vital pharmaceuticals reached Mexico. In turn, German schooners carried Mexican agricultural products like coffee, hemp, cotton, and rice to European markets. Most importantly, this economic exchange had not resulted in a Mexican dependence on Germany.

Another distinctive feature of the Mexican–German trade relationship after the Mexican Revolution was the relative absence of government involvement. There was no need for strong German diplomatic pressure in Mexican government circles since German companies did not own significant property inside Mexico. While U.S. and British diplomatic representatives never ceased to press the Mexican revolutionary government on economic issues, German diplomats in Mexico were not known as representatives of big capital. A deeper involvement of both governments in trade was explored for the first time in 1926, when President-elect Calles traveled to Germany to receive treatment for health problems. He received a warm welcome by German government representatives and much attention from German friends of Mexico. Nevertheless, the government of the weak German Weimar Republic remained too absorbed with domestic issues to become more deeply involved in Mexican trade or development. Still, German merchant traders in Mexico soon received new business associates.

In the late 1920s, German industrial trusts, like the chemical giant I. G. Farben, the electrical manufacturer AEG, and the communication specialist Telefunken, opened their own branch offices in Mexico City. They came as part of a European-wide effort by European export companies to position themselves in a Latin American market that was developing due to increasing import substitution policies. German manufacturers were hoping to gain influence in Mexico in special industrial sectors before British or U.S. companies could once again claim the markets of the Western Hemisphere for themselves. Some board members of the German companies were also hoping that their presence in Mexico and other Latin American countries might slow down Latin American industrialization. Either way, German entrepreneurs were dreaming of selling dies, pharmaceuticals, fertilizers, radios, telephones, and electricity.

The established merchants of the German community in Mexico looked at these newcomers with mixed feelings. Previously, their import and export houses had represented these companies. But they realized that the world depression had changed trade in Latin America forever. In order to strengthen their position vis-à-vis increasing government interference and foreign competition, they had to work together with the representatives of these German companies. If they did not respond to the changes, French, Spanish, and Italian merchant houses would be eager to take over any business they could get.[45]

In 1933, Hitler's rise to power in Germany again changed Mexican–German economic relations. For the first time, political conflicts overshadowed the previously harmonious trade link. From Berlin, Mexican Ambassador to Germany Sánchez Mejorada warned about Hitler's tyrannical actions and the "mystical hope of the German masses in the resurrection of the economic and military power of its people."[46] In Mexico City, Mexican communist organizations were the first to demonstrate against Hitler in front of the German legation.[47] When news about the arrest of the chairman of the German Communist party, Ernst Thaelmann, reached Mexico City, public protests intensified against Germany and German business in Mexico. Soon, Jewish organizations joined in and demanded an end to German anti-Semitism.[48]

For the first nine months of Hitler's administration, Germany continued to be represented by Minister Zechlin, a Social Democrat. Ironically, while his fellow party members were persecuted in Germany, he had the task of defending National Socialist Germany's reputation, filing one diplomatic protest note after the other with the Mexican government, demanding that anti-Hitler protests, movies, and speeches be stopped. At first, his efforts were successful. For example, then Minister of Gobernación José Vasconcelos banned the screening of the film *Via Crucis* in Mexico.[49] Other theaters decided to cut passages that were deemed offensive to National Socialist ideas. Only when Cárdenas assumed office at the end of 1933 did Mexican movie theaters again show anti-Hitler movies uncensored.

The Third Reich arrived in Mexico in December 1933, with the new minister, the fifty-one-year-old Baron Rüdt von Collenberg-Boedigheim. Following World War I, Rüdt had served as German consul to Calcutta and Shanghai.[50] There, he had been introduced first to National Socialist ideas, but like many other Germans, he had waited until May 1933, after Hitler's rise to power, to join the NSDAP.[51] In the fall of 1933 he was reassigned to Mexico City, where he would serve until the break in Mexican–German diplomatic relations in December 1941. Before his departure from Germany, Rüdt was briefed not only by the German Foreign Ministry (AA), but also by the Office of Foreign Organizations of the NSDAP (AO) in Berlin.[52] After the briefing the AO's head, Bohle, expressed his satisfaction with Rüdt. The talk had confirmed that Rüdt belonged to a "new generation" of German diplomats willing to give equal consideration to traditional diplomacy, as well as to the objectives of the NSDAP abroad. Consequently, Bohle predicted a promising cooperation between the AO and the German diplomatic representative in the Mexican theater.

Compared to other German diplomats in Latin American capitals, Rüdt lacked influence in the German Foreign Ministry and the AO. He received most of his instructions from the AA's economic counselor for Mexico, Hermann Davidsen. In turn, his diplomatic reports went to Department III of the AA. From there, they were circulated to other ministries. A direct exchange between Rüdt and German Foreign Minister von Ribbentrop or his undersecretary, von Weizäcker, did not occur until 1939.[53] At no time did Hitler ever address Rüdt directly.

Like U.S. Ambassador Daniels, German Minister Rüdt had to deal with competing German bureaucracies that pursued separate, sometimes contradictory, policies toward Mexico. First, there was the traditional German Foreign Ministry. From the point of view of professional German diplomats, Mexico was seen not as a country in its own right, but first and foremost as a dependent neighbor of the United States. And since the German community in Mexico was small, compared to that of the ABC countries, and the German economic stake in Mexico was small, the AA made no efforts to challenge U.S. hegemony south of the Rio Grande.

The German Economic Ministry was interested in Mexico as part of the Latin American market. It issued a new German trade policy toward the Balkans and Latin America in 1934, which systematically tried to expand its influence into the privately organized German–Mexican trade.[54] The introduction of artificial currency and barter exchanges were the cornerstones of this exclusionary trade strategy.[55] After the publication of Germany's second six-year plan in 1936, state intervention in private trade only intensified. As a consequence, the German legation in Mexico City was staffed with a full-time economic attaché, Hans Burandt. This was a clever choice, since Burandt had been born in Mexico and spoke excellent Spanish. The Ministry of Economy hoped that his presence would further increase barter trade and channel Mexican raw materials to the German industry without the expense of scarce foreign currency. What the ministry did not know was that Burandt was also working secretly for the German military.

The German Navy had instructed Burandt to secretly organize German drilling rights to Mexican oil reserves. Before 1935, the German Navy had imported only small amounts of Mexican petroleum products through an independent U.S. oil dealer, the Davis company. At the same time, the German Navy—having planned a gigantic buildup of German naval power—became concerned about securing a supply of fuel that would feed the engines of this future German armada. It had identified three possible strategies: (a) to develop Estonian oil-shale, (b) to obtain oil concessions in Iraq for currency-free oil purchases, or (c) to participate in the exploration and exploitation of Mexican oil deposits.

The Estonian option fell through because of high costs, and the Iraqi option collapsed due to British opposition. Thus, by 1936 the only option left was Mexican oil. A letter box company was founded to serve as cover for the German Navy's attempt to get a foot into the door of Mexican petroleum exploration: the Gesellschaft für Überseeische Bergbauliche Unternehmungen. In Mexico this company was represented by the Dresdner Bank's subsidiary Banco America de Sur. The documents do not indicate that the Mexican government was aware of the German deception. Soon, two German geologists traveled to Mexico to arrange a joint German–Mexican exploration project.

At first, well-connected individuals of the German community in Mexico tried to profit from the navy's inexperience in Mexico. Politically well-connected German expatriates offered Economic Attaché Burandt the allegedly "largest and most promising available oil concession in America," located right on the Rio Grande, in the border area of Coahuila and Nuevo León.[56] In Berlin, oil experts shook their head over Burandt's naïveté. The undeveloped oil field bordered directly on the United States, not a very promising location for a German operation during the coming war. As a consequence, Burandt and the merchants were excluded from negotiations and the German oil experts continued alone. Only Minister Rüdt remained informed.

Rüdt's task of expanding German state control over Mexican–German economic relations was significantly alleviated by parallel efforts of the Mexican administration. Coincidentally, the German National Socialist state's need for barter trade complemented the need of the Cardenista state to find agricultural markets abroad.[57] Thus, Rüdt's greatest ally in Mexico became the Mexican trade bureaucracy, which was desperately looking for markets for the products of the increasing number of *ejidos* and for a source of technology that would supply Mexico's development without the involvement of shrinking foreign reserves. It seemed that Mexican *ejidos* could provide much-needed agricultural products in exchange for German manufactured goods and technology.

The increasing state involvement in Mexican–German trade relations caused a recall of the anti-Hitler Mexican Minister to Berlin Sánchez

Mejorada. He was replaced by the trade-oriented minister Leopoldo Ortiz. Ortiz had already served in Germany as a consul in the 1920s and was intimately familiar with German markets. His central mission would be to find new markets for Mexican products in Germany.

When he arrived in Germany he found an economy whose interest in Mexico was still "diffuse."[58] But he assured his superiors that he saw many possibilities for improving future relations.[59] Most importantly, Germany could serve not only as a much-needed market for Mexican *ejido* products, but also as a supplier of technology and scientific know-how that would push Mexico over the threshold of industrialization. An expanding German–Mexican trade relationship might play a vital role in the realization of Mexico's Six-Year Plan.

In Hamburg, Germany, Ortiz found a strong supporter for Mexican–German trade expansion in the Mexican consul to Hamburg, Alfonso Guerra.[60] Between 1934 and 1936 Guerra and Ortiz never stopped declaring to Mexico City that German manufactured products and technology could be central to Mexico's industrialization.

The only serious challenge to this economic expansion arose temporarily in 1935, when the Jewish community in Mexico attempted to organize a boycott of all German businesses and goods.[61] After some initial success, the effort fizzled out since it was not picked up by other segments of the Mexican population and was ignored by most ministries of the Cárdenas administration. The boycott encountered its strongest opposition in the office of the Mexican Secretary of Foreign Relations, which was determined to protect Mexican–German trade.[62] The ministry's effort paid off.

Between 1934 and 1936, this state-directed trade expansion moved German machinery, chemical products, and technological know-how to Mexico. In exchange, the German market received rice and cotton. By February 1936, during the accreditation of Minister to Berlin Leopoldo Ortiz's successor, Leonidas Almazán, Hitler became personally involved and expressed his hope that the commercial relations between the two countries would continue to improve. Hitler then followed a suggestion from the German Ministry of Economy and proposed that Mexico and Germany consider negotiating a formal commercial treaty.[63]

The German Ministry of Propaganda focused on Mexico relatively late. During 1934, the selling of the German Third Reich in Mexico was left largely to Minister Rüdt himself. Arthur Dietrich, an early member of Mexico's NSDAP branch, became Rüdt's key aide. In 1935, Rüdt hired Dietrich officially as press attaché of the German legation.[64] Unexpectedly, however, Berlin ordered Dietrich to go to Spain to reunite the divided German community of Salamanca. During the next two years the German legation in Mexico had to make due without its propaganda chief.

An NSDAP branch in the German community in Mexico existed as early as 1931.[65] In the following years, however, it struggled for influence until the arrival of Minister Rüdt provided the prestige of the German state against the opposition of the conservative nationalist leadership. Between 1934 and 1936 the German diplomat Rüdt and the Nazi party focused their efforts on gaining control over the German ethnic community. They intervened little in Mexican domestic politics.

The previous pages have painted a complex picture of German–Mexican relations between 1934 and 1937. Just like U.S. policy toward Mexico, German policies toward Mexico were characterized by bureaucratic infighting and competition among governmental agencies. But unlike U.S. Ambassador Josephus Daniels, German Minister Rüdt had no direct access to Hitler. Rüdt had to manage the conflicting German bureaucratic initiatives with his limited social skills and his lack of personal charm. However, when push came to shove, he had at least sufficient authority over the German community in Mexico.

Before the 1930s France had played a much greater role in Mexican foreign trade. French investors had held significant amounts of Mexico's foreign debt and were involved to a lesser degree in Mexican industry. However, with the advent of the depression, French imports from Mexico began to decline. Mexican imports from France experienced a more dramatic reduction after 1928. As a result, the importance of France for Mexican foreign trade shrank, and soon German traders took over French market shares. France never recovered its position after the depression and remained Mexico's fourth important trading partner, after the United States, Germany, and Great Britain.[66]

In regard to Italy, Mexican planners were interested in Mussolini's economic nationalism. Also, in 1933 it seemed to some Mexican observers that Italy, like Germany, might offer new trade opportunities for Mexico. One year later, in 1934, the Mexican Secretary of Foreign Relations signed a one-year preferential tariff-rate agreement with the Mussolini administration. In turn, Mexico offered most-favored-nation status to Italy. The Italian invasion of Ethiopia put an end to any plans of an intensification of Italian–Mexican trade. The preferential trade agreement of 1934 was not renewed. Italian investors felt little affinity for the Cárdenas administration. When Mexico asked the Italians to settle their special claims, Italian banks and the Italian government refused. They preferred to keep a united front with other European investors, most notably, French bankers.[67]

In contrast, the advances that Mexican planners made toward Japan seemed more promising. From its very beginning, Japan's developmental process had been of interest to Mexicans. Mexican diplomats, like Cárdenas's Foreign Minister Hay, had returned from their tenures in Japan and China hopeful that Mexico might be able to gain a new trading partner in the Pacific.[68] Still lacking, however, was Japanese interest in Mexico. Finally, by 1935 Japanese businessmen were beginning to pay more attention to Mexico. In that year, Mexican imports from Japan increased by 61 percent, most of which consisted of goods for retail and open market trade.[69] In April of the same year, Japanese oil negotiator Yukio Nagamatsu of Choshu Petroleum company made a first attempt to arrange the export of a small monthly quota of oil from the recently founded PEMEX company. Rumor had it that the Japanese Navy was behind Nagamatsu. Two Japanese businessmen tried to gain access to Mexico's oil deposits. At the center of this activity were two companies. The first was the Compania Mexicana de Petroleo Laguna, S.A., which had been founded in Jalapa in 1934, leasing several concessions for ninety-five years for the purpose of exploiting oil lands in the state of Veracruz. On the company's board served Mexico's Undersecretary of Public Works and Infrastructure and the head of the Banco Azucarero. The central businessman behind the scenes was Dr. Kisso Tsuri, who also represented the Mitsui company in Mexico.[70] He owned another company in Mexico, the Compania Mexicana de Petroleo Veracruzana, and some Mexicans were also on its board.[71]

Not surprisingly, Cárdenas's Minister of National Development, Francisco Múgica, was the most ardent Mexican advocate of increased Mexican–Japanese economic relations. Like Germany, Japan was another potential market for Mexican products and a source of technological know-how. It could increase Mexico's independence from the technology of North America and Europe. Later, when Múgica switched to the Mexican Ministry of Communication and Public Works he became the partner of choice for Japanese inquiries about joint ventures in the Mexican petroleum and fishing industry. His undersecretary, Modesto Rolland, served on the board of a Japanese company in Mexico.

In the end, however, Mexican hopes for an expansion of Mexican–Japanese economic cooperation did not become reality. The Japanese government continued to view Mexico merely as part of the U.S. economic sphere of influence, but not as a country with economic potential in its own right.

Mexican economic planners also had an economic interest in the Soviet Union. Already in the 1920s Mexican agrarian reformers had visited the

Soviet Union and studied Soviet agricultural reform and its applicability in Mexico. By the 1930s Stalin's policy of industrialization revived Mexican interest in Mexico City.[72] Again, it was Minister Francisco Múgica who inquired about obtaining Soviet technological know-how, hoping to forge a closer economic bond between the two countries. But because after 1928 Mexican–USSR diplomatic relations remained hostile, and because Mexico had little to export that the Soviet Union had not already produced itself, a Mexican–USSR economic exchange never became reality.[73]

In sum, compared to Mexico's economic relationships with the United States, Germany, and Great Britain, Mexico's linkages with France, Italy, and Japan remained minor.

In the early 1930s the role of the United States in Mexican economic foreign relations was matched only by Spain's importance in Mexico's foreign political relations. Mexico's independence from Spain in 1821 had by no means eliminated the predominance of century-old Spanish social institutions in Mexican society. The Catholic Church, conservative patriarchal family structures, a European class structure, a legal system build around the European concepts of the individual, private property, and capitalism continued to serve as important conceptual pillars of the newly founded Mexican state. Also, Spanish social values, such as the superiority of everything European, and powerful notions of race continued to influence Mexican political thought. The social upheavals of the Mexican Revolution did not succeed in eliminating the importance of this Spanish legacy either. To the contrary, the destruction and violence of the revolution caused Mexico's growing urban population and upper class to project their desire for tranquil times onto an invented Mexican past, in which a renewed commitment to Spanish values and institutions came to stand for order and stability. This *hispanismo* only gained strength when, in 1917, the news of the Bolshevik Revolution further fanned the fears of the Mexican upper class about worldwide social changes.[74] Finally, when in the same year social tensions exploded in Spain, it seemed to a growing number of Mexican observers that modernization, political radical thought, and the increasing rights of workers were now eroding the political culture of the former motherland. When, in 1923, the military coup led by Miguel Primo de Rivera abolished open political participation in Spain and, with support of the Spanish king Alfons XIII, tried to reestablish the pre-World War I social order, many conservatives all over Latin America were breathing a sigh of relief.

Also, the left wing of the Mexican revolutionary nomenclature cared deeply about the events in Spain. For them, the Spanish struggle symbolized an attempt to put an end to the reactionary political tradition of Spain that revolutionary Mexican politicians themselves were trying to overcome in their own country. Thus, when Primo de Rivera's military regime tumbled in 1930 and King Alfons left the Spanish throne the following year, Mexican revolutionary politicians felt a special kinship to the newly proclaimed Second Spanish Republic. In the following years, they were delighted to see the Spanish Republic enact a radical anti-Catholic policy that promised to separate Spanish state and Catholic Church once and for all. In sum, for Mexico's political left and right the political development of Spain served as a mirror for their own political battles. Up for discussion was the national type of social organization and, as Ricardo Pérez Montfort phrased it, "the question of legitimacy of post-revolutionary governments and a defense of their political and economic models."[75]

Under newly elected President Cárdenas in 1934, debate and polarization inside Mexico further intensified. Cárdenas's incorporation of Mexico's peasants and workers into the national political system,[76] the revival of the so-called socialist education, the realization of large-scale land redistribution in the Laguna area and the Yucatán,[77] and the inclusion of Mexico's rich and diverse indigenous traditions in the official image of Mexican nationalism all challenged the core beliefs of *hispanistas*. Whereas peasants and workers supported the Mexican state, hoping to recover from real income losses and rising prices,[78] Mexican conservatives screamed that Cardenismo was moving Mexico toward a socialist or even communist society.

The rhetorical battle peaked in 1936, when Cárdenas decided to break with the conservative political strongman Plutarco Ellias Calles and exile this symbol of the postrevolutionary status quo and renewed conservatism to the United States.

Only three months later, the struggle in Spain gained a new dimension. General Franco challenged the Republican government in Madrid with an armed uprising that started the Spanish Civil War. Almost immediately, Mussolini and Hitler sent troops to Spain to support Franco's insurrection. Only the USSR and Mexico's Cárdenas administration chose to support the Spanish Republican government. Foreign intervention had internationalized the struggle in Spain.

For Mexico's conservatives, Franco's coup came almost too late to undo the social changes that the Republican administration had forced upon Spanish society. Yet, at the same time, German and Italian involvement suggested to Mexican followers of *hispanista* ideas that they were becoming part of an international effort to "stem the red tide." Even better, Franco would challenge liberal politics on the old continent before it could infect further the former Spanish colonies in Latin America. For these conservative Mexicans, Franco's victory was a necessity in order to deal a first, serious blow to the spread of socialist and communist social models inside Europe.

For the Cardenistas, the Franco uprising symbolized the effort of international fascism to gain control over the Iberian peninsula and to prepare a bridgehead for a future infiltration of Latin America. In particular, President Cárdenas feared that a Franco victory could lead to the development of a Spanish version of fascism, that could attract the yearning of Latin American *hispanistas*. To make matters worse, the expansion of fascist states would only invite U.S. intervention, threatening to end the Good Neighbor policy and U.S. governmental respect for Mexican national and territorial sovereignty.[79] By 1936 the front line in the struggle between Mexican conservatives and liberals had been relocated to the battle fields of the Spanish Civil War.

In the following months, Cárdenas, urged by his advisor Isidro Fabela, made Mexico the only country, besides the Soviet Union, that actively supported the Spanish Republicans with arms.[80] In addition, the Mexican administration used the forum of the League of Nations to defend the Republic of Spain and to challenge the major democratic European powers to abandon their disastrous "neutrality" stance vis-à-vis the Spanish conflict.[81] Regardless, Mexico would challenge the weak behavior of great powers against fascism.[82]

Possible strategic consequences of the spread of fascist governments in Europe and Asia had been contemplated by Mexican planners since the early 1930s. Ever since Japan's invasion of China in 1931, Mexican military planners had examined Mexico's strategic vulnerability as a neighbor of the United States. In 1934, Mexican planners decided that a future U.S.–Japanese confrontation in the Pacific was unavoidable. Even worse, it was feared that Mexico would be asked to enter into an alliance with the United States. Due to its geographic location, Mexico could not refuse the request and would be caught in a conflict between the United States and a fascist power. The stakes rose higher when the Japanese stationed both a naval and a military attaché in Mexico. Not even the United States had such a military presence in Mexico. Mexicans had already encountered unidentified ships in Mexican waters, thought to be Japanese ships surveying Mexico's coast. As a consequence, in 1936, the Mexican military fortified the harbor of Acapulco, "presumably with a view to rendering it less liable to a coup de main on the part of the Japanese either just before, or simultaneously with the outbreak of hostilities between Japan and the U.S."[83] When Japan signed the Anti-Communist Pact in 1936, the Mexican ambassador to Tokyo, General Candido Águilar,[84] warned Cárdenas to be careful lest the events in Japan reproduce themselves inside Mexico.[85] Like Spain, Japan was becoming a country where the military was getting out of civilian control and infusing domestic politics with fascist ideas.[86]

These warnings were justified. In Mexico, the attraction of Franco's movement was felt immediately. Three months after the outbreak of the civil war, the influential Mexican veteran's organization Unión de Veteranos approached Undersecretary of Hacienda Eduardo Villaseñor and asked for his support to create a Mexican fascist movement. Pointing to Spain, the group argued that only a fascist movement, leading to the creation of a fascist state, could prevent "Mexican communists and foreigners" from destroying Mexico in a civil war.[87]

Whereas the Unión de Veteranos was still politely petitioning for a Mexican fascist movement, another organization, the Camisas Doradas, was already actively creating violent skirmishes in Mexico. It was lead by ex-Villista General Nicolas R. Rodríguez, who reemerged on the national political scene during the Escobar rebellion in 1927. Later he had founded the Camisas Verdes, who congregated under the simplistic nationalist motto of "Mexico for Mexicans." It attacked unions and their striking members. During the early years of the Cárdenas administration, he created the Camisas Doradas, the Gold Shirts, and added anti-Semitism and anticommunism to the group's ideology, and now worked to prevent the "sovietization" of Mexican society. The growing urban discontent of these years offered an ideal opportunity for Rodríguez to expand his following from rural to urban areas. After 1935, the number of Gold Shirt attacks on striking union members increased.[88] As Ricardo Pérez Montfort has shown, the Camisas Doradas soon gained increasing popular support among alienated small shop owners and small property farmers. When, in 1936, President Cárdenas had to intervene personally in a strike in Monterrey, Rodríguez chose the city to gain support among Mexican entrepreneurs. Following Cárdenas's visit to Monterrey, he received five thousand pesos from local businessmen, which enabled him to open a recruiting office in the city. Eventually it failed, however, due to Rodríguez's lack of organizational skill. The business people stopped their financial support when they saw that Rodríguez failed to stop union activity.[89] Next, Rodríguez focused on Mexico City. Finally, when Camisas Doradas and union members clashed on the Zócalo in Mexico City, the Cárdenas administration banned the organization. And as in the case of Calles, U.S. Ambassador Daniels supported Cárdenas's wish to exile Rodríguez to the United States and thus effectively remove him from Mexican politics.[90]

In 1937, Franco and his followers founded the organization Falange. It began an organized outreach into Latin America, to recruit followers among *hispanistas* and to present Franco's efforts in a more positive light. In Mexico, they were immediately successful. The organization Unión de Clase Media sought affiliation with Franco's organization in Spain.[91] Many other individuals abandoned their previous sympathy for Mussolini's brand of fascism and switched to Franco. In retaliation, Cárdenas ordered on March 22, 1937, all Mexican embassies to provide full support for Republican Spain.[92] Mexico increased its arms support and offered asylum to Spanish diplomats who backed the Republican camp. In the following years, the Spanish Civil War would continue to have a significant influence on Mexican political debates. With the slowly emerging victory of Franco's forces, the attraction of European fascism in Mexico only grew.

Mexico's relationship with the Soviet Union was marked by political ambivalence. Ever since the Bolshevik Revolution of 1917, Mexican politicians had jealously guarded the authenticity and legitimacy of their Mexican Revolution. Nevertheless, the two young revolutionary states entered into diplomatic relations in the early 1920s. Toward the end of that decade, the Mexican revolutionary nomenclature was increasingly worried about the possibility of the Soviet Union increasing its activities in Mexico in order to advance the Soviet fight against the imperialistic United States. By 1927, Mexican–Soviet relations were becoming publicly strained. In Moscow, the work of Mexico's ambassador to the Soviet Union, Jesus Silva Herzog, was made increasingly difficult because of his continuous surveillance by the Soviet secret service. In the same year, the Mexican administration publicly backed the Kellogg-Briand Pact, which demanded that the Soviet Union and China solve their political problems through peaceful means. In reaction, Stalin's administration branded Mexico publicly as an instrument of bourgeois and U.S. imperialism. The official relationship ended after an alleged Soviet document surfaced in Mexico ordering Soviet secret agents to engage in propaganda in Mexico with the goal of fabricating a coup. This coup, it was hoped, would interrupt oil production in Mexico and upset production in the United States. The Mexican Portes Gil administration was glad to find a reason to end the difficult diplomatic relationship, and it suspended Mexican–Soviet diplomatic relations.[93] Since no economic relationship existed between the two states, this step ended all official Mexican–Soviet relations until 1933. Shortly before Cárdenas came to power, Mexican and Soviet diplomats explored possibilities of renewing diplomatic ties. In Warsaw,

Poland, far out of sight of the Mexican public, Mexican and Soviet representatives discussed terms for a renewal of relations.

From the Mexican side, the key issue was the nature of future Soviet activity inside Mexico. Mexican Foreign Ministry professionals demanded that the USSR abstain from spreading propaganda in Mexico, just as the USA had been asked to. A final decision, however, was postponed until Cárdenas took office.[94] The young Cárdenas administration chose to wait.

Indirectly, however, USSR policies continued to influence the Mexican domestic political scene. Moscow's most significant indirect influence on Mexico came through the Popular Front policy. In 1935, at the Seventh Congress of the Comintern in Moscow, the Communist party's foreign organization followed Stalin's orders to redirect their energies to the defeat of worldwide fascism. The defeat of fascism had become paramount to the Communist party's original goal of achieving world communist revolution.

The central tool in this new strategy was the creation of so-called Popular Fronts. These political coalitions joined communist, bourgeois, and social democratic parties in a national alliance.

Soon after the Moscow conference, the Mexican Communist Party (PCM) president, Hernan Laborde, announced the new course to the Mexican Communist Party. Whereas the party had previously opposed Cárdenas's policies "as a policy of alliance and submission to imperialism,"[95] Laborde now issued the call for

> a united front with the followers of President Cárdenas who were in the *Partido Nacional Revolucionario* (PNR) with the hope that once the government party had been cleansed of "reactionary" elements, the United Front could be extended to the PNR as a whole.[96]

Compared to similar efforts in France and Chile, however, the Popular Front tactics in Mexico remained ineffective. As Robert Scott pointed out, the concept of the Popular Front had been designed as a political device for countries with an existing institutionalized multiparty system and therefore did not fit into the Mexican institutionalized revolutionary context. In addition, the party leadership around Laborde lacked a clear-cut policy during the early years of the Popular Front era.[97] At the same time, Cárdenas himself tried to reorganize the Mexican political system into a state-controlled alliance. His reorganization of the PNR into a party of workers, peasants, military personnel, and professionals constituted the formation of a genuine Mexican front in its own right.[98] The Popular Front tactic in Mexico received its death sentence in 1936, when Cárdenas offered political asylum to Stalin's arch rival Trotsky. Immediately, the move split the Mexican political left "between the Communist Party of Mexico and its allies in the

Confederación de Trabajadores Mexicanos (CTM) on one side and Trotsky, some communist dissidents and anti-Stalinist Marxists on the other side."[99] A nationwide Mexican leftist coalition was now unthinkable.

Nevertheless, the Cárdenas administration experienced some unexpected benefits from the Popular Front–era policies. The PCM's support of the newly founded CTM helped to bind Mexican labor to the Mexican state as never before. Later, during the Saturnino Cedillo rebellion, the Communist party backed the Cárdenas administration against conservatives. Moreover, through the CTM, the Communist party became Cárdenas's most committed supporter of his anti-Franco policy. As Donaldson emphasized, this support was "not just words, but the *CTM* held loyalty demonstrations all over the country."[100] This cooperation also extended into the League of Nations, where the Soviet Union and Mexico were the only countries to actively support Republican Spain with weapons and other resources.

A final word about the alleged subversive influence of the Soviet Union in Mexico during the 1930s. Soviet orders played a role in the activities of Mexico's Communist party and parts of the Mexican labor movement, but in hindsight it is obvious that the role of the Comintern in Mexico, as a major subversive threat to Mexico's internal security, has been exaggerated. Compared to the large number of conservatives in Mexico, who spread their views through a well-established network of Catholic circles in the rural sector, the challenge from the left to the Mexican state always remained uncoordinated and small. This was confirmed by Manuel Caballero and Barry Carr, whose research shows the absence of any real Moscow-directed communist attempt that could have subverted the Cárdenas or the Avila Camacho governments.[101] During the entire period, the Mexican revolutionary state defended its power monopoly successfully and kept the Mexican left weak and split. Political activity inside Mexico in the 1930s could not escape the jealous eyes of the Mexican revolutionary nomenclature.

4
1937
The Watershed of Cardenismo

MANY OF THE ARRANGEMENTS DESCRIBED IN THE PREVIOUS TWO CHAPTERS were called into question in 1937. Through an accelerating interplay of domestic and foreign forces, bureaucratic policy professionals and the Mexican president were forced to delay long-term development policies in favor of short-term steps. Whereas "experimentation" had been the central paradigm for the period between 1934 and 1936, by the end of 1937 the new central theme would be "survival." The crisis and challenge to the system was so strong that it ushered in the conservatism of the second half of Cardenismo.

The string of events began on December 8, 1936. On that day, in the Laguna district of northern Mexico, Lázaro Cárdenas officiated over the expropriation and redistribution of this mostly foreign-owned cotton-growing area. The step was part of a government-sponsored *ejido* program that would further integrate Mexico's rural sector into the state-controlled capitalistic developmental process. Inadvertantly, the administration had embarked on a course that would lead the Mexican government to the brink of bankruptcy within twelve months and, consequently, threaten to erode Cardenismo's political support. In the aftermath of the collapse of Cardenismo, a Mexican version of the Spanish Civil War could erupt, transforming the country into a battlefield for the fight between a majority of pro-Franco *hispanistas* and a much smaller, but committed Mexican left. Just as during the Mexican Revolution and on the eve of World War I, by December 1937 it appeared possible that soon a domestic Mexican conflict would offer itself again for external manipulation.

At the time of the *ejido* creation, the peasants of the Laguna region had no capital to finance the planting of their first crop or to purchase the modern technology necessary for success in export agribusiness. Private Mexican investors refused to sponsor governmental expropriations financially. Foreign investors were waiting for Mexico to resume payment on its external debt before they would pump any new money into Mexico. Therefore, Mexico's Minister of Hacienda Suárez stepped in and created the capital artificially through a forced seventy-million-peso loan on the Bank of Mexico.

Suárez expected to earn enough money from a forecasted fall cotton harvest of 150,000 to 175,000 bales to pay back the loan by the end of the year. The loan would appear on the books as a mere short-term financial transaction. The risky forced loan would not be carried into 1938. In the meantime, this investment would get the Laguna project off the ground and, it was hoped, would prove critics of Cárdenas's *ejido* program wrong.

As expected, the infusion of seventy million pesos into the national money supply created an immediate, mild inflationary trend. After years of relative price stability, the average Mexican experienced significant price increases for domestic products and goods.

World commodity prices fell at the same time. The widening gap between foreign and domestic prices encouraged imports into Mexico, thus hurting Mexico's domestic industry. Minister Suárez countered this trend with a 26 percent tariff increase on January 18, 1937. Hopefully, it would increase domestic purchases which, in turn, would lower domestic prices.

The Mexican Ministry of National Economy backed this measure by instituting state control over the distribution of food staples. The goal was to reduce speculation and price gouging. Also, warehouse loans were cancelled, forcing the liquidation of national storages and lowering prices by increasing supply. The import of corn was contemplated for regions with serious food shortages.[1]

During the first three months of 1937, this economic balancing act worked. Wholesale and retail sales reached new high levels, and prospects appeared favorable for the immediate future. Domestic large industries operated at near capacity, employment remained steady, demand was increasing, and stocks were normal. Ironically, the increased money supply provided a stimulus for the national industry and, as expected, the higher tariff increased small industrial production. In particular, the continuing large amount of federal, state-sponsored construction was fueling an unprecedented boom in building and allied industries. Even the Bank of Mexico was able to supply the normal demand for dollar exchange without the necessity of exporting gold.

The only blemish on this economically rosy picture remained the rising costs of necessity articles, a cause of occasional public discontent, and short strikes. But in March 1937 this issue was still seen as a minor problem.

By April 1937, in addition to the *ejido* program, the Cárdenas administration was involved in a large number of infrastructure projects that rivaled the developmental efforts of the Porfiriato. For example, the administration was working on a highway that connected Mexico City with

Nogales at the U.S. border, a highway that connected Mexico with Guatemala, a railroad linking Lower California with the United States and the rest of Mexico, and a railway line through Chiapas. Nationwide, the government financed three large irrigation projects in land reform areas, and one fertilizer plant in San Luis Potosí. Three dams were under construction to generate electricity for Mexico's industry. The government also made significant efforts to accelerate the expansion of a state-owned petroleum industry through the newly founded Petroleum Administration. Finally, it was refurbishing the nation's railroad with seven million dollars worth of railroad equipment.

It is important to realize that for several years into the future the Cárdenas administration had committed a huge amount of federal funds to these long-term projects. Most importantly, returns from these investments depended on their successful and timely completion. Only then would improved linkages between regional, national, and international markets translate into a growing national economy and more tax income for the state.

But no Mexican document of the period considers such implications. Quite the contrary. Government experts assured critics that the pace and cost of state-financed domestic development could be sustained. They pointed proudly at forty million pesos of federal income for March 1937, the largest amount in the history of the republic. Since the government had regular monthly expenditures of 28.2 million pesos, its ability to support ongoing and additional state-funded projects seemed obvious.[2]

Behind the scenes, however, Minister Suárez was searching for future income for the Mexican state. First, he traveled to Washington to ask the U.S. government for future financial support. He presented U.S. Secretary of Treasury Morgenthau with a plan to float Mexican bonds on the U.S. market, since, he stated, the Mexican market could not absorb anymore of them. Most of the money, he promised, would be designated for the improvement of the economy of the Isthmus of Tehuantepec area. The railroad connection over the isthmus, linking the Gulf of Mexico with the Pacific Ocean, would be overhauled to attract freight that was currently passing through the Panama Canal. In addition, he intended to purchase a railroad that would allow direct export of vegetables and cattle from the Mexican Pacific Coast, via El Paso, to U.S. markets.[3] However, Morgenthau remained cautious. Politely but firmly, he denied Suárez's request. To his diary he entrusted the following: "we have helped Mexico enough."

Next, Suárez turned to the British. The Mexican government had been negotiating with the El Águila Oil Company since 1935 over drilling concessions in the Poza Rica region. Although a preliminary agreement was soon reached, President Cárdenas had always refused his final approval. Then, in November 1936, after the creation of Mexico's National Petroleum Administration, Mexico's oil experts had reopened talks with the British. Shortly before May 1937, a new draft agreement was concluded that promised to provide the Mexican government with unprecedented royalties for drilling permits to the British. For example, within ten months, following the official signing of the draft treaty, a royalty of 35 percent would be paid to the Mexican state. In addition, the Mexican government was allowed to drill a certain number of its own wells in the previously British preserve of the Poza Rica oil zone.[4] Within a year, the agreement would have provided the Cárdenas administration with huge amounts of money, which would have allowed a further expansion of state-sponsored development. But the start of the labor conflict between Mexican oil workers and the foreign oil companies made it politically impossible for the Cárdenas administration to sign the promising agreement.

Efforts to find a foreign market for the upcoming *ejido* cotton harvest was another important Mexican activity during early 1937. With the United States experiencing her own severe agricultural crisis, and Great Britain and France protecting their own farmers, the only large European market left that seemed willing to even consider the import of Mexican *ejido* products was Hitler's Germany. Besides, German preference for barter trade suggested that Mexican planners could purchase critical manufactured goods and German technology without the involvement of sparse foreign currency. Not surprisingly, an expansion of German–Mexican economic negotiations took place in the first month of 1937.

In January 1937, upon the occasion of accreditation of the newly appointed German military attaché to Mexico, the German economic attaché Burandt asked for a special audience with President Cárdenas to discuss future German–Mexican economic cooperation. To his complete surprise, he was granted an appointment for the coming week.

President Cárdenas received the German attaché in the privacy of his personal residence, rather than in the public space of the national palace. When Burandt arrived, Cárdenas's private secretary, Licenciado Rodríguez, was absent and presidential adviser Ramón Beteta was asked to leave the room.[5] Still, Cárdenas assured Burandt that there was no need for secrecy since this meeting was "in the interest of the Mexican nation."

After the exchange of a few pleasantries, Burandt turned the discussion to economic issues. He told Cárdenas that Germany was interested in helping Mexico develop its natural resources and its economic infrastructure.

Unlike the United States and Great Britain, which, Burandt argued, were "only trying to hamper Mexican development, Germany had in common with Mexico a struggle for economic independence." Germany and Mexico should complement one another's efforts, trading Mexican raw materials for German industrial goods, and thus avoiding the costly expenditure of foreign currency. In addition, Germany would be willing to import Mexico's agricultural products, to help in the creation of a Mexican rubber industry, and to participate in the reorganization of Mexican mineral production. Burandt also repeated a previous offer for Mexican–German joint ventures in the chemical sector.

Cárdenas was interested in several of these suggestions. First, he mentioned German participation in the creation of a state-controlled small mining sector. Part of this would be a 50 percent German share in the exploration of copper deposits in Baja California. Second, he discussed the state of the ongoing German–Mexican negotiations regarding a joint exploration of the state-owned oil reserves in the Isthmus of Tehuantepec zone. Then Cárdenas told Burandt that he had decided to order a nitrogen plant from the German I. G. Farben company, a crucial component for Mexico's commercial *ejido* agriculture. Bids by British and U.S. competitors had been rejected.

Still, Cárdenas wanted more. He asked for German loans to finance additional government projects. Right away, Burandt interjected that Germany was not in the position to offer currency loans. It could provide only merchandise loans and technology barters. The two men separated with Cárdenas's promise that the ideas they had discussed would be examined in detail by Minister of Hacienda Suárez in the near future.

Indeed, on January, 28, 1937, Minister Suárez followed up and talked again to Burandt about German participation in Mexico's industrialization effort.[6] Accessible Mexican archives do not contain a Ministry of Hacienda study about German–Mexican cooperation. But in the archives of the Ministry of Communication and Infrastructure may be found a detailed memo from the same month that provides us with an in-depth look at Mexican reasoning regarding cooperation with Hitler's Germany.

In this memo, Francisco Múgica, Cárdenas's close friend and Minister for Communication and Infrastructure, agreed with attaché Burandt's suggestion that "the economic structures of Mexico and Germany complement each other in an extraordinary and truly ideal manner."[7] Múgica also pointed out that the Mexican Six-Year Plan could be realized only if Mexico would secure a complementary market for its agricultural and mineral products. Thus, he drew the conclusion that Germany was the

sole country in the world, which, because of its enormous needs for raw materials, could offer such a market and guarantee the total acquisition of the Mexican surplus production.

Next, Múgica cited four reasons for closer Mexican–German cooperation in the future. First, Mexico hoped to free herself from additional financial linkages with the United States; Mexico could use her raw materials and agricultural products to pay for German technology. Second, if Germany would import Mexico's raw material surplus production, Mexico could bypass the constraints of international mineral cartel agreements. Third, Germany was willing to supply much-needed technological know-how and manufactured goods. And finally, Mexican–German cooperation would not translate automatically into a Mexican dependency on Germany. In other words:

> If the presented circumstances are recognized, what could be more logical than the unification of efforts and economic forces of two countries which have never suffered under any collisions of interest for a more extensive and better organized economic collaboration.[8]

This extraordinary document voids any argument that Mexico was dealing economically with Nazi Germany only in the aftermath of the oil expropriation. On the contrary, it suggests that without the oil expropriation German–Mexican economic cooperation would have been far more extensive and diverse, linking the two economies for years to come. The memorandum demonstrates a shrewd calculation by a nationalist member of the Cárdenas administration trying to take advantage of great-power rivalries for the sake of Mexican national development.

Also interesting is the absence of any consideration of political factors in this document. At this time the Spanish Civil War was unfolding, and German–Mexican political relations were becoming chilly due to confrontations between Mexico and Germany on Spanish battlefields. It indicates that Múgica was determined to realize the goals of the Mexican Six-Year Plan at almost any cost. However, this does not mean that he was pro-Germany or even pro–National Socialist. Rather, it displays a Mexican attitude that interpreted the international fight between fascist and democratic powers as an external issue. While Mexico could not avoid it, it could certainly benefit from it.

It is no surprise, then, that throughout the spring of 1937, the exploration of German involvement in Mexican economic development intensified. There were discussions about the acquisition of German electrical generators for a planned federal electrical plant in Ciudad Juárez; the construction, with German help, of a federal paper company in Morelos;[9] and German delivery of the entire rolling stock for a new industrial sugarcane processing plant in Zacatepec/Morelos, including diesel locomotives.[10] In April 1937, the administration considered the involvement of German companies in the buildup of a national electrical organization to supply energy for the growing demands of irrigation and other industrial projects.[11] Even the construction of a German automobile plant in Mexico was discussed.[12]

Also, the Cárdenas administration tried to deepen the Mexican–German economic relationship with diplomatic symbolism. It recalled the Mexican Minister to Berlin, Leonidas Almazán, who had been in charge of Germany, the Netherlands, and Great Britain. He was replaced by the conservative General Juan F. Azcárate, the former chief of staff of Mexican ex-president Rodríguez and former military attaché to Washington. He would serve in Berlin only. Confidentially, Mexican Foreign Minister Hay urged the German government to recognize Azcárate before Mexican "left wing groups could agitate against his nomination."[13]

Indeed, the desired effect was achieved. German Minister Rüdt recommended Azcárate warmly to the German Foreign Ministry as a *"derechista* (right-winger), and as soldier with greatest sympathy for Germany, the *Führer* and the German army."[14] This was mostly wishful thinking. Azcárate was not pro-Nazi, even though he admired the German military machine, an organization that was an exemplar for him as a professional soldier. In particular, the German aviation industry was looking forward to Azcárate's arrival in Berlin,[15] since he had been involved in the operation of Mexican airplane facilities. German airplane manufacturers hoped that his contacts with Mexico's civilian and military aviation would prepare the Mexican market for German aviation products.[16]

In May 1937, Mexican petroleum workers, the elite of Mexico's organized labor, decided to back their demands for higher wages with a strike. From the popular Mexican perspective this strike was not only about wages, but also a symbolic assertion of the power of Mexican workers. The open labor conflict between Mexican workers and the British, Dutch, and U.S. oil companies had a symbolic political value that went far beyond the boundaries of the oil industry itself. This sentiment was reenforced by the hostile, uncompromising behavior of foreign oil companies in the early days of the strike. It reminded Mexican economic planners and citizens alike of the continuing limits of Mexican economic development. The labor conflict opened a wound in the national consciousness that had been closed only superficially in the aftermath of the Calles-Morrow agreement of 1928.[17]

In contrast, the boards of the foreign oil companies cared little about their operations in Mexico. During the last decade, Mexican petroleum had lost its preeminence to Venezuelan reserves. Venezuelan oil was less heavy, easier to refine, and excellent for the engines of European and U.S. automobiles and airplanes. Not surprisingly, foreign companies had invested little in exploration or in facility maintenance of Mexico's petroleum sector in the years before the strike. For them, the oil-worker strike became an opportunity to show other petroleum-producing countries that economic nationalism would not succeed in taking over the riches of multinational companies. For Shell and Standard Oil, the importance of Mexico's petroleum sector rested in its political symbolism, not in its economic potential. British and U.S. managers combined corporate arrogance with financial strength and categorically rejected the demands of the Mexican workers. The petroleum strike became a matter of principle.

For the Cárdenas administration, the strike was an unwelcome dilemma. If the government were to back the workers directly, it could antagonize U.S. foreign capital in the Mexican mining sector that generated most of Mexico's tax income, thus further undermining the fiscal foundations of the state's developmental policy. If it did not intervene on behalf of the oil workers, it would lose the political support of Mexico's organized labor and political left, a critical pillar of Cardenismo support. Besides, if the Cárdenas administration allowed the nation's pride to be damaged it could no longer use nationalism as an effective political tool.

Before these issues could be solved, the economy reacted. National wholesale and retail prices accelerated their rise, and the purchasing power of the average Mexican continued to drop.[18] Overnight, the public economic optimism was replaced by a sense of uncertainty. Panic purchases took place and hoarding increased. In the petroleum-producing areas themselves, the situation was worse. Since the petroleum workers were not earning wages, business plummeted in these normally very healthy zones of economic activity. The sense of uncertainty was exacerbated by a shortage of railroad cars that caused food shortages in several areas of the country. Finally, the Laguna district was hit by bad weather and insect infestation. Updated forecasts indicated that the upcoming *ejido* cotton harvest would fall far behind the original estimates. Immediately, critics of the Mexican administration accused the Cardenas administration of economic incompetence.

Then suddenly, two weeks into the oil petroleum strike, on June 7, 1937, the immediate crisis seemed to reach an end. Both sides agreed to end public escalation and to move their disputes into court. Nonetheless, the Mexican economy refused to bounce back to prestrike momentum.

Despite these serious problems, Minister of Hacienda Suárez and his planners continued their economic course. In June 1937, Mexico's railway system was expropriated by the government. Few people could see that this was an attempt to merge a foreign-owned rail system with a new and expanding national road system, to form an infrastructure that would serve Mexico's national economic needs. For most contemporaries, it was a political move in favor of organized labor. In the paranoid mood of these weeks, some voices mentioned the fear that the Cárdenas administration had begun to expropriate systematically all vital economic sectors of the Mexican economy. Perhaps, it was feared, the Mexican government was turning communist.

Next, the Cárdenas administration intervened in Mexico's fledgling rayon industry to end a chaotic supply situation. By imposing state control on rayon prices, both import and export prices, the Cárdenas administration intended to increase employment in this troubled sector. Once again, the step was interpreted politically, enforcing communist phobias in business circles. Then, at the end of July 1937, Cárdenas left for Yucatán, Chiapas, and Campeche to continue the government's redistribution of agricultural property, in spite of the bad news from the Laguna district. More than ever, the Cárdenas administration needed reliable future income to finance these economic projects and their workers.

Another effort was launched to earn for the Mexican government administration new income. On June 26, 1937, former Minister of Hacienda Eduardo Pani spent almost the entire day at the Mexican national palace, discussing with President Cárdenas a plan to create an independent company that would help the Mexican General Petroleum Administration both to refine its crude oil and to organize the export of the Mexican refined petroleum products. It would provide Mexico with the opportunity to refine its petroleum reserves at home, thus eliminating U.S. and British middlemen. The proposal included the construction of three refineries. Furthermore, Mexico would purchase a merchant fleet that would allow her to market petroleum products independently from the world tanker fleet, most of which was controlled by the seven world oil companies.[19]

By early August, the idea had matured into a draft treaty. The entire production of the Mexican General Petroleum Administration would be sold, at 10 percent below market price, to a private company called Centramer, which would be incorporated with Mexican private capital in London. President Cárdenas gave his approval at the end of the month.[20]

From the very beginning, the key obstacle to this plan remained financing. The Bank of Mexico, while "involved," refused to commit any new funds, which was hardly surprising during this time of financial crisis.[21] Minister Suárez then revealed the existence of thirty-five million ounces of Mexican silver in the Federal Reserve Bank of Kansas. He offered the silver as collateral to U.S. banks.[22] These banks, probably influenced by U.S. oil companies, refused. Also, in London the Centramer plan encountered stiff opposition. El Águila's powerful British mother company, Shell, informed prospective lenders in London's financial market about its displeasure concerning the creation of alternative processing and shipping facilities for Mexican oil. Eventually, all interest on the part of British commercial lenders fizzled. They were in no mood to trade their established, profitable cooperation with Shell for that of a yet unincorporated Mexican company with a lack of financing.

Next, Minister Suárez tried to sweeten the offer. He called the British consul in Mexico City and promised that Mexico would give all of its shipbuilding orders to British companies, providing much-needed employment for the depressed British shipbuilding industry. In addition, he offered the British new drilling rights in the established production area of Panuco.[23] Still, nobody moved in London.[24]

German–Mexican efforts to bring the Tehuantepec oil-region deposits into production and generate revenue had to be postponed. On August 27, 1937, German Minister Rüdt told the Mexicans that, in principle, Berlin had approved the deal. However, he asked for some additional time to consult with a geologist who was to be sent to Mexico.[25] In other words, in the near future, Tehuantepec oil would not be available to earn income for the government.[26]

Within this context the legal outcome of the petroleum strike took on supreme importance. For Mexican businessmen and foreign investors alike, the administration's interventions in domestic industries suggested that, for the immediate future, their decisions should be governed by caution, not by entrepreneurial risk taking. Mexico's private domestic economic sector took a wait-and-see attitude toward the Cárdenas administration. In the coming months their assets would not contribute to a revival of the declining Mexican economy.

For the general Mexican public, continuing price increases indicated that something was seriously wrong with Cárdenas's economic course. Over the previous eight years, prices had increased a total of 16 percent. From May to July alone, they had climbed 4 percent.[27] The petroleum strike also affected the Mexican capital. Occasional fuel shortages slowed down production and delivery of goods in the Federal District, pushing prices up even more. Consumers reacted by postponing purchases of daily necessities for the first time in a decade. Increasingly, psychological factors—fear, worry, confusion—influenced Mexico's economy as much as macroeconomic factors.[28]

During September 1937, fuel shortages in the Federal District caused industries to convert their power plants to using coal or wood. Others reduced their operation to the available supply of petroleum fuel. Mexico's cement industry produced at only 55 percent of normal production.[29] In the oil-producing regions, merchants stopped ordering wholesale goods, depleting their existing stocks.

Then the foreign oil companies decided to move their capital reserves from Mexico to banks abroad. Until access to company records is granted, it will remain unclear whether this was a deliberate move to increase pressure on the Cárdenas administration or a legitimate precautionary move designed to protect company assets against a surprise expropriation.[30] To contemporary observers and to President Cárdenas himself, however, the capital transfer was interpreted as a declaration of war on the Mexican government and the Mexican economy.

To make matters worse, other foreign and Mexican private investors followed suit. For the first time during the Cárdenas administration, a serious capital flight began, pressuring the foreign currency reserves of the Bank of Mexico. Suddenly, Mexican private banks decided to take a wait-and-see attitude. New credit applications were examined with the greatest care and reservation. Many merchants understood the message and ran for safe ground, calling in outstanding accounts and loans.[31] By the end of September 1937, Mexico's economic barometer dropped from "uncertain" to "negative."

Suárez and his advisers had tried to buy time by borrowing more funds from the Bank of Mexico. The Mexican government's overdraft from the Bank of Mexico was increased from 80 to 102 million pesos. While this does not seem very much money to us today, in the 1930s the capitalist planners thought they had reached the limit of responsible government borrowing. Inexperienced with the fairly new tool of deficit spending, they also remained committed to balancing the Mexican budget by the end of the year. The small circle of Mexican bankers and financial experts warned the Cárdenas administration not to undertake more debt.[32] Minister of Hacienda Suárez was impressed by the warnings. In strictest confidence he admitted to his predecessor, Pani,

> the very difficult present financial situation of the government . . . he had to find 20 million pesos before the end of year to balance the budget.[33]

Soon Suárez's central problem would be lack of funds to keep alive state infrastructure and administration work projects. The end of government funds would halt the progress of the projects and cause unemployment that would be attributed to the shortcomings of Cardenismo. To make matters worse, with each takeover of a fledgling industrial sector, the government's financial obligations increased while its assets shrank. Within weeks, the central question was who was willing to provide new funds for the government's infrastructure projects and the contractors and workers employed by them?

By November 1937, the administration's financial situation was bleak. Domestic, U.S., and British investors refused to provide the Mexican government with new financing. The money-producing oil sector was caught up in the labor dispute in Mexican courts. The Mexican mining sector, the other major tax producer for Mexico's government, was firmly in the hands of U.S. investors. Any attack on this sector would be suicidal. Most likely, it would create a united front between U.S. and British oil and mining companies, an alliance powerful enough to neutralize President Roosevelt's pro-Mexico stance of the good neighbor. From there, it would be only a short way to a right-wing coup to end the Cárdenas presidency.

The Bank of Mexico and Mexico's private bankers refused to provide Suárez with any new funds. Suárez and his president were facing months during which the Mexican economy could spiral further out of control. Already, economic and social crisis was leading to an ever-growing number of right-wing protests. Many of them, it seemed, were backed by malevolent foreign interests.

Here it may be beneficial to interrupt the narrative of the economic crisis of 1937 and provide a short excursion into the mushrooming rural and urban opposition to Cardenismo during 1937. Not surprisingly, with the beginning of the oil strike in May 1937 the number as well as the seriousness of opposition movements to Cárdenas increased. Of particular concern to political insiders and foreign observers were the growing connections between these movements and fascist groups in Germany and Spain. Once we add the political activities of these groups to the expanding economic anxieties of the second half of 1937, the steadily increasing sense of danger felt by the Cárdenas administration becomes clearer.

In Mexico's rural areas of the Southwest, the Unión Nacional Sinarquista was becoming the most formidable challenge to Cardenismo.[34] Officially, it had been founded May 23, 1937, in the city of León by a group of young middle-class professionals. Unofficially, this group was only the visible part of a larger, secret organization. The states with the greatest numbers of

Sinarquistas were Guanajuato, Michoacán, Jalisco, Puebla, San Luis Potosí, Querétaro, and the Federal District itself. It was a class coalition of rural participants as base and middle-class individuals as leaders.[35]

Initially called Las Legiones and later La Base, it had emerged in 1934 in response to the anticlerical policy of the Calles administration. At first its program was ideologically incoherent, focusing among other things on the reestablishment of religious freedoms that had been lost during the Cristero rebellion.

Then Cárdenas's leftist social and agrarian policies provided the Sinarquistas with a new antigovernmental focus. They targeted peasants and small property owners who had been left out of the government's land redistribution program. Soon Sinarquista rhetoric condemned the *ejido* program as an imperfect form of landownership. Instead, it advocated the creation of a Sinarquista state, which would give complete ownership to all farmers. Hellmuth O. Schreiter, a German immigrant, had been present at the official founding in 1937. Contemporary observers feared that he was a Nazi agent and transmitted the desires of the German legation to the Sinarquistas. The evidence, however, shows that Schreiter was not that important. Rather, he functioned as a go-between with little influence.[36]

Another powerful rural challenger of Cardenismo was San Luis Potosí's caudillo, Saturnino Cedillo. The Germans had appreciated Cedillo as a conservative restraint inside the Cárdenas cabinet. Until Cedillo's cabinet resignation in the fall of 1937, German Minister Rüdt had tried to use Cedillo as a pro-German influence, but with little success. Still, Rüdt received from Cedillo hints, at least, about the caudillo's political plans. For example, after a breakfast meeting at the German legation, on February 23, 1937, the German Minister reported to Berlin that Cedillo was trying to counter Cárdenas's radical leftist measures, adding that "it seems not impossible that, under certain circumstances, (Cedillo) might preempt (Cárdenas's) measures also with anti-constitutional measures."[37] Five months later, in a personal conversation with Cedillo's adviser, Ernst von Merck, Minister Rüdt was warned to take his family outside the country because of an expected uprising of pro-Calles forces.[38] Neither the surveillance records in the Múgica Archive nor documents in German archives prove, or even indicate, that any German ministry played a role in these plans.[39]

Cedillo himself was a pragmatist and invited support from anybody who could provide it in the most direct and effective way, regardless of ideological affiliation. This was also true for Ernst von Merck, Cedillo's naturalized ex-German adviser. Like his Mexican boss, von Merck knocked on the doors of the German legation, as well as on those of the U.S. embassy, depending on what appeared more promising at a given moment.

However, Cedillo was best received in the U.S. business community. In an autobiographical sketch for U.S. Ambassador Daniels, an embassy employee admitted that Cárdenas's policies

> lead many American business men to encourage the Governor of San Luis Potosí in his revolutionary ambitions and Mexican army officers who where friendly to Cedillo would drop by at the embassy to inquire confidentially whether the U.S. would open the border to the passage of arms, if the Mexican government expropriated the oil companies. As the United States is practically the sole source of arms and ammunition in Central America and Mexico, it is true, in a sense, that every revolution starts "over the border."[40]

Certainly, Daniels's efforts assured that U.S. government forces would refrain from supporting Cedillo. But he did not control the U.S. business community in Mexico. Before the expropriation, well-connected U.S. businessmen had fed officers of the U.S. embassy positive assessments of Cedillo's "anti-communist" efforts.[41] A U.S. military report stated that, in December of 1937, Cedillo approached U.S. and British oil companies and inquired how much backing he could expect from them in case he chose to lead an armed movement against the Cárdenas regime. Cedillo assured the companies that he could count on the support of Governor Yocupicio of Sonora and Governor Marte R. Gomez of Tamaulipas.[42] It is not known whether, or what, the companies replied. Later, in England, internal Shell inquiries led to the conclusion that Cedillo had not received any money from the British oil company.[43]

In the fall of 1937 Cedillo resigned from the Cárdenas cabinet in the middle of the economic crisis and went to San Luis Potosí to organize his rural followers. Immediately, many conservative Mexicans hoped Cedillo would be someone who could stop Mexico's drift to the political left. Indeed, at that time, Cedillo and his supporters were actively plotting an armed uprising against Cárdenas. The Mexican government kept extremely close surveillance on Cedillo. Minister of Communication and Infrastructure Múgica personally coordinated an extensive surveillance campaign against Cedillo, which proved to be the key to his later defeat.[44]

There were other important regional caudillos who had sent clear signs of opposition to Cárdenas during 1937. Ex-president Abelardo Rodríguez, after returning from an extended stay in Europe, refused Cárdenas's invitation to serve as Minister of War.[45] He did not want to be associated with the current administration. Andreu Almazán, the caudillo of the state of Nuevo León, also returned from an extended European trip in July 1937, and at a welcome-back reception he expressed himself openly as an admirer of General Franco.[46]

In this context, we also need to mention ex-president Calles, who conspired from his California exile against Cárdenas.In 1936, Standard Oil and Shell had tried to return Plutarco Elías Calles to the Presidential Palace.[47] But U.S. Ambassador Daniels's refusal to back the conspiracy had protected Cárdenas. Calles also had a German business partner, Alexander Holste, who, on occasion, kept in touch with the German legation. However, the sources show that the Germans did not find Calles influential as long as he remained in California.[48]

The year 1937 also saw the mushrooming of urban opposition to Cárdenas. Of great influence was the national veterans' organization, Unión de Veteranos de la Revolución. Political observers of the era interpreted veterans' agitation as an expression of the feeling of Mexico's standing-army members. At the beginning of the oil-worker strike, the organization published a strong anti-Cárdenas statement in the national newspaper *El Universal,* drawing significant public attention.[49] From then on, the organization sought more direct support of the German legation in Mexico City, but received only tacit backing. Then, in the fall of 1937, when the German legation and the Falange came under repeated attack by the Mexican political left, the Unión offered unsolicited support to the German legation. One letter assured German Minister Rüdt that "even today, important circles of the country hold on to the old respect and friendship to Germany."[50]

The Asociación Española Anti Comunista y Anti Judía had been founded in November 1936, by ex-generals Daniel Rios Zertuche and Gabino Vizcarra Campos. The group counted twenty militant members.[51] In May of 1937, this organization sent a letter to Franco assuring him that the Spanish community in Mexico was 90 percent pro-Franco.[52] Soon it merged with a second pro-Spanish organization, the Liga de Hispanidád Iberoamericana, forming a larger umbrella organization called the Falange Española Tradicionalista.[53]

The Falange's foreign branch organization had been created in Spain in 1937. Its official purpose was to organize all Spanish descendants living abroad in support of Franco and his policies.[54] In Mexico, the organization opened an office of information for "espanoles" in order "to reconnect them with the Spanish motherland." Functioning as an *oficina de trabajo,* it also organized pro-Franco social functions for the Mexican Spanish community. Its Mexican leader was Augusto Ibañez Serrano,[55] but the real control came from Franco's own organization in Spain.[56] The Falange began its propaganda work against Cárdenas in September 1937, when the economic crisis became serious.[57] The organization also had established contact with the Unión Veteranos de la Revolución and a third group called Confederación de la Clase Media.[58]

The Confederación de la Clase Media[59] united small investors and businessmen with Spanish ancestry. The group had been founded on June 21, 1936.[60] Soon it represented a committed corps of fifteen individuals and forty supporters who used Mexico City newspapers to attack Cárdenas's social and economic policy. Their rallying cry was to unite against Cárdenas's "communism."

We also need to mention the Partido Nacional Socialista Mexicana, which emerged in the sources for the first time in 1937 in southwestern Mexico.[61] The extremely scarce source material allows only the educated guess that it seems to have been an exclusive urban fascist party, organized along the example of the German NSDAP. There is evidence that it later had contacts with the Sinarquista movement.[62]

In January of 1937, an Ejército Patriota Liberal had approached the German consul in Mazatlán and asked for airplanes and ammunition for a revolt. It was to be delivered by submarine in order "to help fighting Jews and Bolschewists." It claimed to have asked for support from Japan and Spain as well.[63] Germany never reacted. After that it disappeared from the sources.

Finally, the Camisas Doradas, the famous Gold Shirt organization, and its leader, Nicolás Rodríguez, had enjoyed contacts with German press attaché Dietrich before his departure to Spain. According to Alicia Gojman de Backal, Rodríguez's agitation against Jews and communists had been encouraged by the German legation. Dietrich had also designated the World War I German Military Attache to Mexico, Krumheller, as liaison for the organization.[64] However, this connection must have been arranged by the NSDAP in Berlin directly through the mail, since Krumheller no longer resided in Mexico at that time.[65]

The Cárdenas administration took these organizations very seriously. It had eliminated the threat of Rodríguez by exiling him to the United States in 1936. Calles's potential machinations had been neutralized by U.S. Ambassador Daniels's support. The Mexican Ministry of Gobernación searched the headquarters of the Unión de Veteranos and of the Confederación de la Clase Media. (The archives of the Ministry of Gobernación, it bears pointing out, do not contain information on the results of these searches.) Then Cárdenas publicly called on the Ministry of Gobernación to halt its investigation,[66] assuring the public that "no subversive activity could threaten the state." Most likely, Cárdenas did not want to further challenge the influential veterans' organization in public.

Today, benefiting from a perspective of more than sixty years, we can state that during 1937 most foreign subversive activities within Mexico were still limited to overt propaganda activities. During this year German policy toward Mexico's conservative opposition to Cárdenas remained to establish contact, but not to support violent uprisings.

This policy was based on three arguments. First, for the German Navy and the German Economic Ministry, the positive development of Mexican–German oil negotiations during 1937 suggested a pro-Cárdenas attitude. A destabilization of the current government would probably eliminate German chances to establish a much-needed oil base in Mexico. Second, Mexico's anti-Cárdenas forces were also supported by U.S. and British oil industries, who wanted to keep German influence out of the Mexican oil sector. German Minister Rüdt explained this catch-22 in a memorandum to Berlin, shortly before the start of the Cedillo rebellion:

> On the one hand, we would welcome a movement against leftist radical and even communist extremes that aimed at toppling the present government which repeatedly had been predicted during the previous year. On the other hand, it is to be feared that such efforts are backed by interests which would work toward strengthening the North American influence. It would replace Mexican disorder and chaos, which at least economically has not been negative for us, with American order and silence. At the least the next goal of these forces would be to make life for German competition more difficult, yes, even push it out of the market. Therefore we can support a toppling of the government only with great hesitation.[67]

Third, the German hesitation was reenforced by negative fallout following the discovery of secret German support for opposition groups in South America. German agitation and conspiracies in Argentina, Brazil, and Chile had fueled fears within Latin American governments that subversion was indeed a primary German activity in the Western Hemisphere. Eventually, in May 1938, the head of the foreign office of the NSDAP, Bohle, ordered German NSDAP party branches in Latin America to limit themselves to working inside German ethnic communities.[68] German Minister Rüdt shared this sentiment. When Nazi organizations in Berlin tried to supply Mexican organizations with propaganda through the mail, Rüdt ordered Berlin's NSDAP, by letter, to stop these efforts. Rüdt warned that these activities "would only be misunderstood by the left, besides propaganda works only if done in large style organized by this local legation."[69]

But from within the crisis of 1937 this was not at all discernable. On the contrary, contemporary observers registered great concern that Axis representatives were beginning to coordinate their operations in Mexico. For example, German Minister Rüdt was seen with visiting representatives of the Spanish Falange,[70] and Mexican Falange branch leader Serrano Ibañez was a frequent guest at the German legation.[71] Germans and Japanese also seemed to have established some connections after the signing of the Anti-Comintern pact.[72] If the Cárdenas administration did not succeed in turning the economic crisis around, domestic opposition forces seemed to have found powerful foreign contacts in Germany and Spain, who could be willing to use the crisis for their own objectives. Even if they did not actively topple the Mexican administration, the mere impression of a foreign fascist-supported Mexican movement could mean the sudden end of the pro-Cárdenas United States Good Neighbor policy. Perhaps it would convince some members of the U.S. Congress to once again renew the call for an armed invasion of Mexico. Conceivably, it could become reality under the more benevolent disguise of an intervention in defense of Mexico against foreign fascist intervention. We can now continue with an analysis of the events during the final two months of the economic crisis of 1937.

By November 1937 the Centramer plan from the summer of 1937 had failed. German–Mexican negotiations had not yet produced a signed treaty and the legal battle of Mexico's petroleum workers was unresolved. The Laguna cotton harvest had been disappointing, leaving a huge, permanent hole in the accounts of the Bank of Mexico. Mexico's economy was contracting, and revenue for the state was declining. If this trend continued, the Cárdenas administration would run out of money soon. In November, some observers suggested that the question was not if, but when.

Against this background, the economic professional, Minister Suárez, and the economic nationalist, Lázaro Cárdenas, decided that they had to do the unthinkable and enter into even deeper cooperation with the despised Shell daughter, El Águila, as well as ask the U.S. Treasury for financial help.

On November 12, 1937, Cárdenas announced that he was willing to sign the El Águila draft treaty, which he had refused to sign in 1935 and again in April 1937. Until we have access to more company records or the archives of the Mexican government provide us with additional information about this change of mind, we can only enter into educated speculation about the reasons behind this move. The treaty would give the Mexican Shell daughter control over two-thirds of Mexico's proven oil reserves. In return, the Mexican government would receive 5.6 million pesos for drilling work, 6.785 million pesos for the construction of two refineries, and 3.475 million dollars for the purchase of ten ships, the core of a Mexican merchant marine.[73] In addition, within ten months the Mexican government would gain substantial revenue from new wells that would go into production. From a purely economic point of view this was a good deal. After years of neglect and disinterest, this agreement would force the British to bring their dormant reserves into production which, in turn, would generate tax revenue. Business and commerce in the vital petroleum sector would resume and many Mexicans would have found work in the newly explored oil fields. If the British oil company accepted the treaty the impasse over the oil question would end. Economic recovery would take place. Besides, within the near future, the Mexican government could not have financed an expansion of the domestic oil sector out of its own resources.

In addition, Cárdenas's move might have been a signal to the Shell daughter that the Mexican administration was willing to work with the multinational rather than expropriate its holdings. Perhaps, Cárdenas's concession would have convinced the foreign companies to move their money back into the country and alleviate the pressure on the Mexican exchange rate. In November 1937, the Cárdenas administration had no financial reserves left to take over the British-owned part of the petroleum sector without the investment reserves that the British and U.S. companies had moved abroad. The money for tankers would have created an independent Mexican shipping capacity that could have shipped federally owned oil to new markets. Finally, it was also a clever move, as Lorenzo Meyer suggested, that would have split the united U.S.–British oil company front.[74] Thus indirectly, through the treaty, the Cárdenas administration had succeeded in obtaining investment capital abroad at a time when international commercial lenders were unwilling to give Mexico one dollar or one pound through traditional financial channels. In the worst case, the Mexican administration could have used some of the money for the immediate budget crisis. But this time the British kept the Mexican administration waiting. Until the verdict of the Mexican court, nothing would move.

Next, Minister Suárez asked U.S. companies and the U.S. government for help. He approached the Mexican branch of the First National Bank and offered the reduced Laguna cotton harvest, the Mexican sugar harvest, and privately owned henequen reserves as collateral for a loan of ten million U.S. dollars, but without any success. Finally, he asked U.S. Economic Counselor Lockett whether the U.S. Treasury would be willing to help the Cárdenas administration. Suárez handed Lockett a letter for U.S. Secretary of Treasury Morgenthau in which he assured his U.S. colleague that

"the actual emergency has not been reached, but he was attempting to prepare a way to meet a financial condition which might develop at any time," an issue that should be of decided interest to the ". . . U.S. Treasury, American exporters and American invested interests in Mexico."

U.S. Ambassador Daniels backed Suárez's request and urged Morgenthau to help.[75] Three weeks later, on December 7, 1937, Morgenthau invited Suárez to come for talks to Washington, D.C., under one important condition: the Cárdenas administration had to request U.S. assistance through the confidential, but nevertheless official, channel of the Mexican ambassador to Washington. Secretary of the Treasury Morgenthau did not want to be caught in acts that could be misinterpreted by the enemies of the Cárdenas and Roosevelt administration as a U.S. attempt to exploit the crisis of Cardenismo for their own political goals.[76] Suárez obliged. Publicly, however, it was announced that Suárez would travel to Washington to negotiate the renewal of the U.S.–Mexican silver purchase agreement.

Once in Washington, Suárez used the occasion to visit U.S. bankers and offer them Mexico's future oil taxes for a new loan. He even agreed that the U.S. oil companies could pay their taxes directly into U.S. bank accounts without any Mexican financial intermediary.[77] If this was an attempt to motivate U.S. financiers to pressure U.S. oil companies into resuming production in Mexico, it did not work. Now, Suárez's last hope for help was the U.S. Secretary of the Treasury.[78]

The Mexican Treasury Secretary and the U.S. Secretary of the Treasury met for the first time on December 14, 1937. At the meeting, Suárez presented Morgenthau with a memorandum that stated four requests.[79] First, Suárez asked the U.S. Treasury to purchase the thirty-five million ounces of silver from the Kansas City Federal Reserve Bank, which private banks had refused to touch. These U.S. government dollars for Mexican silver would provide much-needed relief for the balance sheet of the Bank of Mexico. Second, Suárez wanted access to the U.S. government's currency stabilization reserve should the Mexican crisis become an emergency. Third, he asked for an additional five- to ten-million-dollar bridge loan to cover short-term financial problems. Last, he pleaded with Morgenthau to provide him with finances for Mexico's oil reserves:

> We have some important oil reserves in proven fields and if there is any way to get the money we would like to invest it in the development of these oil reserves. We think that we could get only from one of our oil fields for the next year a production of 40.000 barrels a day at least. We have a royalty of 13.000 barrels a day in the deal we made with the Aguila Company . . . So our needs for money, as

far as the government is concerned is for investment, which we consider a sound one, to bring out wells, extending pipes to the pipe lines, stations, pumping stations and refineries. That is our trouble, Mr. Secretary . . .[80]

Morgenthau listened attentively. He replied by asking Suárez to provide him with a detailed statement of Mexico's current federal financial assets and obligations. Before he could make a decision, he wanted to study Mexico's financial situation. The remainder of the meeting was devoted to a discussion of the causes of the current Mexican crisis. Whereas Morgenthau thought that Mexico's economic problem resulted from an unbalanced budget,[81] Suárez suggested that Mexico's trade imbalance and the worsening credit situation were the main culprits. Suárez assured Morgenthau that Mexico's federal budget was healthy. It was the lack of investment, he argued, that had produced Mexico's current predicament.

From a theoretical, purely economic perspective Suárez's interpretation carries much weight. But Suárez failed to mention his government's economic nationalist rhetoric, the risky financing of the *ejido* policy, and the opposition of private Mexican financial institutions. Also, the agitated labor situation and the public decline of confidence in the strength of Mexico's economy had not been mentioned.

Morgenthau and his advisers pondered the implications of Suárez's request in a subsequent meeting. Everybody agreed Mexico was in crisis. But for Morgenthau, the crisis was not so much about Mexico itself as it was about the creation of opportunities for hostile Axis powers to gain a foothold in Latin American economies in crisis. Thus, he suggested the creation of a U.S. technical mission to Latin American countries that would review national budgeting procedures and the operation of national collection agencies. He hoped that a sounder national budgeting process would end the existing crisis and keep Axis financial influence in Latin America to a minimum. In other words, the Mexican crisis provided a unique opportunity to examine Mexico's financial system more closely, to reform it, and to put the economy of the United States' southern neighbor on a more solid footing, to promote "a sounder economic situation in those countries and thereby a strengthening of democratic tendencies in Latin America."[82] However, until such a mission could be organized, Mexico also needed short-term relief.

The next day, Morgenthau discussed the Mexican situation with President Roosevelt. His laconic diary entry gives a sense of the spirit of their discussion. He told the president

that the Mexican situation was desperate; Mexico was busted and that if we did not do something to help them that within a year I prophesy that Italy, Germany and Japan would walk in there and treat Mexico the way they did Spain. That Mexico is the richest colony in the world for those three countries to take over and I wished that he would see Hull and Welles and myself together.[83]

Roosevelt must have given Morgenthau a free hand to take care of the situation because, on the following day, Morgenthau began his political maneuvering inside the maze of Washington's political establishment.

First, at a private reception for Suárez and the Mexican negotiators, Morgenthau explored the idea of overhauling Mexico's fiscal structure. Using medical metaphors, he suggested that

> treating the patient [Mexico] by applying adhesive plaster for a small scratch when the patient was suffering from a serious illness would not accomplish any real benefit. He felt that the general condition of the patient required a thorough examination but at the present time, he reminded Dr. Nájera and Minister Suárez, President Cárdenas of Mexico was the doctor in general charge of the patient. A U.S. Treasury team would be willing to examine Mexico's financial system and put it on a sounder footing if the Mexicans so desired.[84]

Suárez promised to submit the suggestion to President Cárdenas. Within days, Cárdenas gave his approval to negotiate any "possible plan of economic and financial cooperation between the two countries . . . which can be submitted to the consideration of our government."[85] This was a cautious presidential mandate for negotiations without preconditions.

Now Morgenthau's only remaining obstacle was the Hull faction inside the U.S. State Department. Frustrated by years of Mexican land expropriations and unresolved disputes over oil and water rights, Secretary of State Hull and his followers saw Mexico's crisis as an opportunity to extract concessions from Mexico first and help the southern neighbor later. The power of their wrath was mitigated only by the fact that Sumner Welles represented the Department of State at meetings.

During the remaining days of December 1937, Morgenthau skillfully created political momentum inside the Washington bureaucracy in favor of helping Mexico immediately and decisively. Eventually, it defeated any plans of the internationalist faction in the State Department to hang out the Cárdenas administration to dry.

On December 28, Morgenthau decided that the U.S. Treasury would continue its regular monthly silver purchases during 1938. This was not a great concession. Nevertheless, it signaled to the State Department that the U.S. Treasury would not go along with any attempt to ask for Mexican concessions first and then provide help later.[86] Also during 1938, the U.S. Treasury and President Roosevelt refused to use silver purchases as a tool for destabilization.

The next day, December 29, Morgenthau abruptly abandoned the negotiations with the Department of State. For him, the State Department's position had "too many angles to this situation that I do not understand and they do not smell good".[87] He also postponed his original plan of sending a technical mission to Mexico; Mexico's finances needed help now, he decided. Suárez should go home with immediate relief in his suitcase. He planned to purchase the thirty-five million ounces of Mexican silver from the Federal Reserve Bank in Kansas, providing the Bank of Mexico with an immediate and significant infusion of foreign reserves to stabilize the peso exchange rate. These steps would send the message to Mexico's financial circles that Washington was continuing to support the policies of the Cárdenas administration.

Still, before Suárez received the good news, the State Department received a token chance to press the Mexican representatives on issues that were on its wish list. In the presence of Treasury Secretary Morgenthau, Welles was allowed to urge Suárez and Nájera to solve outstanding water, land, and petroleum disputes. Again, the Mexicans proved to be splendid diplomats. On the spot, they agreed to the creation of a bilateral water-rights commission. In addition, the two men called Cárdenas to convey to him the State Department's misgivings about the ongoing oil conflict. Via telephone, President Cárdenas assured Welles that he too wanted a satisfactory solution of the oil conflict. He promised that he would allow the oil companies to receive full justice within the Mexican legal system. He would not object to the company's appeal to the Supreme Court of Mexico.[88] De facto, this decision enabled the companies to obtain a suspension of the decision of the Labor Board, except insofar as the payment of back wages was concerned. Cárdenas had not compromised the stance of his administration, nor had he compromised Mexican law. Yet he had allowed a continuation of the legal tensions that had paralyzed much of Mexico's business in the fall of 1937.

Next, Morgenthau was free to pursue his own Mexico policy. He announced the purchase of Mexico's thirty-five million ounces of silver reserve in the United States. Just as important was the fact that the silver purchase came with no conditions attached. As Morgenthau pointed out, "it's just a straight monetary transaction and I am not going into what use you make of it. There are no strings attached."

The Mexican diplomats thanked Morgenthau profusely.[89] They had been able to sell Mexican silver to the U.S. government at a higher price than they would have received on the official market. They had received U.S. financial help without any strings attached. From the public relations point of view, Suárez could return home with a substantial deal in his pocket. He intended to demonstrate to the people of Mexico "that we have some support, make people feel a little better." At the end of the meeting, Morgenthau could not help but provide Suárez with some final advice on how to operate in a capitalistic system:

> The weakness in your exchange is caused by the flight of capital, both foreign and domestic, because of uncertainty or fears as to your future action in the treatment of capital invested in Mexico. We had the same situation here in 1932 but the actions we have taken have inspired confidence. . . . You have all the raw materials the world needs, but nobody can help you but your own government, It's like our own country. You want people to have a decent living, land, good roads, good schools and you want just what we want, but there is the thing of going too fast, quicker than you can afford it on a capitalistic system.[90]

After Suárez and Nájera left the room, the representatives of the U.S. Treasury were pleased. They had helped the financial situation of the Mexican administration despite misgivings by the U.S. State Department. At the same time, they had protected their own huge silver reserves from a potentially serious devaluation. The Mexican government could have chosen to sell its silver reserve on the open market for a much lower price. A release of so much silver at one time on the free market would have forced the free-market price of silver down even further than it already was. A devaluation of the United States' huge silver reserves would have created a significant loss for the U.S. federal balance sheet.

The numerous, sometimes confusing angles of this U.S.–Mexican Treasury cooperation in December 1937 are summed up best by Secretary Morgenthau himself. After the meeting, he joked with his advisers: "So we're really not doing so much for them, so I thought we might do it—nobly."[91]

Mexican Minister of Hacienda Suárez returned to Mexico City at the end of the first week of January 1938 only to find the Mexican capital in a state of even greater economic tension. The city's bakers had just ended a strike of several days, and Mexico City's middle and upper classes could finally enjoy bread again. The capital's telephone system still did not work; its Swedish owner was refusing to make repairs as long as the government wished to take over the communication system. Even worse, Mexican commercial banks had stopped processing loan applications, and many of their receivable accounts were unpaid. Local contractors who had worked in government infrastructure projects were halting construction, waiting for government money to pay wages and to buy material.

The government's monthly income in January had fallen to a dangerously low twenty million pesos. Federal ministries and government agencies were cutting expenses wherever they could. All federal purchases abroad had been suspended. The Secretary of Foreign Relations was recalling Mexican ambassadors and ministers worldwide, replacing them with lower-paid chargés d'affaires. Some government employees remained unpaid for the first time. In the offices of the Ministry of Agriculture, government officials were negotiating with *ejido* farmers from Morelos who had come to the capital to demand an end to their participation in communal landownership programs because government-sponsored rural development banks had run out of funds to finance their programs. To make matters worse, the Mexico City correspondent of the influential *New York Times,* Kluckhohn, insisted in the Mexican press that the United States had forced Suárez into an agreement during his stay in Washington. It mattered little that the Cárdenas administration denied such an allegation in the U.S. and Mexican press.[92] Few Mexicans could differentiate between policies of the U.S. State Department and those of the U.S. Secretary of the Treasury. For most, there was just the powerful, often abusive neighbor north of the Rio Grande.

The run on the U.S. dollar reserves of the Bank of Mexico continued. The reserves of the Bank of Mexico could reach a level where Mexican banking law required the Bank of Mexico to devalue the peso/dollar exchange rate. This would be a drastic step, with disastrous consequences for the stability of the government. A memo of the Bank of Mexico explained:

> The alteration of the exchange rate would bring with it very serious harms since it means a new demonstration that investments in Mexico are insecure, that is to say, a new reason for capital leaving the country for a large period of time; moreover, it represents an alteration of the real wages of labor, since the purchasing power of our currency, if the exchange rate is raised, would tend to decrease and would be a cause of intranquility in the industrial organization; it also means an increase in the expenses of the government, especially because of the acquisition or expenditures which it has to make abroad, and, finally, a new situation in the distribution of all individual income, for which reason it must be considered in general terms, as a very undesirable measure and must be left for an extremity in which it should be totally impossible to find another remedy.[93]

No doubt the Cárdenas administration feared such a scenario. A devaluation of the Mexican peso would be tantamount to a drastic devaluation of Cardenismo. At that point in time, the Cárdenas administration could not afford it, neither with regard to its supporters or its critics. On January 19, Suárez tried once again to halt the flow of dollars out of the country by further raising import tariffs.

At the end of January the Mexican economy was in a state of severe crisis. Rising prices and supply shortages existed countrywide. In the Laguna district, the government's irrigation works, highways, and railroad construction projects had come to a halt, suggesting to the peasants that the government might renege on its promises. The next planting season was approaching, and funds were needed to prepare for the planting of the next crop. Mother Nature could not wait for the Bank of Mexico to find new resources. In the Federal District, members of the Mexican army wondered about government promises to take care of their needs when construction of the military hospital at the outskirts of Mexico City was suspended.

Suárez was personally humiliated in the second week of February 1938. When he asked Mexican domestic banks to sign promissory notes for seven million pesos to cover federal payrolls into the month of March and to accept responsibility for a two-million-dollar loan from American banks, Mexico's private bankers refused. Now federal work projects in the harbor of Veracruz, along the U.S. border, and at other points in the country had to stop. A growing number of state employees were without pay and were soon unemployed.

At the end of February 1938, Mexico was full of rumors about the pending economic doom of the Cárdenas administration. Some experts predicted that the fiscal disaster could be postponed for a month or two at the most. Nevertheless, it was expected that the financial collapse of the Mexican government was unavoidable. It was obvious that the support of the U.S. administration had failed to translate into a lift for the Mexican economy. The Shell agreement from November also remained unrealized because of the continuing legal dispute with Shell. German–Mexican explorations agreements still were not signed.

Then on March 1, 1938, the Mexican Supreme Court denied all points of the petroleum companies' request for *amparo* against the award of the Federal Labor Board in December 1937. Two days later, the companies were officially ordered to comply with the legal decision by noon on Monday, March 7. This meant that the confrontation between the foreign oil sector and the Cárdenas administration would continue, and as long as the two forces remained deadlocked an improvement in the Mexican economy could not be expected.

In these few months, Mexico's economy had degenerated to a point where economic development could no longer be pursued. Coupled with expanding conservative opposition and their foreign contacts, the developmental course of early Cardenismo had reached an insurmountable impasse, even before the oil expropriation. Regardless of what would happen next in the oil question, the economic emergency had eroded most social and political support for radical Cardenismo. Even the staunchest Cárdenas supporters were rethinking their personal commitment when the government failed to pay wages, left rural banks unfunded, and did not stop the rise in food costs. By March 1938, Cardenismo had to redefine itself or history would redefine Cardenismo.

Together, the impact of deficit spending to finance *ejido* reform, unpredictable Mother Nature, the economic consequences of the oil dispute, and the refusal of domestic economic forces to back Cárdenas's economic plan any further had created a watershed for Cardenismo. Something dramatic had to happen soon, in order to keep the myth of Cárdenismo and leftist Mexican economic nationalism alive. The sword that would cut through the Gordian knot of Mexican politics in March 1938 would be the oil expropriation. This dramatic action would provide the government with a unique opportunity, not only to remove the immediate obstacles that it faced, but also to regain the desperately needed financial resources necessary to support Mexican workers and peasants through national economic development and its related works projects.

ஐ

5

Mexican Economic Self-Defense in a Closing International Market (1938–1940)

THE GENUINE POPULAR ENTHUSIASM AND NATIONALISM THAT EMERGED IN the weeks after the expropriation did not eliminate the Mexican government's desperate need for finances. To the contrary, the state's takeover of the foreign oil industry only increased the government's obligations. Only a rapid recovery of the Mexican economy and a dramatic increase of the government's income would create the financial tools for the Cárdenas administration to resume its political and social projects. Without the recovery of the Mexican economy, even a less radical version of Cardenismo would remain a utopian dream. Thus, before we can examine Mexico's foreign relations after the expropriation as they related to political, diplomatic, and ideological issues, we need to analyze various economic-rescue operations that revived Mexico's domestic economy and, with it, the stability of the government, including its ability to resume national economic development.

While Mexicans celebrated, newspapers editorialized, and politicians agitated, Minister of Hacienda Suárez quietly started the devaluation of the Mexican peso. He and the leadership of the Bank of Mexico suspended all dealings in foreign exchange and freed the Mexican peso from its official exchange rate based on the dollar. The peso was allowed to find its real relationship to the dollar.

Most contemporary observers failed to see that the popular excitement about the expropriation served as an effective smokescreen for the realization of this previously feared, but necessary, peso devaluation and without creating additional anti-Cárdenas feeling among the population. Fortunately, most Mexicans believed that the peso devaluation was a by-product of the expropriation, not an economic maneuver that had been contemplated long before the decision to expropriate the oil companies had been made.

By coincidence, popular reaction reinforced the measures of the government. First, most capital flight ended. Mexicans who had significant savings or assets had already moved their money abroad before the expropriation. Now, demands by average Mexicans who wanted to exchange their small peso savings into dollars also stopped. Popular concern moved its attention from devaluation to inflation.

Average Mexicans certainly suffered from the immediate 20 percent price increase for food and manufactured goods in the aftermath of the devaluation. They tried to protect themselves from its consequences by exchanging their paper money for metal-based coins. If the Mexican peso should devalue below seventeen U.S. cents, the silver content in the Mexican silver peso would be worth more than the nominal value of the coin, providing at least some asset protection.[1] During March alone, Suárez and the head of the Bank of Mexico weathered an estimated drain of 50 percent of Mexico's silver reserves.[2] Still, this was good news because for the first time in six months the pressure on the Bank of Mexico's foreign currency reserves was easing. Consequently, the fall of the peso also slowed, with the devaluation showing the desired results.

The devaluation also functioned as an indirect tariff on Mexican imports. It reinforced existing measures to reduce imports and, in turn, push up orders for domestic manufacturers. The devaluation earned the Bank of Mexico a windfall profit of pesos from its remaining dollar reserves. The bank's significant peso debt was decreasing.

Next, Suárez and his professionals reversed the flow of international currency and forced dollars back into the accounts of the Bank of Mexico. The annual March tax collection continued during the expropriation process. Initially, most foreign companies asked Mexican banks for peso loans to cover their tax obligations, since they had transferred their financial reserves abroad before the expropriation. However, the Bank of Mexico advised all domestic banks that any loans to foreign companies would be viewed with extreme displeasure. As a result, the foreign companies were forced to re-import their dollars into Mexico and exchange them for pesos. The Bank of Mexico exchanged these repatriated dollars for paper pesos, of which the bank had more than enough after the popular run on peso silver coins. This increase in foreign dollar reserves further stabilized the peso exchange rate and generated more windfall profit for the Bank of Mexico, since one dollar was now accounted at 5.0 instead of 3.6 pesos.[3] Suárez had beaten the foreign companies at their own game and forced some of their assets back into the Mexican economy.[4]

Suárez also defused the dangerous confusion that followed the announcement by Mexican Ambassador to the United States Castillo Nájera that the United States would not renew its silver purchase agreement with Mexico after the end of March 1938. Contrary to the assumption of many historians, U.S. silver purchases from Mexico did not end at all. Rather, the U.S.

Federal Reserve and U.S. Treasury Secretary Morgenthau continued to help the Cárdenas administration by purchasing Mexican silver on the open spot market, only now at lower prices. Suárez recovered the income loss by imposing a 12 percent tax on Mexican exports, which targeted the U.S.-controlled mining industry in Mexico.[5] This cooperation between the U.S. Treasury and the Mexican Ministry of Hacienda successfully countered efforts by members of the U.S. Congress and the U.S. State Department to further destabilize Mexico's economy.

As expected, the nationalization of the oil properties ended the fuel-supply shortages for Mexican industry, and domestic industrial production increased immediately. This revival of the economy improved the Mexican government's income so quickly that by July 1938 the Mexican Ministry of Hacienda was again meeting its monthly income targets.[6] By September 1938, Minister of Hacienda Suárez stopped borrowing funds from the Bank of Mexico. The government was making its payroll and was able to cover all its other obligations. By October 1938, Suárez announced officially the end of the government's fiscal crisis.[7] By December 1938, the popular sentiment of economic crisis disappeared, giving way to a more optimistic feeling. During the remaining months of the Cárdenas presidency, the recovery of domestic production and commerce continued and stabilized the Mexican economy.

Suárez's economic skills had averted the dramatic fiscal heart attack of the Cárdenas administration that, most likely, would have been followed by a serious political and social collapse. The successful stabilization of Mexico's domestic economy created a financial base strong enough to face the other critical economic challenge: how to sell the export share of Mexico's now state-owned petroleum production.

The suffocating anti-Mexican boycott by U.S. and British/Dutch oil multinationals, as well as by associated foreign industries, that followed the expropriation is common historical knowledge.[8] However, a closer look at the historical evidence suggests that, at first, the power of the multinationals was more limited than a lionized, nationalistic Mexican historiography would have us believe. Moreover, the Cárdenas administration was banking on the structural forces of the approaching European war to limit the power of international multinationals to strike against Mexico and to create markets for Mexican state-owned oil. And indeed, from September 1938 on, the emerging war in Europe provided the Cárdenas administration with enough breathing space not only to resist the formidable pressures of the oil multinationals, but also to exercise an economic self-defense that forced the multinationals to accept a settlement without the return of the properties. In other words, if the expropriation had not taken place in an expanding scenario of international war, the foreign oil companies could have used their oligopolistic powers successfully to cripple the nationalized petroleum industry. But, as Mexico's planners had theorized before March 1938, in the not too distant future the selfish forces of war would overrule the gentlemen's agreements of capitalism.

As early as 1932, the Japanese aggression in Manchuria had opened the eyes of Mexican policy planners to the expansive nature of right-wing nationalism in Asia.[9] The Italian invasion of Ethiopia, in October 1935,[10] and Germany's occupation of the demilitarized Rhineland, in March 1936, had focused Mexican attention on Europe. From then on, President Cárdenas, his cabinet members, and Mexican diplomats all pondered the implications of a newly emerging international war. In 1936, the Mexican consul in Berlin cabled to Mexico City the message that Goering's second Economic Four-Year Plan was transforming the German economy into a war economy.[11] The Mexican Minister to Berlin, Almazán, reported from the national party convention of the NSDAP in Nürnberg that the fight of dictatorial regimes against the democracies had begun: "here in Nürnberg the cry of war has been pronounced."[12] Three months later, the outbreak of fighting in Spain, as well as the intervention of German, Italian, and Soviet troops in the Spanish conflict, demonstrated to the Mexicans that open violence had become an accepted feature of European politics. Mexican Ambassador to Spain Ramón P. de Negri wrote to Cárdenas that in Spain "the war already exists, although all of the involved parties refuse to recognize its existence."[13] The only remaining question, De Negri added, was when the war would spread to other European battlefields. By September 1937, Cárdenas himself expected the world war to break out in the near future. He wrote to Isidro Fabela, his ambassador at the League of Nations in Geneva:

> The bloody conflicts in Asia and the constant aggression against Spain, the actions in the Mediterranean and the race of rearmament show that the fears of a new great war are not unfounded suspicions.[14]

In early 1938, the Japanese attack on Nanking left a deep impression on the Mexican public and the Mexican leadership. Two months later, Cárdenas, pondering whether to expropriate or not, entrusted to his diary that he had begun to use the approaching great war as a protective shield for the expropriation:

> we took also into consideration the threat of a new world war,

which was developing because of the provocations of nazi-fascist imperialism. It would restrain the governments of the U.S. and Great Britain from attacking Mexico, in the case of decreeing the expropriation.[15]

In short, when the Cárdenas administration envisioned the operation of its nationalized petroleum industry, it saw a petroleum sector functioning within an international context of war.

When the Cárdenas administration calculated possible repercussions in the aftermath of the expropriation, it also considered the relationship between foreign multinational oil companies and national governments. In the United States, Mexican observers registered with great satisfaction that President Roosevelt and American oil companies were opposed to each other after Roosevelt targeted the petroleum companies for a federal tax offensive. In August 1937, Mexican Ambassador to Washington Castillo Nájero assured Mexico City that U.S. petroleum companies lacked support from the White House and could no longer act as they pleased.[16] In contrast, he emphasized, the Cárdenas administration could count on the sympathy of the Roosevelt administration because "it tried to reach the same objectives as U.S. policy."[17]

In London, the relationship between British multinational companies and the British Foreign Office was closer. But in Mexico, the daughter of Royal Dutch/Shell lacked effective diplomatic representation. In the fall of 1937, the London Foreign Office had appointed Sir Owen O'Malley as new British Minister to Mexico. Previously, O'Malley had served in postrevolutionary Russia, civil war–torn China, and the Japanese invasion of China. His imperial racism convinced him that Mexicans were incapable of making their country economically self-sufficient.[18] To make matters worse, everybody in Mexico City knew that the British community in Mexico did not get along with O'Malley, which the new British minister attributed to the failure "of the majority of those affected to handle their affairs with the necessary combination of initiative, vigor, tact and appreciation of local conditions."[19] In the following months, O'Malley remained completely isolated in Mexico City. He himself described his ineffectiveness, in a cable to London in early 1938:

> British property and vested interests are viewed as an obstacle to the realization of Mexican ambitions, which indeed they are, and no way has yet been found of bringing effective pressure to bear on the Mexican government to respect them.[20]

The oil companies' position inside Mexico was further weakened because U.S. and British diplomatic representatives refused to form a united front against the Mexican government. As so often before, at the end of the first week of March 1938, British Minister O'Malley had asked U.S. Ambassador Daniels for cooperation in the oil question. But as before, Daniels rejected the overture, pretending that his instructions did not permit him "to go further than to show personal interest in finding the way out of the deadlock."[21] Even a casual observer of the U.S.–British diplomatic relationship in Mexico could predict that, in case of an expropriation, the oil companies would lack the support of an immediate, effectively united European–U.S. diplomatic pressure group inside Mexico.

In 1937 the Bolivian oil nationalization had given the Cárdenas administration an indication of how the Roosevelt administration, as a government, might react to the expropriation of U.S.-owned petroleum property in Latin America. As in Mexico, Standard Oil had not paid much attention to Bolivian reserves in prior years. No well had been drilled in the previous five years, and Standard was publicly contemplating the sale of the Bolivian properties. Then, during the Chaco War, the Bolivian government charged Standard Oil of Bolivia with tax fraud and illegal export of oil to Argentina, and simply expropriated its holdings.[22] Stephen Randall has argued that the Bolivian case should not be compared to the Mexican step in 1938 because Bolivian oil was relatively unimportant to the U.S. government.[23] Still, I believe that the case was of significance to Mexican observers. It indicated that although a U.S. company was the exclusive target of an expropriation, the Roosevelt administration opted to find a solution through mediation, not intervention. Did this not suggest that the Cárdenas administration's greatest fear in case of an expropriation, a direct U.S. intervention, was even more unlikely when the majority of the expropriated assets would belong to British interests, as was the case in Mexico?

Another important issue was the available shipping space on the eve of the expropriation. Could the Cárdenas administration reasonably expect to sell its nationalized oil products outside the worldwide distribution network of the big oil sisters?

The Cárdenas administration knew that the lack of a national merchant marine and tanker fleet made it dependent on outside shipping sources. In 1936, Minister of Communication and Infrastructure Múgica, calling for the creation of a national merchant fleet, had ordered three tankers from Republican Spain. They would have been available before the expropriation, if the developments of the Spanish Civil War had not repeatedly postponed their delivery. During 1937, Cárdenas ordered ten steamers from the United States—six for the Pacific and four for operations in the Gulf of

Mexico.[24] At that time, the emphasis on steamers still made sense, since the Mexican government itself did not have access to much petroleum. In addition, the previously described Centramer deal would have provided Mexico with more tankers in the near future. Still, when the expropriation became reality, Mexico owned only one tanker. During the expropriation process it seized three more from the foreign oil companies. It lost one again when it was confiscated by a U.S. court while on repair in a U.S. shipyard. But the situation was not as bleak as it appeared at first sight.

In 1937, 1,690 tankers operated worldwide: 60 percent of them were controlled directly by Shell and Standard Oil; 11 percent were owned by Germany, Italy, Japan, and USSR; 28 percent were owned by other major companies or foreign governments; and the remaining 1 percent belonged to independent oil dealers. At the time of expropriation, half of Mexico's oil production was used domestically. This market was expected to continue to exist after the expropriation and would probably expand once Mexico's economy recovered. In other words, Mexico had to export two million barrels of oil, or 60 tanker loads every month, to sell its remaining production. At least on paper, it did not seem too difficult to find 60 tankers out of 1,690, outside the control of Standard and Shell, to market Mexican oil abroad after the expropriation.[25]

Immediately after the expropriation, it seemed as if Mexico still did have international friends who could import Mexican oil. After the expropriation, Eduardo Villaseñor, the head of the Bank of Mexico, traveled to Spain and France to use his personal contacts. Theoretically, Republican Spain was a good destination. The Republican government owned seventeen tankers that could transport Mexican oil around the world if the Republican government was willing to carry the insurance risks.[26] The Republican government owed the Cárdenas administration more than a political favor in light of Mexican support in the League of Nations and Mexican arms deliveries. But after his arrival in war-torn Spain, Villaseñor realized that the losing Republican government was completely absorbed in the civil war and was in no position to help Mexico. Next, he went to France.

In Paris, a classmate of the current Mexican military attaché to France served on the French Army's chief of staff. At first, French General Gamelin agreed to use Mexican petroleum in the buildup of France's strategic reserve for the expected war against Germany. It seemed as though the Cárdenas administration had found a major democratic power to import a significant part of its oil reserves. Then, at the last moment, France's Foreign Minister Bonnet overruled his decision and ordered the French military to stay away from Mexican oil imports. French politicians, facing a powerful Germany, did not want to endanger proven, long-term British oil supplies in exchange for Mexican oil.[27] In the end, Eduardo Villaseñor returned to Mexico empty handed. The efforts of the Mexican administration to export Mexican oil to democratic governments had failed.[28]

Next, in April and May 1938, the Cárdenas administration offered its oil to independent oil dealers. Soon, however, it became apparent that most independent oil merchants preferred to stay away from deals that involved Mexican oil products, and for three reasons. First, since many made their living by shipping extra loads for the big oil multinationals, they did not want to risk their long-term relationship with the oil multinationals for short-term deals with Mexico. Second, many of them owned only a few ships and, therefore, depended on speedy loading and unloading of cargo at port facilities whose main business came from the big oil companies. Third, most international shipments of oil were insured by Lloyd's of London. Few tankers would venture to the open sea without such an insurance policy. Every policy spelled out in detail the cargo of the ship and the origin of its load. If Lloyd's of London informed Shell or the British Foreign Office, independent tankers could be targeted once they arrived in Europe and their cargo could be confiscated via lengthy legal procedures. Since every day in port cost significant docking fees, this was a rather effective way to discourage independent transporters from carrying Mexican oil. For example, Lord Inverforth, himself the former head of the Bank of Lloyd's, learned this lesson in March 1938. He visited Mexico immediately after the expropriation to negotiate the purchase of Mexican oil. Right away, the Mexicans set up a draft agreement and offered an attractive price. Suddenly, direct intervention by Shell and the British government in London convinced him not to sign the final contract.[29] The small independent German oil importer from Hamburg, the Ernst Jung Company, defied the risks and purchased eighty thousand tons of gas oil. Previously, the load had belonged to the U.S. Sinclair Oil Company, which until then had not used legal action to confiscate its expropriated oil once it arrived in European or U.S. ports. Still, Jung's purchase was a onetime deal only, not enough to export half of Mexico's nationalized oil production. Finally, the Cárdenas administration offered its petroleum to any foreign government that was interested, including European and Asian countries with fascist governments. In the first week of April 1938, Gustavo Espinosa Mireles, the head of the newly created Mexican government office of oil exports,[30] invited representatives from Germany and Japan, as well as the United States and Scandinavian countries, to his office in Mexico City. He offered all of them Mexican oil in exchange for hard currency and a small amount of manufactured goods. Since he personally favored German deals, he told the German economic counselor in Mexico, Burandt, that President Cárdenas had secretly agreed to sell oil to Germany, as long as the negotiations would be conducted by a non-German company.[31] None of the governments reacted to the offer.

But Mexican representatives only intensified their efforts. On April 7, 1938, in New York, a Mexican businessman, claiming to act on behalf of a relative of the Cárdenas family, approached the head of the German shipping company Hapag Lloyd and offered Mexican oil in exchange for German goods. The only condition was that the negotiations would have to take place on neutral ground, removed from public attention.[32] At the end of April, a Mr. Rascon contacted the German legation in Mexico City on behalf of PNR President Luis I. Rodríguez, inquiring if Germany would be willing to import Mexican oil. Also, Mexican export chief Mireles offered the German importer Behr & Co. the exclusive rights for oil exports to Germany.[33] Finally, a German acquaintance of Cárdenas from Michoacán asked if Germany would be interested in a long-term export contract. German Minister to Mexico Rüdt backed the Mexican efforts and urged Berlin to accept the offers. But his recommendations, too, seemed to make no difference.[34] Contrary to the existing scholarship, this evidence suggests that the Germans showed a pronounced disinterest in Mexican oil. In April and May 1938, there existed little German governmental interest in exploiting the oil crisis in Mexico. What was keeping Berlin from exploiting this historic opportunity in Mexico?

In 1938, German oil imports were controlled by the German Foreign Ministry and the German Ministry of Economy. And the majority of Germany's oil imports came from Standard Oil and Royal Dutch/Shell. As part of its war preparations, German ministries protected their good relationship with the U.S. and British multinationals, who seemed only too willing to supply the German war machine in the coming years. German industrial and military power depended too much on the goodwill of these multinationals to endanger this relationship with politically risky short-term imports from Mexico.

The only German ministry truly interested in cooperation with Mexico, at that time, remained the German Navy. However, for the Germany Navy the expropriation had been a major setback. Shortly before the expropriation, the treaty concerning joint German–Mexican explorations of the Isthmus of Tehuantepec oil reserves had been ready for signature. Only Cárdenas's signature had been missing. After the expropriation, the exploration of the Tehuantepec area was less important to the Mexican government. Therefore, in the first week of April 1938, the Cárdenas administration informed the German negotiators in Mexico City that the isthmus treaty was on hold. The Mexican government told the German negotiators that the treaty's fate would depend on the future course of negotiations between Mexico and the expropriated companies. These could last "2 weeks or two years."[35] Just when the German Navy was about to reach its original goal—control over an independent oil source in Mexico—the expropriation had destroyed the work of the previous months.

Only then did the German Navy decide to change from a developer of Mexican oil reserves into an importer of Mexican raw petroleum products. Suddenly, the German Ministry of Economics intervened and canceled the navy's budget of 6.6 million British pounds, which had been put aside for oil development.[36] The German rival ministries objected to the idea of the German Navy as a net oil importer.[37] After all, oil could also be imported from Shell or Standard. The navy's budget was reassigned.

Shell and Standard also discouraged the Germans from entering into a deeper relationship with the Mexicans. Dr. Kruspig, a German distributor of Shell oil from the Rhenania-Ossag Mineraloelwerke Hamburg Company, informed the German Foreign Ministry that Germany's situation would not benefit from a potential conflict with the British over Mexican oil imports. To make his point, he arranged a personal meeting with Hermann Goering, where he repeated his threats. Goering, however, was not impressed. Still, in the months to come the German Navy remained without funds. All that it could do was exert political pressure on the other ministries to reverse their position in regard to Mexican oil.[38]

In the meantime, Minister of Public Work and Communication Francisco Múgica offered oil to the Japanese, who declined politely. Oil shipments from California's Pacific Coast to Japan remained cheaper than Mexican crude shipments from the Gulf of Mexico through the Panama Canal. Besides, previously refined petroleum products from Mexico had proven unsatisfactory, as their sulphur content was too high for more sophisticated combustion engines. Until summer 1939, the Japanese government would consider Mexican oil purchases only to correct small trade imbalances.[39]

In sum, three months after the exproriation, very few private entrepreneurs or foreign governments—fascist or democratic—were interested in importing Mexican oil. Fascist governments, democratic governments, and independent oil dealers all preferred to honor existing oil-supply relations, either because of financial reasons or because of alternate supply plans in view of the coming European war. It was not simply the boycott of the oil multinationals that had created a real export crisis for the Mexican administration.

In the middle of May 1938, Minister of Hacienda Suárez was in New York to talk to Standard Oil representatives.[40] During a stroll down Fifth Avenue, he ran into an independent U.S. oil dealer named Davis. Davis had worked with Mexican oil shipments before the expropriation. He owned thirteen tankers and a refinery in Europe that could process raw petroleum. In other words, he could perform exactly the tasks that the Cárdenas administration needed at that point in time, without being pressured by the multinationals.[41] Not surprisingly, Suárez invited Davis to come to Mexico City and meet with President Cárdenas to discuss possible cooperation.

After several meetings in Mexico, Cárdenas and Davis reached an agreement. Davis would buy ten million U.S. dollars of Mexican raw petroleum products. Davis would refine the raw material and sell it to European purchasers, in particular to Germany. Germany, in turn, would credit Mexico with 60 percent of the value of the petroleum products, for which Mexico could order manufactured goods from Germany. Davis himself would pay Mexico the remaining 40 percent of the payments in cash.

This critical agreement provided help for the Cárdenas administration in five areas. First, it allowed the nationalized petroleum industry to continue production at prestrike levels. Second, this, in turn, kept the highly politicized workers of the nationalized petroleum sector employed. Third, it allowed half of Mexico's oil production to move out of the country and keep the Cárdenas administration from drowning in its own oil production because of a lack of storage tanks. Fourth, it enabled the Mexican administration to demonstrate publicly that it was able to operate the petroleum industry successfully. And fifth, the agreement enabled Cárdenas to resist the pressure of the multinationals until the expected European war would change the international situation enough for new markets to emerge. In the meantime, Davis's company would guarantee the transport, refining, and marketing of more than half of Mexico's monthly oil production.[42] During 1938, it remained the first and only significant breakthrough for the Cárdenas administration in its search for export markets.[43]

Cárdenas's approval of sales to Germany through Davis must have been personally very painful for him. He and his government had made every possible effort to avoid selling Mexican oil to Axis countries. In spite of repeated, serious Mexican efforts, all foreign democratic markets had remained closed. The Davis deal was the only way for Cárdenas to mitigate the impact of the boycott by the forces of foreign oil multinationals. Also, the services of the Davis company allowed Cárdenas to tell his own citizens that Mexico was selling oil to an independent U.S. oil dealer.[44] Behind the

scenes, Minister of Hacienda Suárez made sure that the Roosevelt administration was informed about all aspects of the Mexican deals with Davis. In
addition, in the months to come Cárdenas repeatedly offered Mexican oil to
the Roosevelt administration, hoping that the U.S. president would be willing to force open U.S. or democratic markets for Mexico.

The multinationals tried to destroy Davis's deal with Mexico. When his
first shipments of Mexican petroleum went to France and Belgium, the tankers' loads were confiscated as stolen property upon arrival in the ports.
Eventually, these confiscations were declared illegal, but for the immediate
future the damage was done. Private French and Belgian customers needed
dependable deliveries and were not willing to go to court every time they
imported Mexican oil.

Next, Standard and Shell both tried to torpedo the Davis deal inside
Germany. Standard promised Germany a substantial long-term contract if
the import of Mexican oil stopped entirely.[45] But by that time the German
Navy had regrouped and intensified its lobbying within the German administration. At a German inter-ministerial conference on May 28, a compromise had been reached that opened the German market for Mexican oil a
little bit. Direct, open oil imports from Mexico still remained prohibited in
order to save German face vis-à-vis Shell and Standard Oil. Also, the German Ministry of Economy continued to refuse cash to the German Navy.
However, independent oil dealers like the Davis company were allowed to
supply the German Navy as a part of barter deals.[46] In other words, the
import of Mexican oil could resume on a small scale. By the end of June,
Standard Oil agreed grudgingly that Germany could import at least the
amount of Mexican oil that seemed to be "absolutely necessary" for its
objectives.[47] In addition, German courts assured the Mexican consul that
Mexican petroleum loads would not be confiscated.[48] Still, while the Mexican consul in Hamburg advertised to the Mexican government "unlimited
perspectives [sic] for our petroleum" in Germany,[49] the other German ministries refused to supply the German Navy with enough financial resources
to take advantage of the inter-ministry compromise.

In the end, it was only the European war that pushed doors open for
Mexican petroleum in democratic and fascist Europe. During the German
invasion of the Czech Sudeten area in September 1938, Germany experienced a mysterious slowdown in Shell and Standard oil deliveries. During
the same period, oil from Mexico reached Germany without problems.[50]
Suddenly, the German foreign and economic ministries feared that they might
be held responsible if the German Navy lacked sufficient supplies in case
large-scale fighting broke out.[51] From then on, the German ministries ended

their obstruction of Mexican imports, whereupon there began an impressive flow of Mexican oil to Germany through oil middleman Davis. By the end of 1938, Germany had increased the volume of Mexican oil imports through Davis's Eurotank 4.5 times. This equaled a seven-fold increase in value.[52]

It took another four months until the war atmosphere opened the Italian oil market. Previously, Minister of Hacienda Suárez had tried repeatedly to barter Mexican oil for Italian rayon, to help the fledgling Mexican textile industry.[53] Each time, Italian companies refused to barter and insisted on payments.[54] Finally, in April 1939, Italy and Mexico signed a first rayon/oil barter agreement. A second agreement was reached in November.[55] In June 1939, the independent oil merchants Stevenson and Hardy of London decided to defy the multinational oil companies and shipped sixty thousand tons of refined petroleum products on a Norwegian tanker from Davis's Eastern States Refining Company in Houston to the Canary Islands for storage. It was estimated to be about six months of the Italian Navy's peacetime oil reserves. It is not known in what form payments were made.[56] The Mexican oil products were delivered to the newly created Italian state oil company AGIP, which, like Mexico's PEMEX, was also challenging the dominance of Shell, Standard Oil, and other major western oil companies. During the fall of 1939, Minister of Infrastructure and Communication Francisco Múgica arranged an additional delivery of 3.5 million dollars of Mexican oil to Italy for the coming two years. In exchange, Italy promised to pay in the form of three oil tankers, to be delivered in 1940. In November and December 1939, the Italian Navy accepted a total of 120,000 tons of fuel oil from Mexico.[57] PEMEX and other Mexican government agencies were delighted about the Italian–Mexican connection. In January 1940, negotiations about future Mexican–Italian oil deals resumed.[58]

Not surprisingly, German representatives tried to tap this deepening Italian–Mexican oil relationship. The German Navy sent representatives to Rome to negotiate the possible rerouting of German oil imports via Italy. It was suggested that Davis's company could supply Germany through a new bunker station in Italy. Mussolini's administration agreed in principle, but in reality it never materialized. The British watched Italy's imports closely and did not allow more oil to enter Italy than was required for Italy's national consumption.[59] In a memorandum written in March 1940, the British Foreign Office confirmed that since the attack on Poland no substantial quantities of Mexican oil had flowed from Italy to Germany.

About this time, the Japanese also became interested in Mexican oil.[60] In the summer of 1939, Minister of Communication and Infrastructure Fran-

cisco Múgica sold to the Laguna company 367,000 tons of Mexican Poza
Rica crude oil, consigned to the Pacific Oil Company.[61] In return, the Mexican government received much-needed cash. At that time, the budding Japanese–Mexican oil relationship seemed so promising that Minister of Hacienda
Suárez informed the United States that Mexico would make more deals
with Japan if payments continued to be made in cash.[62]

Múgica's Undersecretary of Communication and Infrastructure, Modesto
Rolland, used the occasion to deepen Japanese–Mexican petroleum cooperation through the joint construction of an oil pipeline over the Isthmus of
Tehuantepec. A pipeline connection from the Minantitlán refinery to Salina
Cruz on the Pacific Coast would create a Pacific port for oil exports to Asia,
eliminating the costly journey through the Panama Canal.[63] The Japanese
were willing to finance part of the project. Rolland had applied to Minister
of Hacienda Suárez for a pipeline concession for the Japanese-owned
Veracruzana company in the spring of 1939. But Suárez and Minister of
National Economy Buenrostro had opposed the joint venture between Japan and the Mexican Ministry of Communication and Infrastructure. In the
following months, an internal power struggle between the Ministry of Hacienda and the Ministry of Communication and Infrastructure began. Eventually, Suárez was able to enlist Cárdenas's support. Both men put a stop to
the deal out of fear that it might provoke serious animosity in the United
States.[64]

At this point, one must also consider important changes in the U.S. market setting that occurred due to the expanding war in Europe. On the day of
the German invasion of Poland, President Roosevelt went out of his way to
inform Mexican Ambassador Castillo Nájera that the two governments
would "find a satisfactory solution [to the oil problem] and Mexican–U.S.
friendship would prevail."[65] As we will see in the next chapter, this was a
major departure from the previous diplomatic position of the White House.
Never before had President Roosevelt shown such personal concern and
confidence that a positive solution to the oil crisis would be found. In the
middle of October 1939, Roosevelt reacted for the first time to Cárdenas's
repeated offers of oil sales to the United States. Again, in a talk with the
Mexican ambassador, Roosevelt mentioned "that there would be a large
market in the U.S. able to take all the production of Mexican petroleum."[66]
This had been an even more significant signal from Roosevelt than his statement in early fall 1939, indicating that the White House was becoming
more than impatient with the antinationalist stance of the foreign oil companies. The war in Europe, and a possible U.S. involvement, demanded more
than ever that the U.S. market become open again for Mexican oil.

Roosevelt received unexpected help from the small, expropriated U.S.-owned Sinclair Oil Company. Sinclair Oil inquired in Washington whether it was opportune to leave the united oil-company front and resume direct negotiations with the Cárdenas administration. Roosevelt was delighted and encouraged the talks. Here, a private industry initiative could achieve what he had been unable to do because of domestic political restraints.

The Sinclair talks with Mexico progressed against the background of the Soviet attack on Finland. This unexpected war in northern Europe demonstrated that international violence was no longer easily reducible to a war paradigm of democratic versus fascist countries. Rather, state-organized war, as a viable tool for political reorganization, had become acceptable to societies in all of Europe. And if war continued to spread that unpredictably and that fast, it would soon affect all great powers, neutral ones as well as belligerents.[67] In the not too distant future, the intransigence of the multinational oil companies in the Mexican-oil question could endanger the necessary and desired formation of Western Hemisphere solidarity, a critical U.S. national security interest. Petroleum policy was now no longer exclusively an issue for private industry, but an issue of patriotism and strategic interest.

By February 1940, an agreement with the Sinclair Oil Company was in sight, and soon Mexico signed the agreement. From an economic point of view, the Sinclair agreement was the first document in Anglo-Saxon legal terms that recognized the transfer of the foreign company's property into the hands of the Mexican state. More importantly, it made it impossible to seize petroleum exports from former Sinclair wells in Europe and the United States. Legally, it was no longer stolen goods. This meant that the door to the U.S. market had at least somewhat opened by spring of 1940. The Sinclair agreement became the capstone of Mexico's economic defense in a changing international market. The Davis deal had allowed the Cárdenas administration to survive the immediate aftermath of the expropriation in 1938. The outbreak of large-scale fighting in 1939 assured a strong European market for Mexico, regardless of the multinationals' pressure tactics. After the establishment of the British blockade of the Atlantic, Italian neutrality allowed the continued import of Mexican petroleum products into the Mediterranean area into 1940. Clearly, by January 1940, the idea of an effective boycott by the oil multinationals could no longer be maintained. At that time, the decision of the Sinclair company to reach an agreement with the Mexican government had opened the backdoor into the lucrative U.S. market. The war was redefining international trade relations in such a way that peacetime commercial arrangements and loyalties were superseded by more

immediate needs for raw material supplies. The boycott of the multinationals could not last when nations reasserted state control over international
trade relations.

Between the spring of 1938 and the spring of 1940, the Cárdenas administration, with quiet support from the pro-Mexico faction in the U.S. government, realized the integration of the oil industry into the national economy,
exploited the international needs of war to undermine the boycott of the
foreign oil companies, and found entry into the previously closed, but critical, markets of the United States.

After the Sinclair agreement, the developments in favor of Mexico continued. In April 1940, the Japanese government bought 2 million barrels of
Poza Rica Crude oil, 210,000 barrels of gasoline, and 192,000 barrels of
kerosene for delivery within a year from May 1, 1940. To obtain the Japanese order, the Cárdenas administration made the concession of selling the
oil thirty cents below market price to offset Japan's Panama Canal dues.[68]

At the same time, the power of Royal Shell/Dutch over its European customers was further weakened. France created a special organization for the
direct import of petroleum products for future French war efforts.[69] Indeed,
by the end of May of 1940, during the German invasion of France, it ordered 250,000 tons of Mexican gasoline, 80 percent to be paid in cash plus
two gas deals for June and July 1940.[70] The needs of war had convinced
France to disregard previous objections of Royal Shell/Dutch and import
Mexican oil. The united oil front of democratic governments was now crum-
bling in the United States and in Europe. The expanding war in Europe
systematically undermined the boycott of the oil multinationals in Europe.

The previous examples also show that Mexican oil relations with fascist
countries were not the result of a deliberate Mexican plan to supply the
Axis powers. By no means was it a Mexican attempt to play the German
card against the United States, even though the press, war correspondents,
and some historians insisted on this more dramatic interpretation. On the
contrary, the Cárdenas administration went out of its way to avoid dealing
with fascist powers, and at all times, kept the Roosevelt administration informed about its oil relationship with Axis countries. Mexico's oil policy
was the result of a complex process driven by an emerging international
war economy, in which the nation's need for secure raw material supplies
slowly overruled the proprietary claims of multinational companies. War
was asserting itself over peacetime capitalism.

Outside the petroleum sector, however, the early years of the European war
proved very frustrating and disappointing for the Cárdenas administration.

During 1938 and early 1939, Mexican planners had used their barter credits in Germany in much the same way as they had in previous years. Mexicans ordered machinery and parts for critical national infrastructure projects, in particular, for hydroelectric dams and pipes for irrigation. By February 1939 the Mexican planners recognized that Germany was quick to import Mexican oil, but slow to deliver goods in return.[71] At that time, Minister of Hacienda Suárez admitted to U.S. economic counselor Lockett that barter trade with Germany had become a major frustration marked by slow delivery and complicated financial wizardry.[72] The Mexicans did not yet understand why.

On the very day of the German attack on Poland, September 1, 1939, Minister Suárez asked W. R. Davis to obtain binding assurances from Germany that all Mexican orders in Germany would be delivered on schedule, regardless of war activities. If that proved impossible, Mexico would close its accounts immediately and expect the outstanding balance in cash.[73] In addition, future oil deliveries to Germany would be made for cash only. Then the British economic blockade of the Atlantic was imposed, and all shipments from Germany to Mexico stopped.[74]

During the two months that followed, Suárez received only contradictory replies from Germany. The German Navy pressed for the resumption of oil deliveries, assuring Davis that the delivery of outstanding orders would occur according to plan.[75] In contrast, some German manufacturers simply canceled their undelivered Mexican contracts. Others stopped production temporarily and asked for more money.[76] In Mexico City, German Minister Rüdt painted a promising picture of a growing German market once the expected German victory of the "little blitzkrieg" in Poland had been achieved. He urged ministries in Berlin to promise the delivery of outstanding orders according to schedule, regardless of the companies' ability to do so. He stated that a German confirmation would be good propaganda for the expansion of Mexican–German trade relations once the war was over.[77] Rüdt also urged German manufacturers to bid on new Mexican infrastructure projects, whether they could deliver or not.[78] In the midst of this confusion, the German Economic Ministry tried to forge one official German answer.

Finally, in November 1939, Suárez received a first official word from Berlin. The German Economic Ministry promised the Mexican Ministry of Hacienda a timely delivery of all its outstanding orders, but added that "small lateness must be expected due to transport difficulties and envisioned overextension of German industry due to the war."

But Suárez had decided to obtain an independent evaluation of the situation in Europe. In October 1939, he sent a representative to Germany who toured the German company AEG, which manufactured the desperately needed parts for Mexican hydroelectric dams. During the visit, the Mexican representative made forceful presentations in which he demanded the completion of all contracts. Mexico had paid five million reichsmarks in oil, he remarked, without ever receiving one part in return. Since Mexico had kept its part of the deal, he expected Germany to keep its promises too.[79]

The Germans were even more embarrassed when the Mexicans produced special certificates from the French and the British, which allowed the delivery of Mexican orders through the British blockade as long as they had been placed before the outbreak of fighting. If the Germans had difficulty delivering from Hamburg or Bremen, PEMEX also accepted delivery through Genua, Italy,[80] or other neutral ports.[81] The same message was repeated to the Germans by Mexican Director of the Department of Federal Funds Manuel Alfonso Cortina. In December 1939, he visited Europe to evaluate the manufacturing situation in Germany and Italy. He also stopped by the German Foreign Ministry, where he was received by an unimportant, second-ranking bureaucrat.[82]

Finally, by early 1940 the German ministries admitted to Mexico that barter trade had become impossible—not because of the fighting, but because the German war machine preferred to allocate raw materials for purposes of war only and no longer to trade, regardless of previous agreements. Thus whereas de facto German–Mexican trade via the Atlantic had stopped in September 1939, now it had also ended officially. Most of Mexico's oil deliveries to Germany during 1938 and 1939 remained unpaid throughout the war.

In the months to come, German Minister Rüdt tried to keep Mexican interest in German trade alive with a combination of threats and invitations, repeating over and over again how promising the economic potential of a German-dominated Europe economy would be once the war ended.

From Italy the news was more optimistic in late 1939. A Mexican inspector who toured Italian manufacturers in December 1939 and January 1940 reported enthusiastically that industrial production in Italy continued without a slowdown despite the war. From Genoa, he cabled that "the shipyards in Italy . . . continue to work on the tankers as though war had not been declared in Europe."[83]

Then, in the middle of May 1940, the Mexican–Italian relationship ended as abruptly as the one between Mexico and Germany before the war. Overnight, the Italians canceled all existing contracts with Mexico and all negotiations stopped. The Italian government ordered all ships that happened to be in Mexico to remain in Mexican ports and to await further orders. Rome informed the Cárdenas administration that it might be impossible to deliver the ships currently under construction. Still, it offered the Italian ships that had sought refuge in Mexican harbors as an alternative payment.[84] Thus, in the end, the Italians also had freely imported Mexican oil without delivering the goods that Mexico had ordered.

On June 10, 1940, Italy attacked France. The Italian entry into the European war completely closed the Atlantic for Mexican trade with the Axis. Mexico had lost its European markets, about 40 percent of its prewar exports and imports.

The only possible markets left were the democratic countries and Japan. Since Standard and Shell were still strong in the United States and in Europe, Mexicans decided to explore the Japanese option.

The Japanese government had intensified its overtures toward Mexico during the German attack on Poland. During the fall of 1939, the Japanese Chamber of Commerce in Mexico City and the Japanese legation issued an invitation for a Mexican trade delegation to visit Japan. The trip was to be paid for by the Japanese Economic Federation and the Japanese Association of Importers and Exporters to Latin America. But the Mexican government remained cautious. Relations with Europe were still continuing via Italy.

In the same month, Mr. Yasunosuki, the liaison between the Japanese Navy and the Pacific Oil Company toured the Poza Rica oil zones in Mexico. Allegedly, he was trying to find out how far previous Japanese efforts had progressed to line up deals with the Mexican government.[85] But behind the scenes, discussions about the possible future relationship between Mexico and Japan intensified, especially in light of the currently deteriorating Japanese–U.S. relationship.

From Tokyo, Mexican Minister Villa Michel cautioned the Cárdenas administration that Japan saw Mexico only as a

> maturing natural satellite of the U.S., whose alliance the U.S. needed to preserve . . . Mexico was trying to emancipate itself following racial impulses that were well meant but futile. . . . In this scenario, they try to use us in their difficulties with the White House.

Japan was playing the Mexican card to pressure the United States into a renewal of the bilateral economic treaty. Mexican Minister Villa Michel doubted that Japan was truly interested in any exchange of goods that was beneficial for Mexico. He argued that Japanese interest was

> not in the field of buying and selling, but it appears that it aimed at obtaining concessions and forming societies in order to create a base for the expansion of its export in the Americas. . . . The goods are

produced by Japanese, then shipped by Japanese, imported by naturalized Japanese and sold by the same groups, all of this to the
damage of the Mexican state and consumer.[86]

In an effort to set future Mexican trade policy toward Japan, the Mexican
minister suggested that permanent trade concessions to Japan not be granted.
The Mexican administration was supposed to make sure that it was not used
as an operational base for Japan's trade expansion into Latin America. Inside Mexico, Mexicans should take control of the commerce in Japanese
articles.[87] Still, he pointed out, Mexico could play a more prominent role for
Japan if the United States were to impose a trade embargo on Japan. Then
Mexico could act as a bridgehead for Japanese trade into the United States.[88]
Thus, all in all Michel believed

> that it is appropriate to continue in concrete form our independent
> policy in regard to the problems in the Pacific. Since we have a
> Pacific coast we have an interest in the Pacific from which we can
> reasonably demand great expectations.[89]

In the first two months of 1940, renewed inter-ministry battles between
the Mexican Secretariat of Foreign Relations and the Ministry of Hacienda
delayed a final decision about the delegation's trip to Japan. In the end, the
Ministry of Foreign Relations prevailed and accepted the Japanese invitation. Ambassador Castillo Nájera was ordered to sooth possible U.S. wor-
ries by informing the Americans that similar Mexican missions had been
sent to other countries.

The leader of the trade commission was Ernesto Hidalgo of the Mexican
Foreign Ministry's Comisión Nacional del Comercio Exterior. He saw Japan as an ideal market for Mexican goods, mainly because its economy was
operating at full capacity due to the war with China. He was ready to find a
way for Mexico to benefit from that conflict. Hidalgo was joined by members of key Mexican export industries. They included representatives of the
Banco Nacional del Comercio Exterior, Banco de México, Crédito Minero
y Mercantil, Banco Nacional de México, Banco Nacional de Crédito Agrícola,
Cámara Nacional de Comercio y Industria, Distribuidora Nacional de
Petróleo, Asociación Nacional de Publicistas, and the Asociación Nacional
de Productos de Sal. The group left for Japan in March 1940, "putting
behind them all personal and political differences, from now on being simply Mexicans."[90]

The Japanese government used the visit to engage in propaganda first
and in trade second. First, the delegation received a tour of the large naval
station in Yokosuka. In addition, the impressed Mexicans were lectured on

Japanese efforts to establish a new economic order in Asia. The head of the Mexican delegation received an extremely rare honor. He was received by Emperor Hirohito himself.

In the negotiations that followed, Mexicans explored possible Japanese investment in the Mexican salt, minerals, and fishery businesses, as well as Japanese-Mexican cooperation in the creation of a Mexican merchant and fishing marine. Other Mexican negotiators wanted to acquire Japanese machinery, pipes, construction aids, chemicals for the petroleum sector, paper products like filters and fibers, carbonizing paper, cellophane, and chemical products. In return, the Mexicans offered petroleum, agricultural, forest and silver products, mercury, manganese, antimony, tungsten, molybdenum, zinc, and lead, all essential raw materials for the production of sophisticated weaponry and military supplies.

The negotiations revealed that the Japanese saw the relationship with Mexico predominantly as a way to satisfy short-term raw material needs. Representatives from the Mitsui, Mitsubishi, and Nippon Suisam companies wanted zinc and lead, both materials that they could no longer obtain from the United States. In addition, Japan wanted direct access to a mercury source in Mexico, so that they would not be dependent on purchases by foreign companies in the United States. They also asked to study Mexico's economic, financial, and business conditions. But they made no special efforts to participate in or to further Mexico's industrial development.

The Mexican documents contain little information about oil negotiations. The Mexican representative of the Distribuidora Petróleos Mexicanos reported:

> I limited my activities to cultivate friendly relations with the representatives of the government petroleum department, as well as the directors of the petroleum companies, including the Pacific Oil Company. . . . At the same time we established a basis for the future.[91]

As before, the head of the Pacific Petroleum Company urged the Mexicans to expand port facilities in Salina Cruz so that it could be used for future cheaper exports of oil to Japan. The last line in his report hints at a major oil contract that became public in April 1940.

Nevertheless, when the Mexican trade delegation returned, disappointment was the predominant feeling among its members. They had little to show for their efforts. On the one hand, the representative from the Crédito Minero y Mercantil wrote:

There exist great trade possibilities with Japan, in particular since

the Mediterranean Sea is closed. . . . It is necessary to work the
Japanese market with constant efforts, and understanding of all the
peculiarities of Japanese commerce.[92]

Also, the representatives of the Mexican banks thought that Japan had a
positive desire to trade with Mexico, in particular to trade with products
like petroleum, salt, cotton, rice, henequen, turpentine, and resins. But on
the other hand, and contrary to Mexican expectations, Japan had not promised to help Mexico with the acquisition of desired technology. The delegation had also failed to see how Japanese interest in studying Mexican markets
would be of immediate benefit to the Cárdenas administration. The head of
the delegation admitted that Mexican–Japanese talks might have had more
to do with the ongoing U.S.–Japanese negotiations than with a genuine Japanese interest in helping Mexico. He feared that in the end Japan would
renew the economic treaty with the United States, while Mexico would remain in a position of secondary importance. The Mexicans had failed to
find a way to convert oil deals into genuine economic cooperation and access to technology and manufactured products. The exploration of the Pacific option for Mexico yielded mostly disappointment. Not surprisingly,
the Cárdenas administration canceled all its existing exchange agreements
with the Japanese on October 24, 1940.[93] Japan was not interested in
Mexico's development.

Nevertheless, Mexico had experienced great success in defending itself
economically during the previous two years. It had achieved most of its
objectives, and the Cárdenas administration had strengthened the economic
base for the developmental politics of the postrevolutionary state. The future of Mexican development depended entirely on the Mexican–U.S. economic war relationship. Between 1937 and 1940 Mexico's foreign economic
relations had been reduced to the now pivotal bilateral U.S.–Mexican trade
relationship. Circumstances of the war were about to move Mexico and the
United States into their closest economic cooperation prior to NAFTA.

ॐ

6

Mexican Diplomatic and Propagandistic Self-Defense on the Eve of World War II (1938–1940)

A CRITICAL ACHIEVEMENT FOR THE CÁRDENAS ADMINISTRATION WAS ITS ability to shape in its favor the search for an internationally negotiated solution to the oil expropriation. Three factors came together to bring about Mexican success on the diplomatic front. First, the Cárdenas administration pursued a long-term outlook based on accurate information about the state of the oil industry prior to the expropriation; second, Mexican diplomacy toward the Great Powers and multinationals was controlled by a few, highly experienced individuals whose policy preferences required little coordination, thus avoiding damaging internal bureaucratic turf battles; and third, the Mexicans were fortunate to be confronted by slow, self-important and ineffective diplomatic bureaucracies of the Great Western Powers.

This achievement is even more significant because it was achieved against the background of an expanding foreign propaganda battle inside Mexico. From the fall of 1938 on, nationalist Cardenismo was again weakened by a polarization between Mexico's political left and right, this time fueled by foreign support that eventually could have challenged the ideological hegemony of the Mexican administration. Ironically, this danger to the Cárdenas administration on the eve of the 1940 presidential elections was neutralized early by the ideological fallout of the European war. Unexpectedly, the Hitler-Stalin pact provided the Mexican administration with an important reprieve from foreign and domestic subversive anti-Cardenista activities. It allowed the Cárdenas administration to conclude successfully its diplomatic self-defense, without causing greater fears in the United States about the state of Mexico's internal security.

We need to begin the analysis of this process by examining the weeks before the expropriation. Already, then, international diplomacy provided a protective umbrella for Cárdenas's actions.

In Mexico and its capital, the expropriation unfolded as a process, not as one major event. It was a series of actions during weeks that later, crystallized into March 18, 1938, the day when Cárdenas announced the nationalization of foreign oil property in Mexico.[1] In reality, the three weeks leading up to March 18, 1938, were characterized by confusion, fear, and contradictory behavior inside the Mexican cabinet. On the one hand, the circumstances described in chapter 4 pushed the Cárdenas administration toward the inevitable expropriation. On the other hand, members of the administration were justifiably apprehensive about doing the inevitable, and still continued to find a compromise with the oil companies. On Tuesday, March 1, 1938, the Mexican Supreme Court officially denied the oil companies' injunction against the December 1937 judgement of Mexico's labor arbitration board. Two days later, on Thursday, March 3, the oil companies were notified in writing that they had to comply with the judgment by Monday noon, March 7. The Cárdenas administration used this time not to prepare expropriation, but once again, to find a compromise with the companies.[2] A first meeting between government and oil-company representatives took place on Sunday, March 6. But it failed to produce results. A second meeting took place on Monday morning, March 7, before the noon deadline. Once again, President Cárdenas negotiated directly with the representative of Standard Oil, Armstrong. Once again, Cárdenas made a face-saving offer, and once again, oil man Armstrong turned him down. What followed then is best described by Armstrong himself:

> He [Cárdenas] then asked us if we had considered, and sufficiently considered, the possible consequences of our attitude, to which we replied in the affirmative and again reiterated how much we regretted that circumstances made it impossible for us to meet his wishes and cooperate with him in the manner which we so much desired. The president then told us that the Law would now follow its course; that, if there was anything in which he could be of assistance to us, he would always be willing to receive us, then he terminated the interview.[3]

Even in today's terms, the arrogance of the oil negotiators toward President Cárdenas himself and the symbolic power of his office is surprising. Capitalist Armstrong proved to be a poor representative of his company, lacking any understanding of the Mexican social and cultural norms within which capitalist bargaining took place. Armstrong negotiated like a U.S. capitalist for whom negotiations were about mere facts, not issues connected to personal feelings. In contrast, Cárdenas had made repeated, indirect gestures toward the British and U.S. companies that would have allowed an advantageous compromise for the oil companies. Their economic participation in an industrializing Mexico would have been assured.

Once the Mexican Supreme Court's ruling was made public, Mexican cabinet members were obliged to expropriate for the mere honor of the nation, an idea that was alien to multinational management of the 1930s, but very real and tangible for nationalist Latin American politicians. A Cárdenas administration that could not deliver economically and subsequently suffered public humiliation at the hands of European and U.S. companies would have lost all its remaining viability among Mexico's population. Whereas earlier expropriation had been a constitutional promise, a threat born out of decades of multinational humiliation and an option to recover political and economic power, now it had become inevitable for reasons of national honor. On Monday, March 7, several hours after the passing of the noon deadline, Cárdenas called his cabinet together and declared that the conflict had reached the point where the government was preparing for open conflict.

The enormity of this step provided the Cárdenas administration with much-needed, renewed focus. The immediate concern in the cabinet was multinational sabotage in reaction to the nationalization, not fear of an export boycott. Successful sabotage would have made it impossible to use the petroleum sector as a producer of revenue for the government in the immediate aftermath of the expropriation. Even worse, it would have robbed Mexico's domestic industry of desperately needed fuel. Consequently, preparations were made to prevent a complete shutdown of operations after the expropriation announcement.[4]

The documents show that on Wednesday, March 9, Cárdenas went one step further and explored other possible consequences of the expropriation with his close advisers Mújica and Súarez. On Thursday, March 10, Mújica was put in charge of the public staging of the expropriation. His task was to renew the bond between the Cárdenas administration and Mexicans by composing an expropriation decree "that would stir the heart of the nation."[5] At the same time, Minister of Hacienda Súarez started to prepare the hidden financial rescue operation that, hopefully, would restore the financial power of the state.

Then, on Saturday March 12, the interplay of international war and diplomacy supported the Cárdenas administration's defense efforts for the first time. Thousands of miles away in Europe, the next day had already begun. Along the German–Austrian border, German troops were using the cover of darkness to begin their invasion of Austria. By coincidence, Hitler's takeover of Austria was providing Cárdenas with a major international diplomatic crisis, which immediately absorbed the attention of European political elites and their diplomatic professionals. Against the possible consequences of Hitler's aggression—Allied war against Germany—an expropriation in Mexico in a few days would remain of secondary importance. Overnight, Mexico's expropriation was reduced from a Third World assault on a First World capitalistic industrial sector to a regional issue that interested only area specialists and petroleum professionals. As Cárdenas had hoped, war in Europe was working to the benefit of leftist economic nationalism in Mexico.

In the following days, Cárdenas waited for the passing of last-minute legal deadlines, which again offered the companies final opportunities to comply with Mexico's law. Then, unexpectedly, on Wednesday, March 16, after the Oil Workers Syndicate declared the oil companies to be in the state "of non-compliance," the oil companies reacted positively and asked to resume negotiations. To everybody's surprise, they agreed to pay higher wages. Only weeks before, this offer would have been gladly accepted by Cárdenas, but now the nature of the political game had changed. Preparations for the expropriation had been finished, the state of the Mexican economy demanded the pending peso devaluation, and the expropriation was expected to renew the bond between Mexicans and Cardenismo. The companies had misread the needs of the Cárdenas administration.

On Friday morning, March 18, the physical takeover of multinational property began. Mexican government officials tried to confiscate an El Águila tanker that was taking on oil in Tampico. But when the Mexicans attempted to board the vessel, the British crew cut the ship's lines and escaped into international waters. Later in Mexico City, the Mexican government announced that all contracts between oil companies and their workers were void and that all members of the Oil Workers Syndicate would stop working at midnight. Finally, at ten in the evening, while most diplomats and reporters in Europe, Washington, and Mexico City had already fled their capitals for the weekend, President Cárdenas made the expropriation official in a radio broadcast to the Mexican people.

Múgica's expropriation decree did stir the emotions of the nation. Spontaneously, Mexicans ran into the streets and released frustrations and anger that had accumulated over the last ten months. On Saturday morning, March 19, the expropriation progressed when members of Mexican labor unions, sometimes backed by members of the conservative Mexican military, occupied the oil fields, production facilities, and residential properties in the oil-producing regions. On Sunday, March 20, people who owned a car, operated a truck, or rode a bus pulled into gas stations that were serviced by an enthusiastic labor or government representative. On Monday, March 21, in Mexico City, the Mexican government announced the creation of a Council for Petroleum Administration.[6] In a symbolic gesture, the council members occupied the recently finished El Águila building on the Avenida Juárez in downtown Mexico City. Finally, for the majority of Mexicans who had not yet been personally touched by the expropriation, the Mexican government and the unions organized public demonstrations for Wednesday, March 23, 1938. In every important city in Mexico, state offices and private shops remained closed until after the 3:00 P.M. lunch break. This allowed federal employees, union members, and government supporters to gather for demonstrations at preassigned departure points. Often, their enthusiasm turned the organized demonstrations into genuine celebrations, where members of leftist organizations again fraternized with conservative members of the Mexican army and passersby.

Temporarily, the pronounced ideological cleavages that had existed within Mexico before March 18 were overruled by an exceptional degree of nationalism. Throughout the country, conservative sympathizers noticed with great disappointment how the anti-Cárdenas sentiment of previous months was diminishing. Economic nationalism proved powerful enough to overcome strong regional geographic divisions, class cleavages, and ideological adversities. In retrospect, this popular nationalism was easy to join. One hundred thousand Mexicans found relief from months of serious economic frustrations. Best of all, there were no negative repercussion whatsoever for those who participated. No Mexican demonstrator had to fight a foreign invader, participate in violent antigovernment acts, or battle anti-insurgency troops of the Mexican army. It is no wonder these moments became emotionally so satisfying that often they would be remembered for a lifetime. Indeed, for months it provided an understandable, unifying nationalistic focus for Mexico's fractured society. It created the much-needed emotional support for the fragile Cárdenas administration and diverted attention from the continuing economic frustrations of the current economic crisis.

In contrast, disinterest and confusion dominated reactions to the expropriation in the capitals of the United States and Great Britain. For days, the Great Powers' disbelief and distraction provided critical time for the Cárdenas administration to secure the petroleum wells, to resume oil production, and to initiate the economic rescue operations described in the previous chapter. Each additional day that the Cárdenas administration could hold on to its newly acquired property and deepen nationalist popular feelings reduced the likelihood that the expropriation could be reversed without provoking major civil unrest. For different reasons, though, no government among the Great Powers wanted a Mexico in rebellion on the eve of the next great international war. For all sides, Mexico's oil reserves served their future plans better within a stable, not a revolutionary, setting.

In London, board members of the Shell company were genuinely shocked that Mexico's government had rejected the last-minute compromise and had dared to confiscate British/Dutch multinational property. Right away, the company's leadership tried to mobilize the British Foreign Office for the defense of its Mexican property. But they received little attention, for in the context of Hitler's violent acts in Europe, the Mexican nationalization of the oil companies seemed of secondary importance. In the words of British Minister to Mexico O'Malley, the Mexican expropriation

> seemed rather sensational to the representatives of the El Águilar Company, but excited little interest in the Foreign Office, where, on my return, no one wanted to see me or discuss what happened. In the spring of 1938, everyone in London was too occupied with Hitler and his doings to bother much about anything that happened in Mexico.[7]

In Washington, U.S. government circles were also surprised by the expropriation. On Friday, March 18, when the expropriation became official, President Roosevelt was on vacation in Georgia. Secretary of State Hull had left the State Department and Undersecretary of State Sumner Welles was in charge. After learning about the Mexican events, Welles used the occasion to realize a long-held dream: to establish complete control over U.S. policy toward Mexico. Days before, he had mentioned to a colleague that he was looking for an occasion to remove U.S. Ambassador Daniels from Mexico so that he himself could go "down to Mexico in a few days to fix it all."[8] The expropriation was Welles's opportunity.

In Mexico City, U.S. Ambassador Daniels had missed most of Cárdenas's radio broadcast of the expropriation decree. At 10:15 P.M. Daniels was called by an excited U.S. embassy clerk and asked to turn on the radio, just in time to catch the English translation of the decree. Then a cable came in through White House channels, ordering Daniels, first, to deliver verbally an extremely harsh diplomatic protest to President Cárdenas, and then, second, to leave Mexico City for further consultations in Washington.

Several embassy employees in Mexico City had heard rumors about a pending confrontation between Sumner Welles and Josephus Daniels. Now they pleaded with Daniels to disobey Welles's instructions. They pointed out that once he had left Mexico City, he would never return. The Good Neighbor policy would disappear with him. Eventually, after hours of discussions, Daniels cabled Secretary of State Hull asking him whether he was aware of the possibly grave consequences that Welles's instructions were about to cause in Mexico. He warned that his departure would be interpreted by Mexican opposition groups as a signal that the United States was removing its protective shield from Cárdenas and that his administration was open for domestic and foreign attacks.[9] Fortunately, Secretary of State Hull supported Daniels's position and reversed Welles's instructions. For once, the ongoing power struggle between Hull and Welles in the State Department had been beneficial for Daniels, the U.S. Good Neighbor policy, and the Cárdenas administration. Ambassador Daniels would remain in Mexico City until the end of Cárdenas's presidency and protect U.S.–Mexican official relations from future attacks by private U.S. and other foreign interests.

Still, Undersecretary of State Sumner Welles did not give in entirely. Both Hull and Welles tried to force Cárdenas into reversing the expropriation by inflicting immediate, serious punishment on Mexico. Backed by the hysterical screams of the U.S. oil industry, the two men marshaled the institutional power and prestige of the U.S. State Department to hurt the Cárdenas administration where it was most vulnerable: its financial base.

Independent of the petroleum conflict, the U.S.–Mexican silver purchase agreement of December 1937 was up for pro forma renegotiation at the end of March 1938. Hull and Welles, backed by silver interests in the U.S. Congress, argued publicly in favor of ending U.S.–Mexican silver cooperation. This time, U.S. Secretary of Treasury Morgenthau came to the defense of Mexico. Roosevelt's friend, Morgenthau, opposed the State Department's initiative for two reasons. First, the symbolic power of the cancellation of the silver agreement would hurt the Cárdenas administration's domestic and foreign economic reputation at a time when it was trying to revive its domestic economy. Morgenthau feared that it would force Mexico into financial deals with Axis countries who seemed to be eager to expand into Latin America. Secondly, the refusal to renew the agreement would cause huge amounts of Mexican silver to flood the free silver market and trigger an international silver price decline, de facto devaluating the huge U.S. silver reserves in Fort Knox. The U.S. State Department's hateful obsession with Mexico's economic nationalism would destroy six years of U.S. silver stabilization.

Publicly, Morgenthau displayed an appropriate amount of outrage over the Mexican expropriation. Domestically, it was not good to appear as a friend of the Cárdenas administration during these weeks. But behind the scenes, Morgenthau countered the State Department's efforts as effectively as he could. First, he decided to play for time. After all, the silver agreement would remain valid until the end of March. More than ten days remained in which to weaken the State Department's latest initiative. In response, on

Thursday, March 25, the State Department enlisted the help of Nevada Senator Pittman, chairman of the powerful Senate foreign affairs committee and
the self-appointed head of an elusive silver committee, to challenge
Morgenthau publicly.

Still, Morgenthau emerged from this intra-bureaucratic battle with a pro-
Mexico compromise. The two ministries agreed that U.S. silver purchases
from Mexico would not be cancelled. The negotiations for its renewal would
only be "deferred." In addition, Morgenthau had gained the concession
that this compromise formula should be presented to President Roosevelt
for final approval first. Thus Hull, Welles, and Morgenthau used Roosevelt
to decide the future of U.S.–Mexican silver cooperation. All men agreed
that the result would be made public in a press conference in the middle of
the following week. The same evening, a cable from Washington, D.C., to
Georgia suggested the reexamination of "certain U.S. financial and commercial relationships with Mexico."[10] The word *cancellation* was not mentioned. The last phrase of the cable read laconically: ". . . unless you advise us
to the contrary."[11]

However, on Friday, before Roosevelt had made a decision, Sumner Welles
called Mexican Ambassador to Washington Castillo Nájera and informed
him of the State Department's plan.[12] Right away, Ambassador Castillo
Nájera, who was not aware of Morgenthau's stance, contacted Mexico City
with a warning about the shaky future of the silver purchase agreement. In
Mexico City, the rumor was leaked to the Mexican press, who interpreted it
as an official decision to end the U.S.–Mexican silver purchase agreement.
The next morning, on Saturday, Mexico's newspaper headlines screamed in
big, fat letters that the U.S. government was ending its silver purchases from
Mexico to punish Mexico for the oil expropriation. In the official jargon, it
was branded an "imperialist plot" against small, vulnerable Mexico. In crude,
black and white strokes it was hammered into the minds of the excited
Mexican population that the Good Neighbor policy had been only a disguise for the continuing imperialist underpinnings of the neighbor to the
north. Sumner Welles's ego trips in Washington, D.C., had provided another powerful stimulus for the Cárdenas administration to reinforce the
simplistic economic nationalism that had reunited many Mexicans with
Cardenismo.

In reality, the only victim of Sumner Welles's action became the U.S. government and the plummeting value of the silver reserves of U.S. citizens.
The following Monday, the international silver market reacted to the Mexican rumors, and the pressure on the silver price on the free market increased.
Morgenthau was unable to maintain the artificially high silver price. To

make matters worse, at a noon press conference on Monday, Secretary of State Hull suggested "that the jurisdiction of silver belonged to the U.S. Treasury," blaming Morgenthau for the crisis situation. Now, contrary to reality, Morgenthau appeared as a member of the anti-Mexico faction in the Roosevelt administration. He had lost face in U.S. financial markets and in the Cárdenas administration at the same time.[13] Years of silver price stabilization and financial support for Mexico were destroyed by the State Department's attempt to wrestle control over U.S. policy toward Mexico away from Ambassador Daniels, the U.S. Treasury, and pro-Mexico forces in the White House.[14]

Until today, conventional wisdom has it that the United States canceled its silver agreement with Mexico to retaliate against the expropriation.[15] However, as pointed out in the previous chapter, Morgenthau's purchase of Mexican silver continued on the open market, and Minister of Hacienda Súarez recovered the difference in price through an export tax that mostly affected the silver exports of U.S. companies from Mexico. Moreover, Roosevelt eventually followed Ambassador Daniels's suggestion that the Cárdenas administration could expropriate if it was willing to pay immediate compensation. In sum, the official response of the Roosevelt administration to the oil expropriation had been contradictory and confused. Intra-bureaucratic turf battles by the diplomatic professionals in Washington had done more damage to their own assets than to Mexico itself. Certainly, U.S. government actions had not been of any help to the U.S. oil companies. The structural setup of Roosevelt's foreign policy—continuous competition among federal bureaucracies—had worked in favor of Mexico and against the U.S. government.

The U.S. oil companies decided to play for time. In the months to come, familiar tactics of 1930s multinational corporate culture were employed: legal maneuvers in Mexican courts[16] and dreams of domestic anti-Cárdenas coups.

Time, indeed, was the U.S. companies' only ally. First, in the absence of a foreign military intervention, an expected successful conservative rebellion against Cárdenas might put a more pro-foreign business president into the Mexican presidential palace, who might be willing to reverse the expropriation. Second, the U.S. presidential election was only two years away. Perhaps in late 1940, a newly elected pro-business Republican President would be willing to pursue a more aggressive anti-Mexico policy. And third, the expropriation had eliminated the dominant British position in the Mexican oil sector. Mexico's geographical proximity to the United States and the expected closing of the European economic markets, once a British economic blockade over the Atlantic was reestablished, would guarantee the continued influence of U.S. industry over Mexican economic development. Over time, it would be U.S. technology that would develop the expropriated British oil fields in Mexico. The only question was when and under what terms. U.S. companies were not eager to restore the British influence of British oil interests in Mexico. Consequently, after March 1938, U.S. oil companies increased economic pressure on Mexico. Constant economic harassment was supposed to soften up the Cárdenas administration for upcoming negotiations.

The British/Dutch company, in contrast, understood that it needed to reverse the course of events in Mexico sooner, rather than later. The longer the Cárdenas administration operated the oil fields and brought formerly British reserves into production, the more the Mexican government's position would solidify and make permanent its hold on the newly acquired industry. After the initial shock, Shell's state of angry helplessness was crystallizing into a general emotional consensus that the company, somehow, needed to keep "the ball rolling" in Mexico.[17] But when planners tried to translate this vague idea into specific action, all strategy meetings ended with the same result: British players lacked the power to pressure Mexico directly.[18]

In the midst of this state of frustration, British Minister to Mexico O'Malley saw an opportunity to regain ground in Mexico for England and for his own career. He was only too eager to erase the humiliation of the expropriation and to prove to his superiors and Mexicans alike that British diplomatic skill was worth something. He suggested launching a traditional barrage of tough diplomatic notes against the Mexican government. The goal was to discredit the Cárdenas administration's promise of prompt and fair compensation for the expropriated companies. If the world could understand that currently Mexico was unable to pay immediate compensation, then, according to Mexican law itself, the expropriation was illegal. The properties would have to be returned. To add power to this diplomatic offensive, O'Malley suggested publishing the British notes in the press, a crass violation of international diplomatic custom. Minister O'Malley was certain that the notes would reveal to Mexicans and foreigners alike that the Mexican government's legal justification for holding on to the oil properties was false. At the least, he hoped, the note exchange would force the Cárdenas administration to return to the bargaining table.

The publication of the first and second British notes failed to move the Mexicans. The Mexican government merely repeated its invitation to meet anytime with British representatives to assess the value of their former properties and to negotiate compensation payments.[19] The British notes also failed to achieve O'Malley's goals. In the eyes of the Mexican public and international diplomatic circles, the Mexicans still appeared as reasonable partners who were only too eager to come to an agreement with the expropriated companies.

Next, O'Malley changed course. He realized that rather than attack the Mexicans directly, he should attack indirectly, by challenging the United States' official position vis-à-vis Mexico's expropriation. Currently, the Roosevelt administration's "in principal" approval of expropriation in exchange for immediate compensation was providing a quasi-political U.S. protectorate for the oil nationalization. If O'Malley could prove that Mexico was unable to pay *prompt* compensation, then the U.S. position would become indefensible and Cárdenas would lose this critical concession from the White House. Therefore, O'Malley's third note would focus on Mexico's inability to pay immediate compensation. As he wrote to London, the

> Mexican attitude regarding compensation is fundamentally disingenuous and prejudicial to British interests, and if we can counterbalance this without giving offence to the U.S. we should do so.

Again, a parallel publication of the third note in the Mexican press would give the message to lay people and professionals in Mexico and the United States alike that the Mexican government was lying. In other words, negotiations with Mexicans should be about the return of the properties, not about the amount of compensation.[20]

There was more. O'Malley told the British Foreign Office that if the third note would fail again to show results, London should resort to even tougher measures of diplomatic warfare by calling him back to London. After that, only the outright rupture of Mexican–British diplomatic relations would remain in the British weapons arsenal of British diplomacy. Either way, O'Malley was convinced that the third note would force the Cárdenas and the Roosevelt administrations to take a stance more favorable to the British in the oil conflict.[21]

Inside Mexico City's diplomatic circles, the possibility of a British rupture of diplomatic relations with Mexico was already hot cocktail-reception talk. Most diplomatic observers delighted in speculations about when the British Lion would punish the disobedient Mexican nationalists with this extreme diplomatic weapon. Ironically, the London Foreign Office objected strongly to O'Malley's idea. Rightly, it feared that such a step

> might merely result in giving the United States a freer field than they already possess to extract, if they are so minded, what settlement

they can from the Mexican Government on behalf of their own interest to the detriment of our own.[22]

The British government's Oil Board seconded this position:

> The Mexican Government should not be placed in a position where they could claim victory for themselves and appear to the world as having succeeded in despoiling the oil companies of their properties without detriment to their national interest.[23]

The diplomatic professionals in London were not interested in leaving the Mexican diplomatic arena to exclusive U.S. dominance.

The infamous third note was presented by Minister O'Malley in person to Mexican Foreign Minister Hay on May 11, 1938. Hay read it on the spot and discovered to his great surprise that the note asked how Mexico could promise immediate compensation for the expropriation, if it could not even pay its outstanding debts to domestic bondholders. Immediately, Hay asked O'Malley to reconsider the note and omit any reference to Mexico's internal debt, and thus avoid injury to diplomatic custom. When O'Malley refused, Hay ended the meeting abruptly.[24]

Finally, the third note had touched a raw Mexican nerve. Indeed, at that time Mexico had few reserves to service foreign or domestic debts. In London, the Foreign Office celebrated the strong note; it "evidently gave the Mexican Minister of Foreign Affairs a nasty jolt." John Balfour, the Foreign Office's head of the America Desk, envisioned that the latest Mexican offer,

> when viewed against the background of the Mexican government's failure to honor their previous obligations to pay compensation in respect of outstanding claims, will presumably lose much of its force![25]

Certainly, O'Malley's argument made sense for those unfamiliar with the financial games of domestic and foreign debts. It appeared possible that the Mexican government was lying and that Roosevelt was choosing to overlook this fact. The White House's tacit support for Mexican economic nationalism was now becoming problematic.

Mexican cabinet members realized the serious implications of the third note. No Mexican administration could afford to give in to the note's argument. If Mexico was forced to pay immediate compensation in cash, it would lose millions of pesos earmarked for the resumption of industrial development which was critical for the political survival of the Cárdenas administration. The British attack had to be countered strongly.

President Cárdenas conferred about a response with Mexican Ambassador to Washington Castillo Nájera, Foreign Minister Eduardo Hay, and advisers Raul Castellano and Licenciado García Téllez.[26] During the meeting, it occurred to one of them to turn the tables on the British. The Cárdenas administration should recall the Mexican Minister from London before the British resorted to a fourth humiliation of Mexico. It was expected that British international diplomatic reputation would demand immediate reciprocity. As a result, the British representative would remove himself from Mexico, and the effective British diplomatic harassment of the Mexican administration from within Mexico would end. After that, the United States would remain as the lone diplomatic representative of the expropriated oil companies in Mexico, and the differences between U.S. private business and the U.S. administration could be exploited for Mexico's benefit. For months, if not years, the British would be eliminated from influential diplomatic representation in Mexico. In short, the multilateral issue of the oil expropriation would change into a de facto bilateral U.S.–Mexican issue.[27]

The following morning, Mexican Foreign Minister Hay called British Minister O'Malley to the reception room of the Mexican Foreign Ministry. There, Hay presented the puzzled British minister with a cheque for the amount of Mexico's revolutionary debt to Great Britain and informed him that Mexico was withdrawing its diplomatic representative from London. This time, the nasty jolt was felt in the British camp.

Upset, O'Malley stormed back to the British legation. Once again, the Mexicans had successfully humiliated the British presence in Latin America. Even worse, they had played the diplomatic game better than the former imperial power, England. He realized that London's Foreign Office would have no choice but to recall him in order to save face. After only nine months, his tenure in Mexico City was about to come to an end. When the news of the Mexican note reached London, British Foreign Minister Lord Halifax had already left for the weekend. There would be no official British reply until the following week.

As expected, the British government recalled O'Malley. To add insult to injury, the U.S. State Department refused to represent Great Britain in Mexico City.[28] Instead, the Danish government took over the representation of British diplomatic issues in Mexico. The United States also indicated strongly that it was not interested in meeting with O'Malley when he traveled through Washington and New York on his return trip to London.

Today, it is difficult to fully grasp the symbolic impact of this Mexican diplomatic victory. Here, a government run by Latin American leftist economic nationalists had been able to expropriate major British economic assets without any immediate punishment. Then it had slammed the diplomatic door in the face of Britain's Foreign Office for the second time, with-

out any negative consequences. Furthermore, from an international diplomatic perspective, this had been the first time in a century that a country
had dared to break off diplomatic relations with Her Majesty's Government.[29] European ethnocentric diplomatic pride was deeply offended by the
fact that these successes had been achieved by Latin American nationalists
with Native American ancestry. The Cárdenas administration had created
an inviting precedent for other emerging nationalist countries.

From the Mexican perspective the action had been highly successful. First,
the British/Dutch oil companies had been deprived of any effective diplomatic representation inside Mexico after expropriation. Second, with the
withdrawal of the British minister, British general diplomatic representation
in Mexico had been eliminated. Third, before talks about compensation
had ever begun, Cárdenas had begun to shape their future format. Now, it
would be U.S. representatives who negotiated with the Mexicans first. Once
again, the Cárdenas administration had exploited the subtle but constant
U.S.–British competition in the Mexican petroleum conflict in order to re-
shape the multilateral oil issue into a bilateral U.S.–Mexican affair. Fourth,
the incident gave the Mexican government another opportunity to use the
Mexican press to further reinforce the nationalistic bond between Mexicans
and Cardenismo. To the general Mexican public, it seemed that, once again,
Cárdenas and his planners had stood up heroically against foreign intimidation and defended Mexico's domestic sovereignty. When O'Malley finally
left for England, the ocean passage gave him ample time to reflect on his
Mexican experience. His final comments suggest how O'Malley had been
blinded by his own racist misconceptions. O'Malley wrote that he felt

> unmixed satisfaction, as I saw the lights of the capital recede, that I
> should in all probability never revisit a place where I had endured so
> much mental and physical discomfort. Mexico City is a combination
> of the sinister and meretricious. It represents a rather macabre
> answer to a problem biologically insoluble. I find it impossible to
> believe that the mingling of Spanish blood with the blood of the
> numerous tribes of degenerate Indians can make any permanent
> valuable contribution to humanity. For all the sunshine and glitter of
> their habitation the people of Mexico City seemed to me to have lost
> the innocence and beauty of animals without any prospects of
> learning to understand the life of spirit. While therefore one could
> sympathize with their difficulties and with their somewhat jejune
> attempts to raise their standards of life and culture, it was with
> rather the same sense of escape that I said good-bye to them as I
> experienced on terminating a journey through Russia in 1925.[30]

The next step in Mexico's diplomatic self-defense focused on the U.S. administration. Until now, research about the U.S.–Mexican relationship during this period has been based mostly on the documents of the greatest enemies of Mexican economic nationalism—the U.S. State Department. Not surprisingly, efforts of revenge, punishment, and extreme diplomatic pressure dominate current historiographic understanding of the U.S.–Mexican relationship during this period.

To this picture, we need to add another high-level Mexican–U.S. relationship that unfolded while completely hidden from most contemporary observers. An expanding personal letter exchange between U.S. President Roosevelt and President Cárdenas about the oil issue counterbalanced the constant threatening diplomatic gestures produced by the U.S. State Department. Second, it provided Cárdenas with the opportunity to pull Roosevelt into the process of finding a political solution to the expropriation by exploiting his domestic political vulnerabilities. The evidence suggests that between 1938 and 1940, the Cárdenas administration was much less shaken by U.S. State Department threats and company reprisals than we previously assumed. This pivotal presidential relationship suggests a very different U.S.–Mexican relationship than that provided by the records of the U.S. State Department.

A first direct contact between Cárdenas and Roosevelt, which moved beyond a traditional exchange of pleasantries between heads of state, occurred in 1936 over the issue of Mexican arms purchases in the United States for Republican Spain. The politically sensitive issue was solved when Cárdenas yielded to Roosevelt's domestic political needs and withdrew Mexican orders for arms purchases in the United States.[31] But Cárdenas also used the exchange to suggest to the U.S. president that peace in Europe and Asia be maintained by using the Pan-American Conference System as an arena for arbitration. Roosevelt, at that time, did not react to Cárdenas's suggestion.

A pattern was developing here. Cárdenas addressed Roosevelt on a particular issue of bilateral concern and, in addition, tried to involve him in an effort to avert the approaching international war. Probably, Roosevelt did not take Cárdenas seriously as a statesman who was trying to be proactive and sincere in his efforts to avoid the coming world war. On the other side, Cárdenas overestimated the independence of the U.S. president in foreign affairs. Nevertheless, this exchange became a blueprint for communication that intensified after the oil expropriation. The next important exchange occurred after the oil expropriation, in September 1938. On the occasion of the German annexation of the Czechoslovakian Sudeten area, Cárdenas wrote to Roosevelt and suggested an economic boycott against all aggressor nations involved in a belligerent conflict. Cárdenas hoped that it would deprive the belligerents of raw materials, the prerequisites for the continuation of the destructive international arms buildup at that time. If Roosevelt accepted the Mexican offer, Cárdenas added, Mexico could end immediately all deliveries of raw materials—that is, oil—to the German Third Reich.[32] In this letter, Cárdenas established a first link between oil deliveries to Germany and diplomatic choices that Roosevelt was facing in the future. It was a clever attempt to change the discourse of the multinationals' boycott against Mexico. Also, for the first time Cárdenas had tried to pull Roosevelt as an arbiter into the conflict between multinationals and Mexico. He suggested that for the sake of international peace, Roosevelt's intervention in the oil boycott was desirable. In essence, Cárdenas was suggesting that it was up to Roosevelt to force the multinationals to allow the resumption of Mexican oil deliveries to the U.S. market. He had begun to redefine the debate over oil-company compensation from legal issues (ownership and compensation) to political issues (maintenance of peace and raw material supply for Axis powers).

The 1938 crisis passed, and once again large-scale war in Europe was postponed. This time, however, Roosevelt at least thanked Cárdenas for his letter, while declining to follow his ideas "because the immediate danger of a declaration of war in Europe had been avoided."[33] This strategy began to show results in early 1939.[34] By then, the next U.S. presidential election was only one year away. In the electoral contest, the delivery of Mexican oil on U.S. tankers and under the eyes of the democratic U.S. administration was becoming a political embarrassment for any presidential candidate of the Democratic party. How could the Democrats argue convincingly that they were fighting against international fascism, when a U.S. company with ties to Democratic senators and congressmen was openly supplying Hitler with oil? Few U.S. citizens understood that Standard Oil had supplied Hitler with petroleum products for years. But the U.S. press coverage of Davis' oil deals with Germany was creating a public-relations dilemma for the Roosevelt administration.

Roosevelt's White House hoped to be relieved of this embarrassment soon by supporting negotiations between the Cárdenas administration and a representative of Standard Oil, Donald Richberg. The talks were scheduled to begin in March 1939. In Paris, financial and business representatives from Great Britain, France, Netherlands, Belgium, and Switzerland gathered to provide support for the multinationals from the European continent. Using intimidation, they urged Cárdenas to accept Richberg's offer. He was warned that Mexican exports to the Axis would end soon because of the expected beginning of the great war. If Cárdenas agreed to Richberg's offers, the Europeans promised him 100 million dollars in technical aid, technical advisers, and additional funds.[35]

These efforts failed. Cárdenas categorically rejected any return of nationalized property to multinational control, even if it was sweetened with significant foreign investment. The Richberg negotiations went nowhere. Suddenly, it looked as if the presidential candidate of the U.S. Democratic party would be plagued with the Mexican oil problem during the fall of 1939.

At that point, Roosevelt abandoned his reserved attitude and intervened in the Richberg negotiations personally. First, he too tried intimidation. If the Richberg negotiations were to fail, he warned Mexican Ambassador Castillo Nájera, domestic pressures in the near future might force him to give in to punitive actions against Mexico, threatening the continuation of the Good Neighbor approach.[36] In the case of a Republican victory in the next year, Roosevelt warned, a compromise with the oil companies would be even more unlikely, and the return of an interventionist anti-Mexican U.S. policy possible.[37] Therefore, a compromise agreement with Richberg now, Roosevelt argued, might be better than a possible defeat of all Mexican gains after November 1940.

The U.S. State Department echoed Roosevelt's threat. It repeated to Cárdenas the argument that during the upcoming U.S. election campaign, the Mexican issue would be too hot for Roosevelt to touch. Secretary of State Hull even went so far as to call the Mexican case the Roosevelt administration's "most serious situation in international affairs, including the situation in the Far East."[38] Finally, almost in despair, the Roosevelt administration hinted at a possible credit for Mexico that Cárdenas could use to cover initial compensation costs that would result from an agreement with Richberg.[39] But all U.S. administration efforts failed to convince Cárdenas. The Richberg talks ended without a solution. The impasse over the settlement of the Mexican oil conflict would continue into the fall of 1939, and most likely into 1940.

It was less personal courage or revolutionary commitment that stood behind Cárdenas's categorical refusal to compromise; rather, it grew out of a sober, realistic evaluation of the petroleum industry's position before the expropriation. In 1937, Mexican planners had put together an excellent evaluation of the state of the foreign oil companies. Based on this study, the Mexicans perceived the multinationals as a group that, in reality, had planned to reduce its involvement in Mexico, not to expand it. For example, before

the expropriation the Sinclair company had offered the Mexican administration its Ojital fields free of rent for two years.[40] Also, the Standard and
Shell operations were in no better shape. As Cárdenas wrote to Nájera:

> Standard has too much production, and does not want more Mexi-
> can production; Sinclair, to a large degree, has given up the internal
> market; Shell, which produces in the U.S., Venezuela and other
> countries, would benefit when its subsidiary Mexican Eagle would
> continue its predominance in Mexico, however without increasing
> her production more than is convenient for the American interests. [41]

These insights suggested to Cárdenas that the companies' sudden interest
in the revitalization of Mexico's petroleum industry on the eve of the Richberg
talks was insincere. Whatever doubts Cárdenas and his planners had, they
were removed by the secret surveillance of negotiator Richberg himself.
Donald Richberg's phone conversations with oil company representatives
from Mexico's finest hotel were monitored by the Mexicans, and his private
meetings were observed. Ironically, there was no need for the cloak-and-
dagger game in Mexico City. Richberg himself, in private, repeatedly admitted to Mexicans that the leaders of the oil companies were not interested in
a settlement in 1939. They were merely filibustering, he confessed.[42]

Cárdenas could afford to remain tough in the diplomatic game and let
time and world war work for Mexico's interests. By the summer of 1939
enough Mexican oil had found markets in Europe and Asia to keep the
multinational boycott tolerable for Mexico. After one year of petroleum
production under government control, it had become politically impossible
to take the properties from Mexico without violent intervention. On the eve
of the great European war and one year before the U.S. presidential election, the Democratic administration in the White House would not engage
in a military intervention in Mexico. Besides, the Mexican domestic economy
had stabilized and the integration of the expropriated companies into
Mexico's economy progressed. In 1939, it was the Cárdenas administration
that was strong. The U.S. White House needed a positive political solution
rather sooner than later, and the British continued to be excluded from real
influence in the oil question.

Roosevelt was personally angered about Cárdenas's refusal to come to
an agreement with Richberg. Indeed, he and the Democratic party were the
real losers in the Richberg talks. U.S. reporters began to focus on individual
Democratic representatives in the Congress who were in close contact with
U.S. oil man Davis. Across America, the continuation of oil shipments to
Germany through Davis raised the question of Roosevelt's resolve to keep
Hitler from receiving critical raw materials. Within Washington political

circles, the growing innuendos and rumors about Davis and his political connections began to wear on the Democratic party's fabric.[43]

Next, Roosevelt accused the Mexicans of failing to return political favors. As he pointed out to Mexican Ambassador Castillo Nájera, he himself had repeatedly squashed anti-Mexican movements in the U.S. Congress. He had avoided the blockage of U.S. silver purchases from Mexico. He had also resisted pressures from within the Democratic party to take drastic measures against Mexico. Why, he asked the Mexican ambassador, could Cárdenas not have come to an agreement with Richberg?

Roosevelt's anger impressed Castillo Nájera so much that momentarily he had doubts whether the Good Neighbor policy toward Mexico would survive much longer. He reported to Cárdenas that Mexico's friends in the U.S. Senate had considered the Richberg offer reasonable and thought that Mexico should have accepted its terms. He warned that "our friends are not very disposed at defending us, the only one who shows good will is Roosevelt and with less resolution Welles."[44]

Again, Cárdenas reacted with diplomacy, but not a change in behavior. He wrote Roosevelt a personal letter stating again his reasons for ending the Richberg talks. The letter included another offer to ship all of Mexico's oil to the United States, if Roosevelt would only want to make room for it in U.S. markets.[45] Through Ambassador Nájera, he communicated to Roosevelt that the question of the future of the Mexican oil industry remained of highest national importance to Mexico and the properties could not be returned. In the end, Roosevelt calmed down, even admitting that Richberg's compromise would have meant a return of the expropriated properties to the multinationals.[46]

Then the rising confrontation between the Allies and the Axis powers in Europe further strengthened the Mexican position. From mid-August 1939 on, members of the Roosevelt administration changed their public discourse about multinational companies and the boycott of Mexico. For the first time, the U.S. administration blamed the oil companies publicly for the failure of the Richberg talks.[47] Right away, Cárdenas reenforced this change in Roosevelt's stance with a new letter. One week before the German attack on Poland, the Mexican president repeated to Roosevelt that the multinationals remained the central obstacle to a solution in the oil negotiations. At any time, Cárdenas assured Roosevelt, Mexico would enter into long-term oil contracts with either the United States or Great Britain.[48] Cárdenas would not allow Roosevelt to forget that the U.S. president could play a major role in the solution of the Mexican issue if he would intervene against the multinationals.

After the German invasion of Poland, Roosevelt's involvement became more direct. Whereas previously he had tried to stand between the companies and the Mexican government, he now assured Ambassador Castillo Nájera that the two governments would "find a satisfactory solution and Mexican–U.S. friendship would prevail."[49] In addition, he ordered his administration to review systematically all U.S.–Mexican bilateral issues and improve relations between the two countries wherever possible. Eventually, he hoped, a solution to the oil issue would follow.

By the middle of October 1939, the war produced another major change in Roosevelt's attitude, in Mexico's favor. For the first time, the U.S. president reacted to Cárdenas's oil offers and promised the Mexican ambassador "that there would be a large market in the U.S. able to take all the production of Mexican petroleum."[50] Right away, Castillo Nájera repeated Mexico's familiar position: oil barter deals with the Axis would continue only as long as necessary; the Cárdenas administration was hoping for a quick settlement of the oil question; it was willing to pay prompt compensation and desired long-term investment agreements with U.S. companies in the Mexican petroleum sector.

The eventual breakthrough in the oil negotiations in the winter of 1939, due to the changing attitude of the Sinclair company, has been described from the economic point of view in the previous chapter. The Sinclair agreement was also a significant diplomatic and legal victory. It created a first legal agreement with an expropriated oil company that de facto and de jure recognized Mexican state ownership over former multinational property. It had validity in Mexican and Anglo-Saxon courts, which would allow a successful legal defense of future oil imports from the Sinclair properties into the U.S. market. Finally, Mexico had demonstrated to the capitalist world that one could reach an agreement with the nationalist Mexican administration, and contrary to the assertions of Shell or Standard Oil in 1938, the Cárdenas administration was able to pay compensation immediately. The validity of the expropriation under Mexican law had been established. Additional advantages were outlined in two memoranda by Ambassador Castillo Nájera and Minister of Hacienda Súarez. Castillo Nájera advised Cárdenas:

> I realize that the price is a little bit high, but it is advantageous for us to conquer an external market that is not touched by fraud and that would remove the obstacles with which we had to deal sometimes before . . . besides, one needs to consider that the agreement with Sinclair will remove at least partly the political problem and convert it into a purely economic conflict.[51]

In Mexico, Minister of Hacienda Suárez backed this suggestion:

The convenience to sign a contract with the Sinclair interests for the political order cannot be doubted. Not only would it break the front of the North American oil companies, also it would demonstrate to world opinion that the Mexican government wishes and is able to pay indemnization as its laws requires. . . . The diplomatic triumph would be great, and the consolidation of the Mexican attitude in matters of the expropriation would be cemented even before the termination of the actual presidential period.[52]

Another important aspect of the Sinclair agreement was that it was received enthusiastically by both the Mexican and the U.S. administrations. Through Cárdenas's adviser, Ramón Beteta, Mexicans were told that U.S. administration members could not show open support for Mexico's success, since it would cost them decisive votes in the upcoming elections. But behind the scenes, the pro-Mexico faction within the U.S. administration celebrated. Undersecretary of State Welles congratulated Ambassador Castillo Nájera on the success of the negotiations.[53] Roosevelt's leftist Secretary of Agriculture and future Vice President Henry Wallace was more outspoken. He told Beteta that the United States should follow Mexico's example and regulate U.S. petroleum companies. Indeed, it did provide Roosevelt with relief. The opening of the U.S. markets would allow Cárdenas to rely less on Davis's oil company in the immediate future. U.S. press scrutiny of links between Davis's oil company and members of the Democratic party would lessen. The Sinclair agreement spared Roosevelt from a more public involvement against the oil companies during the election year.

In sum, Mexico's diplomatic self-defense against foreign governments and multinationals after the expropriation was as sophisticated and skilled as its efforts to protect Mexico's economic needs. Cárdenas had been able to exploit the circumstances of the approaching war to redirect the course of compensation negotiations from a multinational to a bilateral issue. Equally as important was his ability to maintain White House support against the oil companies throughout the entire period. Eventually, the combination of Cárdenas's tough stance during the Richberg negotiations and U.S. domestic political pressures forced President Roosevelt to join the side of the Mexicans. From a geostrategic perspective, Cárdenas's letter exchanges with Roosevelt had convinced the leader of the most powerful democratic nation that Mexico was not playing the German card against the United States, unlike Pancho Villa and President Carranza during World War I. Thus, on the eve of the next world war, Cárdenas's correspondence with Roosevelt also protected Mexico's security from weary U.S. military war planners, by reassuring Roosevelt that Mexico was not falling under German influence.

In the end, these efforts also assured Cárdenas's central goal: to gain official legal recognition of the Mexican state's control over the nationalized properties and to discredit the multinational propaganda that Mexico was unwilling and unable to pay compensation. Western diplomatic tools and pressure politics, U.S. State Department and multinational intimidations, financial carrot-and-stick approaches, the boycott of Mexico's oil exports, and the presidential wrath of Roosevelt had failed to make the Mexicans blink.

These Mexican economic and diplomatic achievements need to be viewed in another context of domestic Mexican history between 1938 and 1940. Diplomatic and economic gains were achieved against the background of renewed ideological polarization, this time fueled by foreign propaganda forces.

Cárdenas's success in reviving broad popular support for Cardenismo through economic nationalism did not mean that the considerable conservative opposition that had existed before March 1938 simply dissolved. In the first weeks after the expropriation, opposition quieted down, shocked by the emotional power of nationalization celebrations. But beneath the renewed enthusiasm for Cardenismo, there lingered yearnings for a return to national politics based on *hispanista* values. In this situation, from the end of April 1938 on, the fermenting rebellion of Saturnino Cedillo became the focus and hope for a revival of national conservative forces.[54] Perhaps the caudillo from San Luis Potosí could achieve for Mexican conservative forces what the expropriation had done for Cardenismo.

This is not the place to repeat the exhaustive research by Ramona Falcon and Dudley Ankerson on this important rebellion.[55] What remains to be examined, however, is the question of foreign involvement in the planning and execution of the Cedillo rebellion.

Cedillo had enjoyed links to the German legation in Mexico City long before his uprising began. At the time when Cárdenas forced him into open rebellion, German Minister Rüdt had left the Mexican capital for a visit to the United States. In Mexico City, First Secretary Northe had remained behind, in charge of the German representation. His reports to Berlin suggest that, at that time, the German legation did not welcome Cedillo's move. He wrote that

> from the German perspective the outbreak of the rebellion can only be regretted. First, the resulting insecurity damages trade in general and therefore, trade with Germany too. Second, it provides the opportunity for continued attacks on Germany. Third, however, it

would be regretted, if the often very healthy ideas that Cedillo represents would disappear from Mexican politics due to a possible early give-away (Kompromittierung).[56]

At that time, German government representatives were hoping for a trade expansion with the German state, not a civil war that might only benefit U.S. economic interests. Later, after Cárdenas's destruction of the Cedillo movement, the German Foreign Ministry conducted an internal investigation to determine whether any German ministry had supported the warlord from San Luis Potosí. The investigation failed to identify any German involvement.[57] Moreover, the Cárdenas administration itself assured the German legation that continued public accusations of German involvement in the Cedillo uprising were really part of a leftist anti-fascist propaganda campaign.[58] Mexican Undersecretary of Foreign Affairs Ramón Beteta apologized to German Minister Rüdt, stating "that the isolated smear campaign against Germany is in no way representative of the position of the Mexican government and people."

Repeatedly, the existing literature has identified Cedillo's German-born chief of staff, Colonel von Merck, as a likely conduit for German influence. The sources in German and Mexican archives, however, show that von Merck established contact with Berlin only *after* the failed rebellion.[59] In a letter written by Colonel von Merck himself to a supporter in the United States, Cedillo's chief of staff displays the very domestic conservative nature of the Cedillo rebellion. Von Merk wrote to a friend in San Antonio:

> what we want is that communism in Mexico, which the government unconsciously supports and which is gaining importance in Mexico, ceases to exist. I believe in nothing absolute, neither the Nazis nor the Fascists who want to bring their doctrines to Mexico, which are perhaps good for Germany and Italy, but not for Mexico. We don't need to import anything to Mexico, not from Russia, Germany or from Italy, nor from any other nations; we want a national nationalism, a Mexican one, nothing exotic. The politics of Europe is of no interest to me, only Mexico.[60]

Once again, the strong domestic orientation of Cedillismo was confirmed. In addition, the U.S. and British governments refused to support Cedillo in any form. In April 1938, the U.S. embassy refused to see von Merck, in order to avoid any appearance of complicity.[61] In September of 1938, Cedillo's sister tried to establish contact with the British Ambassador in Washington "to give him the true facts regarding the situation in the state of San Luis Potosí." She too was rejected.[62] British, U.S., and Mexican diplomatic archives also do not contain conclusive evidence about active support for

Cedillo by the foreign oil multinationals.

When Cedillo, the greatest hope of foreign conservative forces for a turn to conservatism in the Mexican presidential palace, confronted the Cárdenas government, his foreign ideological sympathizers had abandoned him. Dudley Ankerson and Ramona Falcon's interpretation of the Cedillo rebellion as a domestically inspired, planned, and executed insurrection remains valid. By no means were Cedillo or his supporters agents for foreign fascist designs. Their contacts with anybody who might be willing to support Cedillo against Cárdenas was motivated by an opportunistic pragmatism.

After the failure of the Cedillo rebellion, out of sight of contemporary observers, a more potent, foreign force mobilized against Cárdenas. In October 1938, Plutarco Elias Calles's representative, Joseph Eller, arranged a New York meeting between New York's Deputy Commissioner of the Department of Welfare Byrnes MacDonald and State Department Counsel Berle. During the talk, MacDonald identified himself as a Calles emmissary who wanted to topple the Cárdenas administration. He suggested to the Roosevelt administration that the time was right for Calles's immediate intervention in Mexico. Calles claimed the support of ten divisions located in or near the Mexican capital, as well as the backing of Vincente Lombardo Toledano and his union members. Fortunately, for the Cárdenas administration, the pro-Mexico U.S. State Department Counselor Berle rejected the request, even though the Calles emissary hinted at the return of some of the expropriated oil properties.[63] Inside Mexico, Cárdenas's vigilance and tactics had dashed the hopes of Mexico's domestic right. Abroad, the support of the pro-Mexico faction around President Roosevelt once again protected Cárdenas from the conservative, exiled leader of the *maximato* period.

After the destruction of the Cedillo rebellion, Mexican conservatives again turned to General Franco's fascist movement in Spain as their preferred point of political projection. At the same time, Franco's organization, Falange, intensified its propaganda efforts in Mexico. By the second half of 1938, when the nationalism of the expropriation began to wear off, the Francista propaganda in Mexico became so strong that the Spanish Minister in Mexico, who still represented the official Republican Spanish administration, had to ask for more money from Spain to counter the increasingly fascist Spanish image. According to FBI records, the Falange's expense on propaganda was substantial. Franco's secret service in Mexico spent forty thousand pesos per month. Falange militias required an additional forty thousand pesos monthly. The Falange supported Mexican anti-communist groups with fifteen thousand pesos per month, and additional propaganda required forty thousand pesos. These expenses were covered, according to the FBI, by monthly payments of 125,000 pesos from Falange members inside Mexico and 10,000 pesos from Spain.[64] By the end of 1938, Mexican rightists had regained their strength and were looking forward to repeating in Mexico "Franco's defeat of communism in Spain."[65]

The Cárdenas administration took this Falange challenge very seriously. Immediately after the Cedillo rebellion, Mexican agents searched the Falange offices.[66] The Mexican archives contain specific information about the group from this time forward. The Ministry of Gobernación estimated that out of forty-seven thousand individuals with Spanish ties living in Mexico, forty thousand had joined the Falange. Three weeks later, a U.S. military intelligence report forwarded information from the Ministry of Gobernación that counted sixteen hundred militant activists among thirty thousand Falange members.[67] The search had also produced evidence that the Falange cooperated with Germans and Italians in committing acts of subversion and espionage in Mexico.[68] Falange communications with branches in Cuba and Washington had been intercepted, but their code remained unbroken. But contrary to demands from the Republican Spanish embassy in Mexico, union leader Vincente Lombardo Toledano, and other political groups of Mexico's left, the Cárdenas administration could not simply suppress the Falange. In the months to come, while Franco concluded his coup in Spain, the Falange continued to operate inside Mexico and fan the renewed polarization between Mexico's political right and left.[69]

Germany was the second largest propaganda force in Mexico during 1938. Its activities expanded significantly during this year, adding to the spread of pro-fascist foreign propaganda inside Mexico in the aftermath of the expropriation. Whereas the Falange focused on Mexican conservatives and those with Spanish ancestry, German propaganda focused on the small, but influential, group of urban Mexican professionals and members of the Mexican military. Germany tried to achieve its goals through educational channels. In 1938, 730 students enrolled in German government–sponsored language courses. In addition, the German legation tried to give Mexicans a flavor of national socialist culture at an "evening of culture." For several hours, German cultural clubs performed, members of the NSDAP party branch lectured or showed propaganda movies, and students of the local German schools performed plays. After completion of the language course, outstanding Mexican students received the special gift of a book from the German legation. At home, Mexican students could satisfy their interest about Germany by listening to German shortwave broadcasts in Spanish.[70]

German Minister Rüdt himself worked the circles of the Mexican scholarly establishment. As a member of the prestigious Mexican Sociedad

Mexicana de Geographía y Estadística, he lectured about German–Mexican affairs to Mexico's academic elite.[71] But this platform did not provide access to most of the nation's natural scientists. Thus, the German legation and the NSDAP branch created a new German–Mexican scientific association—the Humboldt Gesellschaft—as the hub of an extended German–Mexican scientific exchange.[72] After one year, however, the organization failed to attract a substantial number of Mexicans. Mexico's professionals and natural scientists were not fooled by National Socialist science, and remained within the boundaries of traditional scientific organizations.

Germany was also interested in Mexican physicians and pharmacists because "they belonged to the upper class." Mexican medical students were attracted to German medical science with the help of scholarships to Germany. The Mexican military was another target of German propaganda. Traditionally, Mexican soldiers regarded German esprit de corps and military equipment as exemplary. For the first time, an advanced German course was offered in the Mexican military elite school, Escuela Superior de Guerra. One member of its faculty, a naturalized German, was an early member of the Mexican branch of the NSDAP party. For those who could not read German, a new publication was created that reprinted German articles about military issues in Spanish.[73] A first German–Spanish dictionary for military terms was published. Finally, Mexican doctors or military officers traveling to Germany received German governmental and industrial support. For example, when the Mexican military's General Tejeda toured Germany, the Ibero-Amerika Institut in Berlin provided a personal tour guide and a well-stocked expense account for his trip; the effort paid off: Tejeda placed a substantial order of two million pesos for educational material for a new military school. Mexican scientists received attention from the representatives of the German chemical trust, I.G. Farben,[74] which also supported tours of Mexican visitors through Germany.[75] Pro-German journalists who wished to visit Germany received special support from the head of the German Chamber of Commerce, Richard Eversbusch.[76]

The Mexican government took note of German propaganda activities during that time period. But unlike against the Falange, the Cárdenas administration did not intervene. As Undersecretary of Hacienda Eduardo Villaseñor argued, the Cárdenas administration saw the central German objective of its work in Mexico as gaining control over the German community in Mexico and influencing U.S. policy, but not toppling the Mexican government.[77] No doubt, Germany and Spain were controlling the Falange; but so far, all direct German efforts to manipulate domestic Mexican groups like the Vanguardia Nacionalista, the Camisas Doradas, or Partido de

Salvación Publica had failed to produce any serious threat to Cárdenas. In 1938, Mexico was willing to defend itself against subversive threats to the government, but its police was neither trained nor equipped to do counter-intelligence work for the United States.

To a certain extent, the activities of foreign pro-fascist forces inside Mexico after the expropriation were counterbalanced by anti-fascist propaganda from European democratic governments, European anti-fascist exiles, and their allies among the Mexican political left. The French government focused its efforts on professional groups, such as businessmen, scientists, and the military. The cultural organization Alliance Francaise sponsored eleven language courses in 1938, in which two thousand Mexicans were enrolled. During the year, nine French lecturers toured Mexico, presenting a total of thirty-one lectures, more than two each month. Some of Mexico's union activists were addressed by Leon Jounaux, the general secretary of French unions at the Latin American Peace Congress and the Latin American Labor Congress in Mexico City. The French government gave the Mexican military school and the Mexican Geographical Society extensive gifts of books. The Mexican military received three scholarships for military postgraduate work in France. Two civilian scholarships were coveted by thirty-three Mexican applicants.

One of the greatest successes of French propaganda in 1938 was the Mexican Ministry of Education's decision to declare the French Fourteenth of July a Mexican holiday. On this "Day of Democracy," all Mexican schools remained closed and the Mexican Minister of Education addressed five thousand students in the capital's soccer stadium. The celebration closed with the singing of the Mexican and French national anthems.

A new friendship society, Mexico–Francia, was founded. The organization had ten departments that organized events in literature, music, economy, architecture, theater, and movies. Mexican Undersecretary of Hacienda Villaseñor served as president of the Mexican chapter. Finally, a new French elementary school was opened, teaching children from kindergarten through the seventh grade; about two hundred children enrolled in 1938.

Czechoslovakia focused on inter-institutional exchanges and cultural propaganda. Fourteen Czech institutions maintained ties with organizations in Mexico, and the Czech embassy in Mexico City convinced the Cárdenas administration to name a street in the capital after a Czech politician. The Czech Minister in Mexico and his deputy gave nine public lectures in connection with showing films about Czechoslovakia. A world-famous Czech cellist played a concert series with seven performances in Mexico City. Some of these events attracted over a thousand spectators.

European anti-fascist exiles who had sought refuge in Mexico produced some of the most effective anti-fascist propaganda during 1938. After the CTM Congress in February of 1938, a small but highly motivated group of German and Austrian exiles had met at the Hidalgo theater to commemorate the fifth anniversary of the German Reichstag burning. At the meeting, it was decided to form a German-exile Popular Front in Mexico to challenge head-on Third Reich activities in Mexico. The group was joined by Social Democrats, a member of the former German Republican organization, and Austrians.

This group was able to generate effective propaganda because of its support from communist and socialist Mexicans who worked for the Mexican Ministry of Education. They provided the European exiles with access to the prestigious Mexico City Palace of Bellas Artes. There, they held a six-part lecture series that presented to Mexicans non-fascist German voices and discussed non-fascist German literature and culture. From May 1938 on, the organization now called Liga Pro Cultura Alemana remained a very painful thorn in the side of German propaganda. In the years to come, it would focus a constant spotlight on the activities of the German legation in Mexico and, thus, neutralize many of its schemes.

At first, German Minister Rüdt predicted that the group would remain short-lived. When some members of the German ethnic community in Mexico visited the group's lecture series, Rüdt published a warning in the German newspaper in Mexico and the Mexico City NSDAP branch sent spies to future lecture events to keep the German community away from anti-fascist propaganda. Next, Rüdt protested in the Mexican Foreign Ministry against the Mexican Ministry of Education's support for the group, demanding an end to their use of Bellas Artes. But the Foreign Ministry told him that it had no influence over the activities of the "red ministry of education."

Contrary to Minister Rüdt's hopes, the group lived on.[78] On September 13, 1938, the Liga sponsored another well-publicized evening of anti-fascist speeches in Mexico City. This time, the head of the Partido Revolucionario Mexicana (PRM), Luis I. Rodriguez, gave a presentation about the history and development of the NSDAP, sharply criticizing the Nazi movement. Once again, diplomatic protests by the German legation brought no consequences.[79]

The Liga's greatest propaganda success, however, was achieved in October of 1938. A German immigrant from Silesia, who had married a woman of Spanish ancestry, had written to the NSDAP race department in Berlin asking for his wife to be declared an Aryan woman. In response, Berlin sent him a questionnaire, asking to prove that his wife's family was free of Indian ethnicity as far back as 1800. The man was seriously offended by the request and, as revenge, forwarded the document to the Liga. The Liga copied the NSDAP letter, put a headline reading "Mexicans, do you know that you are a race of second class?" on the top of the page, and distributed it all over the city.[80] Its impact in Mexico City was so strong that Minister Rüdt, who had just returned from a visit in Berlin, was forced to publish rebuttals in the Mexican papers *Novedades, La Prensa, El Universal,* and *Excelsior.* It was too late. While many urban Mexicans had sympathies for far-right political stances, the German racial concepts had touched a raw nerve in a social group strongly influenced by mestizo culture.

Mexico's CTM and union leader Vincente Lombardo Toledano also supported the efforts of the Liga. Vincente Lombardo Toledano became so irritating in his anti-fascist propaganda that Minister Rüdt developed a deep personal hatred for the union leader and wanted him restrained by Mexican courts. After an anti-Hitler speech by Lombardo Toledano in November 1938, Rüdt demanded that the Mexican Foreign Ministry support him in his efforts to take Lombardo Toledano to court, and Rüdt pursued this idea with great determination until the end of that year. Finally, Mexican Foreign Minister Hay managed to convince Rüdt to withdraw his lawsuit with the argument that his action "would make Toledano the hero of the masses and provide further occasion for attacks on Germany."[81]

Republican Spaniards in Mexico also conducted a major propaganda campaign against Franco and the Falange. As in the case of the anti-fascist Germans, anti-Franco exhibitions, lectures, film, conferences, and concerts received important backing from the Cárdenas administration. Mexican leftist political groups, some Mexican unions, and intellectual groups like the La Liga Escritores y Artistas Revolucionarias, El Bloque de Obreros Intelectuales, El Frente Populár Español, and Universidád Obrera joined Spanish Republican anti-Franco propaganda activities. Their greatest success came when they convinced President Cárdenas to open the "Casa de España en México," which became home for many of Spain's leading exiled intellectuals and a center for non-fascist cultural and intellectual work.

Taken together, the activities of the CTM, Mexico's political left, European anti-fascist exiles, Mexican Jewish organizations, and the French and Czech government provided the Cárdenas administration with an indirect anti-fascist propaganda program.[82] But compared to the Mexican right's financial strength, the benefit of a pro-Catholic religious environment, and the traditionally conservative value system of Mexican society of the 1930s, propaganda by the left and democratic countries could do little more than expose the fascist activities to public scrutiny. It failed to gain lasting popular goodwill within the wider Mexican society.

To make matters worse, by the spring of 1939 General Franco emerged as the clear winner in the Spanish Civil War, providing more fuel for the cause of Mexico's *hispanistas*. The impact of his victory further affected Mexico's society when Mexico's Catholic Church issued a letter of support for Franco on April 2, 1939, and published it in the newspaper *La Semana*. Mexico City's Spanish Club celebrated Franco's success on April 4, 1939, in the Spanish casino, together with German and Italian fascist sympathizers. At the end of the party some drunken members moved on to the local CTM and yelled, "Death to Communism and Viva España!" The next day, the CTM and Vincente Lombardo Toledano renewed their public protest against the Falange.[83] With Franco's victory and the sharpening propaganda contest between pro- and anti-fascist forces in Mexico threatening to unload its destructive energy into the streets of Mexico, President Cárdenas decided to take a more drastic public stance against the pro-Franco forces. In the coming days he would expel three leading Falange members from Mexico. For the first time, the Falange had been challenged publicly by the Mexican administration.

Franco's victory and Cárdenas's first direct confrontation with the Falange initiated a debate about future activities inside Mexico. In subsequent months, a struggle ensued between Ibañez, Mexico's domestic Falange leader, and his superior in Washington D.C. Before the two men resolved the struggle over future direction, the European war itself created a new ideological framework that would settle the issue for them. More importantly, it neutralized the power of the Falange in the remaining months of the Mexican presidential campaign. Once again, the European war provided breathing space for Cardenismo.

On August 23, 1939, the publication of the Hitler–Stalin pact created an official state of tolerance between European communists and fascists that was incomprehensible for most deeply Catholic—that is, anticommunist— Mexicans. While the leadership of the Mexican left urged its rank and file to follow Moscow's line of argumentation, Mexican Falangists were spared such a deep insult to their intelligence. Still, in October 1939, the Franco government ordered international Falange groups to refrain from any activity that could be construed as a violation of Spanish neutrality. In Mexico, the ideological implications of the Hitler-Stalin pact and Franco's order paralyzed the Falange. The paralysis was deep enough for U.S. intelligence to argue that the influence of the Falange as "an active force for propaganda and infiltration of German and Italian influence has declined; until Germany clearly wins or disassociates itself from USSR there is no hope for a resurgence."[84] In September 1939, during a conference between a representative of the Mexican Ministry of Gobernación and a member of the U.S. embassy, the U.S. officer gained the impression that the Mexicans had become relaxed about the Falange threat.[85] Twenty days later, Undersecretary of Hacienda Eduardo Villaseñor confirmed that threats from the right were under control.[86] The Mexican Falange, as a social movement, had been substantially weakened by the Hitler-Stalin pact and had stopped being a threat to Cardenismo. After October 1939, Mexico's Falange leader, Ibanez, withdrew into a small office in the Portuguese legation of Mexico City, where he represented Franco's Spain as a consular official, shuffling paperwork, and officiating over documents for people interested in moving to Franco's Spain.

The German legation in Mexico City also reacted with shock to the announcement of the Hitler-Stalin pact. Eight days before its announcement, Minister Rüdt had returned from a trip to Germany without having gained any prior knowledge of what was to come.[87] But unlike the Falange, German groups continued their propaganda activities, only now within the new paradigms of the Hitler-Stalin pact. The demonization of Stalin, the Soviet Union, and the Mexican left stopped overnight.[88] Roosevelt and the United States became the new target.

Among Mexico's leftist groups, the Hitler-Stalin pact had similarly destructive consequences. Most of the leadership of Mexico's left adopted the official line of the Comintern, namely that the Hitler-Stalin pact was necessary to keep the Soviet Union out of a war fought between opposing imperialist forces. Perhaps this idea would have been tolerable for loyal party members. But in addition, Mexico's leftist leadership also asked the rank and file to support the "peace policies of the Soviet Union," a cynical euphemism for the Soviet Union's war against Poland and Finland in the fall of 1939.[89]

It was a grave mistake. For many Mexicans—those for as well as those against the Mexican left—the Soviet invasion of Finland in the early winter of 1939 symbolized not an expansion of the communist world, but an imperialistic attack on a smaller, weaker neighbor. The Finnish–Soviet clash served as a symbolic projection screen for Mexican nationalist fears concerning the United States. It was a reminder of what it could mean to live as the neighbor of an imperialistic world power.

The rank and file of Mexico's leftist organizations did not agree with this interpretation of how to keep international peace, and many felt betrayed in their previous, dedicated efforts to fight European fascism. Many left the Mexican Communist party. Inside the CTM, Vincente Lombardo Toledano's support for the official Moscow line provided the impulse for many smaller unions to leave the CTM in a time of already increasing tensions over the CTM's support for Avila Camacho as the official presidential candidate.[90] Mexico's Ministry of Gobernación informed U.S. intelligence forces that it expected many more communist members to leave the Mexican Communist party, and eventually membership did drop to two to three thousand.[91] As long as the Hitler-Stalin pact remained in place, communism would be no serious threat to anybody in Mexico.

A second, very serious blow to Mexico's left came when Trotsky and his Mexican followers disseminated the rumor that communists and Nazis had formed a coalition in Mexico to prepare a coup against the Cárdenas administration in the context of the approaching presidential elections. This rumor had first emerged in the U.S. Congress's Dies Investigative Committee, and it gained widespread popular attention on October 2, 1939, through a *Ultimas Noticias* newspaper article with the title "Ofensiva Contra los Stali-Nazis." It created a pro-Allied propaganda monster that, in the end, almost convinced Allied governments that its own propaganda were fact.[92] In November 1939, the artist and sometimes Communist party member Diego Rivera reenforced existing fears when he stated that Mexico was already in the hands of the "Communazis."[93] Right away, conservative Mexican anticommunist senators of Mexico's Congress jumped on Rivera's bandwagon and demanded the dissolution of the Mexican Communist party and the denunciation of its members as traitors to the country. Against the background of the Soviet invasion of Finland, they argued "that taking orders from Stalin and to agitate in such a manner as to be subversive in character and to undermine the framework of Mexican Governmental procedure" was un-Mexican![94] The debate received new fuel on April 13, 1940, this time during the German invasions of the Benelux countries and France. Again, *Ultimas Noticias* published an article about "outstanding members of the Comintern in Mexico." Quoting Diego Rivera, a German exile, and other confidential agents as sources, the article claimed that the Comintern's goal in Mexico was to foment a civil war through agitation, with the intention of distracting U.S. attention from Europe and, subsequently, preventing the United States from entering the European conflict. Most importantly, it claimed again that Russian and German agents were working together to start a revolt in Mexico.[95] At the same time, Comintern representatives arrived in Mexico and purged party members, including Secretary General Hernan Laborde and his aide, Valentin Campa.[96] Today we know that this was related to the Mexicans' opposition to the planned murder of Trotsky.[97] Yet in the heated environment of the presidential elections and the German advances in Western Europe, these rumors deepened confusion, fear, and a sense of ideological betrayal among Mexico's left. It would take the Mexican left many years to recover from the era of the Hitler-Stalin pact.

The Hitler-Stalin pact also ended the public clashes between Mexico's right and left. A German agent later told the FBI that both groups had exposed to each other their organizational structure and operations. He reported that when Hitler invaded the Soviet Union in 1941, great fear existed inside the German legation in Mexico City that the leadership of Mexico's Communist party would disclose its knowledge about the fascists in public.[98] On April 1, 1941, a highly confidential U.S. source gained access to the confidential vault of the CTM for three hours. After examining its content, he brought a copy of a letter to the U.S. embassy, revealing that it had been written by Christian Zinsser, an alleged German Gestapo agent. It had been addressed to Vincente Lombardo Toledano and read by Fidel Velázquez.[99] In the letter, Zinsser established a link between the Mexican Nazi organization, individuals inside U.S. labor unions, and some individuals inside the CTM. This, however, remains the only document that proves a more intimate cooperation between the two opposing camps, going beyond a truce in the ideological warfare that had taken place between 1938 and 1939. Also, an internal German investigation in Berlin about possible German secret service ties to Lombardo Toledano remained negative.[100] This suggests that the lone letter in the CTM vault might have been proof of local working arrangements that had taken place without orders from Berlin.

In the final analysis, the Cárdenas administration was the great beneficiary of the ideological confusion that resulted from the Hitler-Stalin pact. First, the Mexican state gained a reprieve from leftist–rightist domestic struggles. Second, its organization would not be altered, neither by fascist nor by leftist political interests. With the two extremes of Mexico's political spectrum paralyzed, the Cárdenas administration could concentrate the state's resources on the election of the conservative candidate, Avila Camacho, as the next Mexican president.

The paralysis resulting from the Hitler-Stalin pact reassured U.S. military planners that Cárdenas was indeed in control in Mexico. The southern border of the United States seemed to be relatively safe from communist or fascist attacks in the immediate future. Domestic fascist sympathies, which had played an important role in Norway, Belgium, the Netherlands, and France, would not be able to open the door to a pro-fascist president south of the U.S. border. The rumors about communist–Nazi cooperation strengthened Cárdenas's foreign image as a guarantor of the path toward greater democratic politics south of the border. To many members of the U.S. Congress, Cárdenas's condemnation of the Soviet attack on Finland in the League of Nations and his support for Finland in the Mexican public reinforced his image as a reasonable, pro-Allied Latin American politician who was not under the influence of the Comintern. Whatever Cárdenas was, he appeared not to be an ideological zealot.

This important achievement must not be underestimated at the beginning of World War Two. In September 1939, Gus Jones, a former Texas Ranger and FBI station chief in Texas, had been invited by the Cárdenas administration to come to Mexico City. Quietly and without official authorization, he instructed Mexican secret agents in the creation of a Mexican counterintelligence group in Mexico City. Over 400,000 pesos were raised for Jones and his men to equip twenty-five cars with radio systems. For the first time, a sophisticated surveillance system of foreign secret activities existed in the Mexican capital that was superior to Spanish, German, Italian, and Japanese systems. Gus Jones remained in Mexico City and headed the Mexico City FBI office. In that capacity, Jones not only reported about foreign activities in Mexico, but he could have also reported about unwelcome Mexican activities. The presence of his eyes and ears in Mexico reassured the FBI, J. Edgar Hoover, and other influential U.S. policy makers that the situation inside Mexico was satisfactory. The Mexican administration was in complete control and there was no need for U.S. military planners to contemplate an occupation of Mexico as a preemptive move against a possible invasion of foreign fascist forces.

After the fall of 1939, foreign propaganda in Mexico refocused its attention from domestic political discourse to manipulating Mexican perceptions about the developments on European battlefields.

A major change occurred when European democratic powers put aside their previously competitive attitudes within the Mexican newspaper market. Members of Mexico's ethnic French, Polish, Dutch, Belgium, Greek, and Jewish communities organized a united propaganda front against international fascism. Propaganda had graduated from an advertisement for national achievements to a tool that presented the cause of the Allies in Mexico. Initially, French commercial houses in Mexico carried the financial lion's share of the propaganda. Soon, however, the British sent a representative from the Ministry of Information to Mexico, who took over the financial and organizational leadership of this newly created Franco British Publicity Committee.

Under the leadership of French researcher Jacques Soustelle and British Consul Ifor Rees, the committee set up a wire service to supply Mexico City papers with British ANTA government news wires. Mexican provincial papers were supplied with wires from the *Servicio Mundial*.[101] During the first half of 1940, the victories of fascism on the European battlefield set obvious priorities of Allied propaganda work. A British memorandum defined the goals in the following words:

> to convert as many Mexicans as possible to the British cause and to supply those already converted with enough information and news to back up their convictions . . . and . . . to convince the Mexicans that we will win the war and that it will be a good thing for them if we do.

Allied propaganda should demonstrate

> to all classes and all factions that this war is a war of the human race as a whole against a false conception of superiority and against an attempt at world hegemony by the self styled master race of Germany.[102]

As during 1937 and 1938, Allied propaganda in Mexico remained focused on educated, professional, and mostly urban clientele. Lawyers, doctors, dentists, professors, schoolmasters, state and federal government officials, engineers, municipal presidents, priests, religious families, barbershops, hotels, hospitals, clubs, army officers, and publishing institutions were the main propaganda targets.[103] Every week, ten thousand households or individuals received a newsletter called *Talking Points*. Priests, the military, and teachers were targeted with special editions. An additional forty thousand addresses received mailings from the Allied committee at least once in a while. The mailings tried to be very sensitive about the different political preferences of Mexico's small urban middle class. A British memorandum explained:

> catholics must be made to believe that catholicism will gain with a British victory;
>
> left wingers, that their particular type of radicalism will benefit;
>
> conservatives that the best part of the status quo will be preserved;
>
> local politicians that England will, at the worst, meddle less in internal affairs than Germany;
>
> businessmen that Mexican trade will benefit form a British victory;

the man on the street that we stand for an ordinary and decent
way of living.[104]

In addition, a wide variety of Mexican newspapers was provided with
special articles about the Allies at war. Articles for the *Gaceta de la Guerra,
Candil, Ultimas Noticias,* and *Claridades* targeted the general public; articles for *El Nacional* were aimed at government bureaucrats; *Novedades*
articles courted Catholics and conservatives; *Documentos y Comentarios
de la Guerra* provided food for thought for intellectuals. For direct, strong
attacks on Germany and the German legation in Mexico City, the propaganda committee used the publication *Candil.*

By the end of 1939 the efforts of the Allied committee showed some
modest results. Thirty-nine of its articles about the war had been published
in major Mexico City newspapers. By April 1940, 480 articles had appeared
in Mexican provincial newspapers. Photographs were offered for the first
time in February 1940, and caricatures became available soon thereafter.[105]
But offers of Allied free wire services and newspaper articles could not match
the Axis's clout in the Mexican print media at that time.

Axis propaganda had an easier forum to begin with, because Germany
was winning every invasion of a foreign country during 1939 and 1940. In
addition, German companies in Mexico dominated newspaper advertising
in important consumer goods and manufacturing sectors like chemicals,
pharmaceuticals, machinery, typewriters, calculators, and photo equipment.
German press attaché Dietrich forced all German advertisers into a advertisement pool, and rewarded or punished Mexican newspapers with German ads depending on their stance toward the German victories in Europe.[106]
In addition, he enjoyed significant financial backing to buy the loyalty of
Mexican journalists, a far more direct and effective method of influence
than merely offering free newspaper articles. After all, the reason to exist
for the Mexican press was profit. In 1939 and early 1940, German propaganda money talked in Mexico's newspaper business. Then, during the German victories in Belgium, Holland, and Norway in the spring of 1940,
German propaganda in Mexico suddenly weakened. German ministries in
Berlin had to rearrange their funding priorities under the pressures of war,
and they moved their money into the German propaganda channels of the
newly conquered countries.

During March of 1940, German Minister Rüdt three times requested
special funds for propaganda activities from Berlin, without receiving a reply. By April he angrily wrote to Berlin:

Due to the lack of sufficient funds day after day we are losing
ground, one newspaper after the other gets lost and yields to hostile

financial pressure. An activation of press and news activity is especially impossible. It would be a dangerous error, to believe that influence on the press can be achieved through offers of material, personal contacts, tea parties or similar things. In this country all newspapers and most journalists expect cash for cooperation, as obviously the other side is offering plentiful.[107]

At the same time, Allied propaganda in Mexico increased its financial help, reorganized, and incorporated new techniques. The frightening German victories in Europe had convinced Allied forces to spend more funds on propaganda abroad. Thus when German payments declined, Mexican journalists were only too happy to switch to Allied financial sources. In addition, Allied Europeans organized propaganda committees outside Mexico City that more easily manipulated Mexican regional and local papers. By the summer of 1940, committees existed in Puebla, Monterrey, Guadalajara, Tampico, Mazatlán, Vera Cruz, and Campeche.[108] A new technique learned from Madison Avenue's advertising agencies also proved powerful. From spring 1940 on, Allied propagandists chose one or two simple themes to sell to the Mexican public in concentrated publicity campaigns. The first campaign that received continental dimensions was the fifth-column campaign, which was highly successful. By May of 1940, Allied propaganda had gained access to every Mexican newspaper, with the exception of *El Popular* and the first edition of *Ultimas Noticias*.

After the saturation of the newspaper-article market, the Allied propaganda committee aimed at breaking into Mexico's editorial columns. At *El Nacional,* which had been pro-Allied from the beginning, the Allies did not have to work too hard. The paper had not yet been taken over by the Mexican administration, and a subsidy of one thousand pesos per month bought control over its editorial column three times a week. The owners of *Excélsior,* who also controlled *Ultimas Noticias,* also received an Allied financial offer. The Allied request was backed by a well-organized, temporary withdrawal of British and French advertisement, and soon the editorial managers of both papers invited Allied representatives back for further talks. Compliance with the allied requests was rewarding. The formerly pro-Franco paper *Novedades* was rewarded with Allied advertisements. A smaller publication received two hundred new subscriptions for distribution in barbershops and in dental and medical offices.

The propaganda battle over the Mexican magazine business was more expensive. At first, the British had tried to create their own Mexican magazine called *Noticias Graficas.* The effort failed and cost fifteen hundred British pounds in the process. The Germans had gained a foothold in the existing

magazine *Todo*. A concentrated advertisement boycott by the Allies against
the magazine caused its eventual collapse and forced the Germans to look
for new avenues in the magazine sector. Next, the German legation targeted
the magazine *Timon*. Its financial needs, however, were so large that it forced
Germans to cut back in other propaganda areas.[109]

The German victory in France further intensified Allied propaganda efforts in Mexico. Finally, the U.S. government became involved and encouraged U.S. business in Mexico to make contributions to the Allied propaganda
committee, and thereby making its financial clout stronger. Most importantly, President Cárdenas himself joined the cause of the Allies. He invited
key Mexican journalists to the national palace and demanded a pro-Allied
attitude from their newspapers and magazines. He also expelled German
press attaché Dietrich from Mexico and ordered the closure of the magazine
Timon.[110] The German propaganda network in Mexico had lost its key or-
ganizer and a major propaganda vehicle.

German propaganda in Mexico never recovered from these blows. After
Mexico's presidential election the major remaining German newsletter, *Diario
de la Guerra*, ceased publication and German propaganda moved to mostly
small extreme-right-wing papers. By then, Mexico's urban professional
groups were gaining most of their news about the war in Europe from Allied sources. By the end of 1940, Allied propaganda averaged 300 published
articles per month in Mexico City alone. The Allied effort peaked in November of 1941, with 518 published articles. Similar success occurred in
provincial papers. Within one year, the Germans had been defeated in the
international battle for Mexican hearts and minds.

In sum, the development of the foreign propaganda battle after 1939
reenforced the message to Allied powers that, unlike during World War I,
the Cárdenas administration supported the cause of the Allies without hesitation. Moreover, Mexican tolerance of the organization of the anti-fascist
foreign propaganda efforts in Mexico by European interests, from the fall
1939 on, allowed the Cárdenas administration to support the Allied cause
without endangering its commercial links with Germany, Italy, and Japan.
The same arrangement allowed Axis governments abroad and conservative
Mexicans at home to believe that the Mexican government was a victim of
imperialistic Allied propaganda pressure that could not be refused without
consequences. After the German victory over France, once the economic
shift toward Mexican economic cooperation with the United States had
become obvious and Mexico's European markets lost, Cárdenas could act
against Axis propaganda more publicly. This veiled attitude had served the
interests of his administration well during 1939 and 1940.

Most importantly, the expulsion from Mexico of the German propaganda chief, Dietrich, on the eve of the presidential election was another strong message to Germany, the U.S. administration, and conservative domestic groups declaring that the Cárdenas administration would act without hesitation whenever domestic political stability was endangered.

ॐ

7

The Modernization of the Mexican Military
under Cárdenas

National Goals vs. Foreign Constraints (1934–1940)

THE CHANGING INTERNATIONAL ENVIRONMENT OF THE 1930S AFFECTED the Mexican armed forces in contradictory ways. The institutionalization and professionalization of the formerly revolutionary forces continued, even accelerated. An increasingly bureaucratic military leadership was determined to diminish the importance of the military as a domestic political player and to assert the monopoly of violence in the hands of the state.[1] Since conflicts were increasingly solved by institutional political means, the military was losing its key role within the postrevolutionary state. In other words, by the 1930s the Mexican armed forces, as an institution, was in need of a new, permanent mission as part of the postrevolutionary state.

This process took place within an international environment preparing for large-scale war. By coincidence, the international drive toward war offered the Mexican military a new justification for technological modernization and, just as important, a new external mission. The new mission was the defense of Mexican territory against the consequences of international war, which conceivably would occur in the form of a preemptive U.S. invasion declared necessary to avoid a fascist takeover or to protect Mexican shores from an Axis invasion. At the same time, the Second World War promised to help the postrevolutionary state by further reducing the role of the military in domestic politics.

And yet, as this chapter will show, the very same international drive toward war kept the Mexican military from acquiring modern technology and reorganizing its troops against a foreign aggressor. The result was that by the time of the German victory over France in 1940, the Mexican military was unprepared for the protection of Mexican borders against a foreign enemy. Therefore, it was extremely vulnerable to U.S. military designs that advocated a takeover of the defense of Mexican territory through a largely well-intended, but politically naive, preemptive invasion.

President Obregon had charged General Amaro with the creation of a national fighting force loyal to the Mexican state.[2] Amaro's task was "to change the army from a vehicle for advancing one's political aims into a nonpolitical institution which would restrict itself to the military tasks of defending the nation against internal and external threats."[3] In 1925, recruitment policies were instituted that reduced the overall size of the army.[4] In 1926, Amaro created a regulatory code that institutionalized military promotion, discipline, retirement, and benefits.[5] In 1928, President Calles's creation of the national party, the PNR, weakened the personal influence of regional military leaders in national politics.

New military education policies reenforced these efforts. At a remodeled Colegio Militar, recruits were taught a new curriculum that focused on professionalization. Enlisted soldiers from the revolutionary period were presented with a skills test that eliminated many of them from army payrolls. There would be less and less space for revolutionary soldiers in a professionalized Mexican military. By the end of the 1920s, Amaro had established a basic legal and organizational framework that could serve as a base for the military's future professionalization.

Bureaucratic centralization of the military's administration was the chief task of the early 1930s. First, the Mexican Ministry of War asserted itself as the central state agency for all national military administrative matters. In 1933, President Rodríguez asked the Mexican Congress for eight months of special powers to legislate independently on all military matters. His Minister of War, Lázaro Cárdenas, used the opportunity to create a Servicio de Intendencia (accounting and fiscal management) and the Dirección General de Materias de Guerra (arms and equipment acquisition), limiting for the first time the procurement power of regional military commanders. As Mexican president, Cárdenas put the acquisition of military armament entirely in the hands of the Secretary of War. He also instituted a rotation policy for regional military leaders that kept them from forming a regional military power base.[6] The improvement of social and living conditions for junior officers was supposed to deepen their bond with the Mexican state.[7]

Indirect measures changed the orientation of Mexican armed forces. General Amaro had sent younger Mexican officers abroad to gain knowledge about foreign armies and military practices. Upon returning to Mexico, their knowledge contributed to discussions about Mexico's future military mission inside the rebuilt General Staff.[8] Also, military scholarships to German and French armies offered Mexican military planners a deeper insight into international military developments. In addition, Mexican military attachés, stationed in the capitals of the world's major military powers, pondered the implications of international military developments for Mexico's situation. Finally, the historical lessons of U.S. naval invasions of Mexican territory and 1920s U.S. gunboat diplomacy in the Caribbean and Central America suggested an additional, external mission for Mexico's military forces in a postrevolutionary state.

A first recognition of a real or imagined military threat from the United States was Plutarco Elías Calles's efforts to establish a Mexican coast guard/ navy during the *maximato*. In 1932, the Spanish Republican government provided the Mexican government with a loan of seventy million pesetas for the construction of five transport vessels and ten gunboats.[9] In addition, the Mexican government began preparations in 1932 for the construction of a naval base at Magdalena Bay. Additional operating bases were to be established at Tampico, Puerto Mexico in the Gulf of Mexico, and at La Paz and Acapulco on Mexico's Pacific Coast. These were not only efforts to establish refueling stations for the newly ordered ships so that they could monitor all of Mexico's coastlines; it was also a signal to U.S. policy makers and congressmen to end their fantasies about acquiring naval bases through purchase, lease, or force in Mexico.

By 1934 a new facet of a foreign orientation for Mexico's forces emerged. No longer was it just the neighbor to the north; now there was also the possibility of an international war in the Pacific that could affect Mexico. A 1934 Mexican military study examined the possibilities of a war between the United States and Japan and its consequences for Mexico. Military planners explored the idea of Mexican support for the Japanese, and in their conclusion, they advised strongly against it. Otherwise Mexico

> would be annihilated without a single American soldier putting foot upon our soil. How? By the United States Navy and Air Force, for both of our coasts would be bombarded by the navy and the air force would destroy our defenseless inland towns in the same way.[10]

In Washington, Mexican military attaché Azcárate considered the longevity and sincerity of the U.S. Good Neighbor policy and declared it would probably be short-lived. In his words, Mexico had to develop its military forces in protection against a United States expected to be hostile. To accomplish this task, Azcárate urged Mexico City to "Europeanize the organization [of the Mexican army] in order not to defraud the high mission that the revolution had entrusted it."[11] All these scenarios involving foreign enemies required a modern Mexican military that could deter or confront foreign forces.

In October 1934, President Abelardo Rodríguez had recognized this need when he announced that the army's combat units would undergo a "gradual organic change in accordance with the necessities of modern warfare."[12] On July 31, 1935, a little more than half a year later, President Cárdenas codified the new direction in his administration's *Plan Sexenio Militar*.[13] To be

precise, the majority of this military development plan still focused on domestic measures and social security programs for the Mexican military, but
it also contained a second component that directly addressed the future
needs of a Mexican military that had to operate within an external context.
Now, new military technology for the Mexican army was necessary:

> A military organization, although its numbers of men may be high,
> cannot have an acceptable combat efficiency if it does not possess a
> reasonable amount of modern equipment. . . . Automatic rifles are
> needed for the infantry and cavalry. Modern warfare demands them
> and they are used in all armies except our own.[14]

The military six-year plan promised the Mexican navy new ships; the
Mexican air force was to obtain new airplanes, improved service facilities,
and air-defense capabilities. The Mexican army was to be mechanized with
armored cars, trucks, and vehicles carrying machine guns. The Mexican
infantry and cavalry would trade its old rifles for automatic weapons, hand
grenades, cannons, mortars, and related accessories. In addition, the creation of a chemical-warfare unit was envisioned.[15] These weapons were designed to fight a foreign force or to deter a foreign aggressor. The period
when the Mexican military focused exclusively on squashing domestic peasant rebellions had come to an end. While the institutionalization of politics
inside Mexico cost the military its revolutionary mission at home, it was
slowly appropriating a new external one.[16]

To plan the technological modernization of an army was merely a bureaucratic paper exercise. But to realize it within a period when the Great
Powers were preparing for war proved much more difficult for the Mexicans.

Armament producers in the United States were the first choice of Mexico's
small air force. In the approaching international war, an expected re-cre-
ation of the British economic blockade of the Atlantic would make supplying Mexican military forces with critical spare parts from Europe very
unlikely as well as vulnerable to pressures from the Axis powers. Besides,
U.S. airplane manufacturers offered favorable credit terms during a time of
limited Mexican state funding. In 1935, an offer of U.S. credit meant that
the Mexican air force could modernize immediately, improve its military
position vis-à-vis the United States, and pay later. Moreover, Mexico already owned some U.S. airplanes, and Mexican officers had received training in U.S. institutions. However, U.S. military representatives discouraged
U.S. manufacturers from sharing sophisticated airplane technology with a
southern neighbor who was deeply distrusted.[17] In 1933, the U.S. Secretary
of War had increased the military staff of the U.S. embassy in Mexico City

to observe more closely countries "with which we may become involved in war, or against which we may be compelled to take punitive measures."[18]

Regardless, after the publication of the Plan Sexenio Militar in 1935, Mexican military buyers approached U.S. companies to explore possible cooperation. Colonel Agustín C. Castrejon, the commander of the Mexican First Air Regiment, visited U.S. military attaché Marshburn in the U.S. embassy. Castrejon informed Marshburn that President Cárdenas had ordered him to purchase about sixty military planes. The Mexicans wished to study the latest test data of U.S. military planes, in particular attack planes.[19] As expected, the U.S. military refused to cooperate, and the performance tests of the newest U.S. airplanes remained top secret. Colonel Castrejon received only very general information, and in the end, he had to be content with the purchase of ten older, used military planes, plus six airplanes for Mexico's mining industry.[20]

During 1937 two developments ended all remaining Mexican hope for a future U.S.–Mexican armament cooperation in the air force sector. First, in January 1937, some of the U.S. planes Mexico had bought the previous year appeared on the docks of Veracruz ready for shipment to Spain to support the cause of the Republican side. In the United States, this Mexican support for the Spanish Republican cause with U.S. weapons caused a political scandal, raising pressing questions about U.S. neutrality in the Spanish conflict. And although Cárdenas gave in to Roosevelt's request, cancelled the delivery to Spain, and promised not to send U.S.-made weapons to Spain in the future, the incident had placed Mexican arms purchases in the United States under a new, suspicious light. From now on, U.S. neutrality legislation would limit Mexican military purchases in the United States.[21] Then, on December 17, 1937, the U.S. State Department restricted the passing of information to foreigners about matters related to airplanes in order to discourage international rivalry in armament matters. Finally, after March 18, 1938 the U.S. weapons industry was no longer willing to offer loans to the Mexican air force. Within two years, Mexican efforts to modernize its air force with U.S. technology had come to an end.

The frustrated U.S.–Mexican military cooperation was easily exploited by European weapon producers who were only too eager to deepen their existing ties with Mexico's armed forces. Contacts between Mexican and European military forces had intensified in the previous years. As early as October 1934, the French military attaché had visited the Mexican Minister of War and held discussions with the head of the Mexican Military Study Commission. He left Mexico with an order for two batteries of anti-aircraft cannons and heavy weapon systems for Mexican gunboats that were under construction in Spain. In October 1935, rumors circulated in Mexico City that the French naval attaché in Washington was about to make another visit south of the border.[22]

The Mexican navy had formed closer ties with German naval circles. Already in 1932, a Mexican–German agreement had been signed to regulate future exchanges of naval visits.[23] In 1933, the German manufacturer MAN had equipped Mexican coast guard–patrol boats with new engines. In 1934, Mexican naval stations were equipped with engines by the same company.[24] In the same year, the German cruiser Karlsruhe docked in Acapulco for its first visit after Hitler's rise to power.[25] The Mexican political left and labor unions, opposing Hitler's policies in Europe, protested strongly against the visit. But as German Minister Rüdt claimed, President Cárdenas himself ordered the police chief of Mexico City to make sure that no disturbances would disrupt the visit. The cruiser's crew visited the Colegio Militar, where German sailors were warmly welcomed by their Mexican colleagues. Some of the Colegio's officers expressed the desire to receive a commission to the German armed forces. Afterward, the captain of the Karlsruhe reported to Germany about the warm reception: "I had the impression that opportunities exist for us in Mexico to become active in the military sector."[26] A second German naval visit took place in February 1936, when the German cruiser Emden stopped in La Paz, Baja California. This time, the governor of Baja California, Juan José Domínguez, a Callista, extended surprising courtesies to the Germans. The German ship practiced torpedo shooting in the bay of La Paz![27] Again, the German visitors were impressed with the pronounced pro-German attitude among their Mexican hosts. In recognition of the Mexican admiration for Prussian military tradition and in view of increasing French and British competition,[28] the German military high command expanded the jurisdiction of the German military attaché to Washington, von Boetticher, to Mexico City in 1936.[29]

German–Mexican military relations improved further during 1937, when economic relations between the two countries promised to enter a new expansive phase. First, military attaché Von Boetticher paid his accreditation visit to Mexico City in January 1937. After laying a wreath at the Statue of Independence and visiting the U.S. military attaché to Mexico, von Boetticher was received by Undersecretary of War Avila Camacho and other high-ranking Mexican military officers.[30] The next day, he toured the Escuela Superior de Guerra, where German courses had just been introduced into the curriculum. During a visit to the Colegio Militar, he noted the pro-German attitude among military circles.[31] The visit concluded with a reception with President Cárdenas, where von Boetticher emphasized that he and Mexican

President Cárdenas understood each other "as soldiers."[32]

Mexico's military attaché to Washington, Azcárate, was reassigned as Mexican Minister to Germany in early 1937. In the following two years, Azcárate, the former chief of staff of President Abelardo Rodríguez and the owner and head of Mexico's premier Mexican aircraft manufacturer, tried to link Mexican–German economic expansion with Mexican–German military cooperation. As a conservative representative of Mexico's military institution and not at all attached to the politics of Cárdenismo,[33] he put the interests of his institution above the anti-fascist policy of his president. From that vantage point, the Mexican Ministry of War only followed in the footsteps of the Mexican Ministry of Hacienda, Foreign Relations, and Public Works and Infrastructure.

In early 1937 a first representative of a leading German airline manufacturer traveled to Mexico to introduce German aviation products to the emerging Mexican civilian and military aviation market.[34] In June 1938, a special plane of the Bavarian company Messerschmitt passed through Mexico City and provided a demonstration for the head of Mexico's small airline industry.

After the oil expropriation, other fascist countries joined the competition over the Mexican aviation market. In September 1938, the Japanese air attaché informed Minister Azcárate that Japan would be willing to sell airplanes to Mexico. The Ministry of War ordered him to obtain a catalogue and prices and wait for further details.[35] In December 1938, the director of the Italian Fiat company made a strong presentation to the chief of the Mexican air force, offering Fiat airplanes in exchange for oil.[36]

In the end, German efforts seemed to win. In February 1939, Mr. Hogemann, a German airplane-industry representative, arrived in Mexico City accompanied by oil man Davis. Immediately, rumors about the nature of Hogeman's visit ran wild.[37] On the evening of February 16, 1939, Davis and Hogemann offered to Minister of Hacienda Suárez the purchase of seventy German planes, paid for with long-term credits and oil barters.[38] In addition, the two men explored the possibility of helping the Cárdenas administration establish an airplane-construction facility in Mexico. With German help, Mexico could become an airplane exporter and supply the Latin American market.[39] The Germans offered to station German military and technical advisers in Mexico to train Mexicans.

This was an incredible offer that would have opened the Latin American aviation market to Germany. More importantly, it could have led to the creation of several Latin American air forces trained by German military advisers. If the Mexicans accepted this plan, the German military would have gained a major inroad into the most pivotal military branch of future wars. Perhaps German advisers could play an important role when it came to undermining U.S. efforts to influence Latin American armies in favor of U.S.–Western Hemisphere military cooperation.

It is interesting that Mexican Minister of Hacienda Suárez even considered the offer and did not refuse it on the spot. He asked the German representative and the oil man Davis to await the outcome of a discussion with President Cárdenas. At that point, Cárdenas asserted the politicians' control over Mexico's military bureaucracy and rejected the German proposal categorically. No German influence would be allowed in the Mexican-aviation sector, even if it meant rejecting the establishment of a viable Mexican air force manufacturing site in Mexico. From then on, Mexican–Axis military cooperation was never mentioned again in Mexican sources.

Consequently, by mid-1939 the Mexican military was still without most of the items mentioned in the Mexican military developmental plan of 1935. The Cárdenas administration used the German deal to apply strong pressure on the U.S. government. The U.S. military attachés in Mexico had already warned about the implications of the German advances in Mexican aviation circles.[40] President Cárdenas added pressure by briefing U.S. Ambassador Daniels about the German proposal[41] in great detail. He challenged the continued unwillingness of the United States to help the Mexican armed forces.[42] Next, the U.S. embassy in Mexico City was deluged with unofficial visits by Mexican military and civilian representatives who repeated over and over again the Mexican desire to purchase ninety to one hundred U.S. planes. The Mexicans also pointed out that the U.S. military was supplying Great Britain and the Soviet Union with information about U.S. airplanes. They demanded equal treatment. The United States should share its confidential information also with the Mexican military.

For the first time, Mexican efforts showed some success. U.S. Ambassador Daniels and the U.S. naval attaché to Mexico joined the Mexicans and argued against the U.S. State Department and in favor of their request.[43] The U.S. naval attaché to Mexico even went so far as to urge Washington to provide Mexico with a 2.5 million-dollar credit for the purchase of the planes. Otherwise, he feared,

> the construction of a well equipped aircraft factory here would further the known ambitions of Mexico to sell aircraft to other Latin American countries, which if under German supervision, would harmonize exceedingly well with the suspected plans of the Nazi Government in the penetration and control of Central and South American countries.[44]

The U.S. commercial attaché to Mexico warned the State Department, in August 1939, that oil man Davis had assured him that if the United States would not sell airplanes to the Mexicans, he would do so eventually.

On August 10, 1939, the chief of the Mexican Military Technical Section, General Juan Rico Islas, the chief of the air force, Alberto Salinas Carranza, and the chief of civil aviation, General Gustavo Salinas, made a joint appearance at the U.S. embassy. They asked to purchase thirty U.S. planes as soon as possible—fifteen fighter planes and the rest convertible transport planes. In addition, they were interested in fueling and repair trucks for military squadrons as well as radio equipment, both for military and civilian aircraft. The Cárdenas administration offered a 20 percent down payment in cash and asked for a credit for the remaining 80 percent.[45] Ambassador Daniels backed the confidential request and asked the U.S. State Department to treat it as unofficial in order to avoid any political repercussions inside Mexico.[46]

The German attack on Poland and the subsequent French and British entry into the war changed the international context for the modernization of Mexican armed forces. Overnight, military and defense issues gained a new importance and urgency within U.S.–Mexican relations. Suddenly, the U.S.–Mexican border became the southern front of U.S. territory that required protection and defense against a possible Axis invasion. From the point of view of U.S. military planners, the state of readiness of the Mexican army was a matter of national strategic importance. From the point of view of the Mexicans, the Mexican military was unprepared and ill-equipped to provide any protection against a foreign aggressor at that time. It was a very dangerous situation because it legitimized a possible justification for a preemptive occupation of Mexico to deter Axis subversion or invasion attempts. Now more than ever, the Mexican forces had to acquire modern military technology from the United States, only now to deter U.S. military planners from taking over the defense of Mexican territory.

At first, the war in Europe revived Mexican hopes. The German invasion of Poland motivated the U.S. Congress to lift the arms export embargo, and at least legally, U.S. weapons could be exported to Mexico in the near future. Indeed, on October 17, 1939, Undersecretary of State Sumner Welles informed Mexican Ambassador Castillo Nájera that in two weeks the U.S. army would receive permission to sell surplus arms and the State Department was willing to organize a credit for the desired Mexican purchases.[47]

The Mexicans were forced to accept that they were becoming part of U.S. defensive considerations, whether they liked it or not. On October 19, 1939, Mexican Ambassador Castillo Nájera received a map from President

Roosevelt that showed the locations of four clandestine German shortwave radio stations inside Mexican territory. Roosevelt asked the Mexican government to investigate these operations and to "do what is necessary".[48] Another nine days later, on October, 28, 1939, U.S. Ambassador Josephus Daniels asked the Mexican Foreign Ministry to allow U.S. airplanes to fly future reconnaissance missions over Baja California and Sonora without prior consultation with the Mexican government. There it was. The absence of a viable Mexican air force and a national Mexican air-defense system motivated U.S. military planners to take over the defense of Mexico. In addition, U.S. popular opinion about Mexico turned fearful when the Senate's Dies Committee explored the possibility that the Hitler-Stalin pact had created a fascist–communist subversive threat in Mexico, which was trying to overthrow the Cárdenas government in the course of the upcoming Mexican presidential elections. Now in times of war, military realities were challenging cherished peacetime political concepts.

Then the frustrating news came that Mexico could not expect U.S. arms and airplanes in the near future. They were desperately needed for the defense of democratic forces in Europe.[49] Also in the future, Mexico would remain without critically necessary modern military technology.

In the end, President Cárdenas refused all requests from President Roosevelt and Ambassador Daniels,[50] and declared Mexico's neutrality in the expanding European war. The nationalist politician Cárdenas was determined that Mexico's self-determination and territorial sovereignty must not become a victim of developments in Europe, long before a credible Axis threat had ever been proven to exist in Mexico.

Nevertheless, these developments had put the new mission of Mexican armed forces against foreign threats on the front burner of Mexican military planners. The Soviet invasion of Finland provided an additional illustration of the Great Powers' disregard for the rights of smaller countries during times of war. It reenforced a sense that these were dangerous times for countries that shared borders with the Great Powers.

In the spring of 1940, the German blitzkrieg successes in Norway, Belgium, the Netherlands, and Luxembourg forced Mexicans to reexamine their national-defense strategy. All of this occurred at a time when domestic political tensions were already high because of the approaching presidential elections. Against this context, the supportive role of domestic pro-fascist political organizations, crystallized in the concept of the fifth column, provided the greatest fear for Mexican policy makers. In the words of Ambassador Castillo Nájera, fifth-column rumors in Mexico could serve as a pretext for a U.S. military intervention. He urged President Cárdenas to reject this type of "protection," which "served only the extension of U.S. imperialism."[51]

In retrospect, Mexican suspicions about U.S. military desires toward Mexico were justified. In August 1940, a document of the U.S. Department of the Navy declared that the unfolding war offered a chance not only to obtain bases for short-term defenses, but also to establish long-term bases at Magdalena Bay and in Acapulco for the postwar period. In the words of U.S. navy planners, a base in Acapulco

> would have peace-time value as temporary base for certain types of planes in transit to and from Panama Canal. . . . Magdalena Bay is ideal in many ways as an operating base for the U.S. fleet in peace time and, in addition, is of value as a staging point for patrol planes to and from the Panama Canal. . . . In addition to the above noted advantages of Magdalena Bay, a lease on that harbor held by the United States would preclude the lease to other foreign interests for development and fishing rights that would be inimical to the interests of this country.[52]

Also the memo stated frankly that

> in case Mexico fails to cooperate in hemispheric defense, U.S. Naval forces would be handicapped in protecting the Western Pacific, without Mexican ports. We would probably have to use the desired bases with or without consent of Mexico.[53]

This was a call for the invasion and occupation of Mexican territory in case the Cárdenas administration refused to cooperate. In October 1940, this strategic plan became official policy of the U.S. War Department. Secretary of War Stimson requested of the Secretary of State that work begin toward the acquisition of Magdalena Bay and Acapulco Harbor as a long-term lease for the U.S. Navy.[54] Fortunately, at that time Mexico was cooperating with the United States and the White House did not want to pressure the Mexican leadership in any way before the inauguration of Avila Camacho.

Mexican military bureaucrats adjusted to the current atmosphere by resubmitting very familiar armament shopping lists. Only now they argued that airplanes and trucks were needed to discourage an expected uprising by Mexican conservative and fascist forces after the elections. In April 1940, the Cárdenas administration asked the United States to supply thirty-two seventy-five millimeter guns, fifty thousand rifles, fifty to one hundred observation planes, eighteen pursuit planes, and all the necessary ammunition to prepare against the event of an uprising.[55] In essence, this request resembled those from previous years, and only the justification had now changed. Mexican and U.S. sources do not show that the Cárdenas administration ever received any of these weapons.

In late spring, President Cárdenas issued first military orders that reacted to the spread of war in Europe and its implications for the Western Hemisphere. He introduced the draft and began the training of military reserves. A national defense counsel was set up for the study of national-defense questions and to develop contingency plans.[56] But the strength level of active Mexican military forces remained at prewar levels and would stay there until an emergency would require change.

The combination of external and domestic pressures created a lively debate within the inner circle of the Cárdenas administration about what Mexico should do in the near future. Two options emerged. On one side stood President Cárdenas, his ambassador to Washington, Castillo Nájera, and his ambassador to the League of Nations, Isidro Fabela. These men counseled military distance from the United States. Their thinking was shaped by long-term scenarios in which the United States and Mexico had irreconcilable differences, which made it impossible for them to work as close allies during the Second World War. Among them there existed a sense that the Second World War was not a Mexican war and that it was a burden imposed on the Mexican nation by the Great Powers' geopolitical games. In particular, Ambassador Isidro Fabela, who had worked closely with President Venustiano Carranza during World War I, insisted that Mexico should always maintain a European option and never enter into an exclusive alliance with the United States.

On the other side stood representatives of the Mexican military who were interested in the war as a unique opportunity to satisfy their dreams of world-class military technology as well as strengthening the importance of the Mexican military in the Mexican state by participating in World War II. For them, an alliance with the United States was the most direct way to accomplish these goals. Their professional orientation interpreted the U.S. military for the first time as fellow soldiers, not as a potential invader. Certainly, cooperation with the United States would be problematic, but desirable from a short-term perspective.

During this half-year, Cárdenas, Castillo Nájera, and Fabela tried to play for time and assert themselves against suggestions of a closer U.S.–Mexican military alliance. For example, when the suggestion was made to enter into a U.S.–Mexican alliance so that Mexico would not become a battlefield in a possible war between Germany and the United States, Castillo Nájera ruled out such a step, arguing:

Certainly it would be easy to convince the people of medium intelligence and culture, capable of reason . . . but it would be much more difficult to bring to the consciousness of the majority of our countrymen the utility of such a step. Unfortunately, the people are guided by instincts and by feeling and do not conform with certain acts. . . . It would be indispensable to organize an active campaign that would try to create among the masses a special psychological state so that they would accept a war pact.[57]

Mexico's ambassador was right. Only two months before the Mexican presidential elections, any formal alliance with the United States would have offered a special propaganda opportunity for Mexico's extreme political left and right to discredit the campaign of the official presidential candidate, Avila Camacho. To Cárdenas, Castillo Nájera wrote:

> Fortunately, cooperation with the Teutons or the Yanquis are not the only alternatives that are open to our fatherland. We can preserve our sovereignty, participate in the defense of the continent and cooperate with all the countries that participate. If it is necessary, we will defend the integrity of the territory to the degree that our forces allow, fighting against whatever "foreign enemy."[58]

And yet Mexican Defense Minister Castro insisted in a cabinet meeting that Mexico's fate was linked to that of the United States. He expected Mexico, which required U.S. military hardware, to enter the war on the side of the United States. The closest bilateral cooperation with the United States was unavoidable:[59]

> it is convenient for us to find ourselves in a perfect alliance with the United States, because its destiny will also be ours . . . we are in a position in which we can obtain advantages for later, even to the extent of defending ourselves against them.[60]

In turn, the politician Isidro Fabela wanted no close alliance with the United States. He wanted to mobilize Mexico militarily only to protect it against the United States. In a later cabinet meeting, he explained bluntly:

> I applaud the fact that the President of the Republic implemented the draft; because this is an act of major transcendence, not because I believe in a German attack, but because we need to arm ourselves in order to defend ourselves against the very same United States. . . . one needs to create the largest possible army, one needs to create soldiers and rifles, one needs to exploit the occasion that is offered to us by the U.S. Therefore, in reality, we will appreciate this moment to arm ourselves and defend our sovereignty and our territorial integrity, in case the United States wants to force its defense against our will. A war with the United States is always possible.[61]

The debate over an alliance with the United States turned from argument to reality shortly before the German victory over France, and also before the Mexican presidential elections. Confidentially, the Roosevelt administration asked Ambassador Castillo Nájera to enter into informal negotiations about a possible U.S.–Mexican military alliance. Against the background of the German victories in Europe, Castillo Nájera and Cárdenas played along. A first bilateral U.S.–Mexican meeting was held on Tuesday, June 11, 1940. Cástillo Nájera represented Mexico. Representatives from the U.S. State Department, the U.S. War Department, and the U.S. Department of the Navy presented the U.S. concerns.

The U.S. representatives wasted little time with pleasantries. Point blank, they asked the Mexicans if they would cooperate in the defense of the Americas, and more specifically, how far they were willing to go in regard to a military alliance. The U.S. planners appreciated Mexico's professionalization efforts, but they feared that in an emergency the Mexican army could not prevent or repel an invasion of Axis forces. For that purpose, the United States needed naval and air bases in Mexico to defend the Western Hemisphere. From a purely military point of view, the American evaluation of the Mexican forces situation was entirely correct.

But Castillo Nájera thought, first and foremost, as a politician, not as a soldier. He discounted U.S. fears of an Axis landing in Mexico in the near future. Instead, he insisted that it would take at least three more years for the conflict to reach the Western Hemisphere—once the fighting had ended in Europe. Moreover, Mexico's ambassador tried to paint the rosiest possible picture of the Mexican military. He assured U.S. negotiators that the Mexican army was well prepared for the tasks lying ahead. If necessary, the Mexican army could mobilize within three months 200,000 men of good quality. In case of an external attack, he promised, this number could be increased to 1 to 2 million soldiers. In addition, the Cárdenas administration was considering replacing the voluntary recruiting system with the draft. He assured his U.S. partners that the Mexican army had no urgent need of supply and was well equipped to maintain internal peace.

When the U.S. soldiers kept pushing, Castillo Nájera became upset. He warned of the political repercussions that would arise if Mexico allowed U.S. forces to operate inside Mexico. Even a simple public debate about these questions inside Mexico, he stated emphatically, would create the impression that the Cárdenas administration had joined in an alliance with the United States and would do great political damage in Mexico.

Still, the U.S. representatives showed little sympathy for possible domestic political repercussions. When the meeting concluded, Mexico was asked to send military representatives to the United States for future, more detailed discussions.[62] Then, in the evening, at an informal Washington party, Undersecretary of State Sumner Welles asked Castillo Nájera again if the Cárdenas administration was willing to enter into a defensive pact with the United States. By then, he had had several hours time to digest the events of the day and talk to President Cárdenas on the phone. He replied to Sumner Welles that Mexico would enter into an alliance with the United States only within a Pan-American context.[63]

In the following weeks Mexico's presidential election gained predominance on the bilateral agenda. This provided Cárdenas with an opportunity to develop a distinct Cardenista reply to the U.S. military requests. Cárdenas planned to protect Mexico's territorial sovereignty during the world war by creating a Latin American hemispheric defense force, consisting of troops from all Latin American nations. He envisioned the creation of a military force big enough to match that of the United States and capable of counterbalancing U.S. hegemonic military desires. He explained to Castillo Nájera:

> the only justification for an alliance between the most powerful nation of the world and the developing people of this continent will be the elevation of the Latin people to the category of high powers with moral character. [The United States] would be protected in part by the material and technical richness of its allies and supported by modern forces which organize themselves locally, with dedicated cooperation of those most capable.

For Cárdenas, then, defense policy during World War II was first and foremost the defense of the Americas against all imperialism—the one from outside and the one from inside the Western Hemisphere (that is, the United States). A central aspect of this design was the avoidance of U.S. military and naval bases outside U.S. territory. Instead, Latin American countries would contribute their own bases to the defense of the Americas. Mexico would allow the use of its bases only in case an American country entered into war with a country outside the Americas. Even then, the bases would be constructed by Mexicans, manned by Mexicans, and operated by Mexicans, and they would always remain under the sovereignty of the Mexican government. Cárdenas was sincerely interested in defending Mexico against the Axis powers, but it would have to be on Mexican terms and not as a junior partner of the United States.[64] In addition, Cárdenas insisted on a linkage between defense and national developmental issues. Latin America should not finance the war for the United States, he argued. Instead, any alliance should be founded on the

new principles of international law that are favorable to the settlement, industrialization and economic evolution of the weaker countries in relationship to those which are stronger and more prosperous.[65]

After the Mexican presidential election, bilateral U.S.–Mexican military talks resumed. Two Mexican military representatives, Brig. Gen. Tomas Sánchez Hernandez and Major Eduardo Huttich Palma, went to Washington for discussions. These two officers traveled to Washington as representatives of their institution, having been asked to present Cardenista positions. While they were as committed to the protection of Mexico's sovereignty as Cárdenas, they were not interested in postponing or avoiding cooperation with the United States. Quite the opposite: they were eager to bring about closer U.S.–Mexican military ties to further their institutional interests. In short, a military institutional policy toward cooperation with the United States emerged that saw the expected entry of the United States into the war as a unique opportunity for the institutional strengthening and recovery of a certain independence from civilian control.

On July 19, 1940, the two Mexican negotiators met with U.S. colonels F. S. Clark, E. M. Almond, and M. B. Ridgway for two sessions. The topic of the morning discussion was again the nature of the threat to the Western Hemisphere. General Sánchez started out by arguing that an immediate invasion of the Western Hemisphere was only a theoretical threat. Then various scenarios of possible Axis attacks on the Western Hemisphere were discussed, and the Mexicans insisted that Mexico's geographic position would always allow sufficient time for a fortification of its coastline before an invasion from the Atlantic could take place. Also, the threat of a fifth-column movement in Mexico was played down, as was the threat to the Mexican Pacific Coast by the Japanese.

The U.S. representatives, in contrast, wanted to discuss the Mexican commitment to bilateral defense cooperation in uncomfortably direct terms. The Mexicans were confronted with the question whether U.S. planes could use Mexican airports as stopovers during their flights to Panama. In addition, the United States wanted to know if Mexico intended to commit troops to war theaters.

The Mexican negotiators had no authority to make such specific commitments. Henceforth, General Sánchez merely assured U.S. negotiators that President Cárdenas wanted honest cooperation. Mexico not only wanted to be a part of the hemispheric defense, but intended to take part in it actively. In regard to the actual commitment of troops, Sánchez thought that, until now, it was not expected that this case would ever present itself. However, in case it would be necessary—for example, in the form of combined Mexican–U.S. troop cooperation—there would be enough time to discuss the necessary plans in the future. Then the groups parted for lunch.

At first sight, the Mexican negotiators had maintained their traditional caution, played for time, and avoided immediate agreements. But if we take into account previously discussed ideas, one notices that the Mexican military representatives had not refused joint U.S.–Mexican combined operation in principle. Neither did they limit Mexican participation to a multilateral Latin American force. No moves were made to contain the military might of the United States in the coming war.

In the afternoon, the Mexican delegation became more direct. Already, in the morning, they had stated that the real German threat to Mexico was an economic one, as manifested by the exclusive barter deals of the past, which would resume after the war. Mexico wanted to create and maintain a professional army for hemispheric defense, but it feared the economic impact of this step. He warned that Mexico's

> defense will depend to a large degree on the Mexican capability to equip and maintain its forces without creating an economic disequilibrium. This could be exploited by the Mexican people for causes of discontent and could be easily exploited by elements interested in destroying continental unity.

Then Sánchez admitted the bleak state of Mexico's defensive capabilities. The majority of Mexico's rank and file and reserves were useless. They had received no training and could not maintain order. Currently, Mexico's force was capable only of maintaining internal peace. Only weeks before, Mexican Ambassador Nájera had portrayed the Mexican armed forces as an organization ready to mobilize fast in case of an external threat. Now, General Sánchez admitted that a professional Mexican army that could fight external forces remained to be created.

Then Sánchez asked point blank what the U.S. delegation thought about a rehabilitation of Mexico's economic situation in an effort to improve Mexican military effectiveness. General Sánchez saw a better chance for Mexican participation in hemispheric defense

> in case the United States was willing to grant credits simultaneously for the acquisition of armament and machinery that would allow Mexico to develop certain economic and military aspects of its economy.

U.S. representative Clark replied that this was certainly an appropriate idea, but it was outside the competence of the U.S. War Department.[66] Then the two groups adjourned.

These meetings had staked out the core issues of future Mexican–U.S. war cooperation. The U.S. Navy and Air Force wanted the immediate use of bases in Mexico. The Mexican government wanted to extract as much economic aid from the United States as possible. More importantly, the fact that military representatives had talked with their counterparts had changed the atmosphere of U.S.–Mexican defense talks. The Mexican military did not harbor any of the strong anti-imperialistic feelings of the Cárdenas generation. If the terms were right they would be interested in close cooperation with the United States. For the remainder of Cárdenas's term in office, sources concerning U.S.–Mexican military cooperation are scarce. Cárdenas's diary covers the entire five months on four pages. Therefore, educated guesses allow only the reconstruction of a rough sketch of events and decisions.

Cárdenas and Castillo Nájera's distrust of U.S. motives with regard to hemispheric defense continued during Cárdenas's remaining months in office. At the end of September 1940, the announcement of the Berlin-Rome-Tokyo Axis was expected to increase the likelihood that the United States would enter the war openly and decisively in the more immediate future. Castillo Nájera continued to urge Cárdenas to find a form of military alliance that "allows us the conservation of our autonomy and the freedom to take defensive measures by ourselves."[67] Also, Mexican fears about the volatility of U.S. policy continued. Ambassador Castillo Nájera declared in October 1940 that Mexico was facing the most serious international situation since the war of 1847.[68] Cárdenas remained determined not to rush into any agreement. Still, in October he insisted that Mexico had ample time to solve the outstanding issues with the United States before the war would come to the Western Hemisphere. Again, he pushed for the creation of a strong Mexican navy and air force. Otherwise, he restated, Latin America's insistence on defending its sovereignty would remain an illusion and Latin American countries would have no other choice but to allow the United States to enter its territory.[69]

And yet the Mexican and U.S. administrations engaged, in the fall of 1940, in their first bilateral defensive cooperation in the aftermath of the Mexican presidential election. Mexican and U.S. diplomats, military forces, and secret services, as well as the two executives, kept the Almazán rebellion, as described in the next chapter, from mushrooming into a more serious challenge to the Cárdenas administration. Although for different reasons, both administrations hindered foreign powers from exploiting this period of political transition in Mexico to create turmoil south of the border. The U.S. government and its military enforced a strict arms embargo against Cárdenas's opponents. The Mexican military demonstrated that it was able to enforce its domestic power monopoly and monitor its coastlines.

Furthermore, U.S.–Mexican military talks were postponed due to elections in both countries, but they were not cancelled. After Roosevelt's re-election in November of 1940, the U.S. administration selected permanent U.S. military representatives for the continuation of talks; and the Mexican side selected military representatives after the inauguration of President Avila Camacho. When the U.S. government proposed to make a public announcement of when and where their commissions would resume meeting, the Avila Camacho administration asked for the talks to remain secret.[70] Once Avila Camacho was inaugurated, however, the Cardenista Latin American defense approach was shelved and the United States and Mexico entered into their closest military cooperation since the creation of the two nations. The professional relations between the two military forces had overcome the fear of politicians on both sides about cooperation.

The developments in the international environment had changed the course of Mexican professional military development. The circumstances of war provided the Mexican military with renewed importance and some space for independent action within the postrevolutionary state. At the same time, the armament policies concerning world confrontations prevented the Mexican military from acquiring the technical capacity to defend itself realistically against an external army. Overnight, Mexico was again confronted with the possibility of U.S. forces operating in Mexico's territory, either with Mexican blessing or by the power of naked force. Fortunately, the institutional self-interest of the Mexican armed forces made the desire for cooperation with the United States strong enough to overcome the fears, suspicions, and plans of political leaders on both sides. Seldom had the Chinese proverb that saw great risks also as great opportunities been more true.

8

From Cárdenas to Ávila Camacho

The Rise of a Conservative Developmental Strategy, the Almazán Rebellion, and the Presidential Inauguration of 1940

THE SEARCH FOR A PRODUCTIVE RELATIONSHIP BETWEEN AN EMERGING international war economy and Mexican national economic development links the presidencies of Lázaro Cárdenas and Ávila Camacho. This quest established a continuity between the two administrations that is not easily discernible from public political rhetoric until Ávila Camacho becomes president in December 1940. And yet the conservatism of Avilacamachismo was developed and nurtured by Mexican bureaucratic planners from March 1938 on.

At its core was a new technocratic language of economics that redefined the state's interpretation of individual Mexican lives. Before the expropriation, official rhetoric had granted Mexican lives a subjective, political, and social quality that was tied to sectoral interests. After the expropriation, however, official rhetoric elevated individual lives into an emotional, but politically vague, nationalist realm that, purposely, deflected class struggles. In addition, Mexican planners reinvented the Mexican as a politically neutral, statistical economic unit becoming part of the nation's developmental process. From above, a political and social conservatism decreed a depoliticized and more unified workforce, ready to exploit the expected economic stimulus of World War II.

After the oil expropriation, the oil industry was the key economic asset of the administration, critical for the generation of income and the resumption of economic activity that could revive national economic development. In addition, the Mexican state was no longer the mediator between Mexican labor and foreign companies, but the proprietor of Mexico's oil industry and the employer of its workers. This role change initiated a change in perspective toward national development and labor issues among Mexican state planners. First, it emerged in state documents concerned with national economic development. Thereafter, the new tone and language was applied in labor negotiations between the Cardenas administration and state-owned companies. Finally, under President Ávila Camacho, it became the official conservative political rhetoric.

The new discourse about labor, national economic development, and economic activity appears for the first time in the immediate aftermath of the expropriation, in letters to Cárdenas and memoranda of the presidential study commission.

For example, in May 1938, Cárdenas's radical leftist Minister of Communication and Infrastructure, Francisco Múgica, toured the oil properties around Tampico to assess the industry's situation and the mood among oil workers in the fields. In a letter, he reported to Cárdenas that the most serious problems he encountered were the export situation, the administration of the industry, and the leadership of the oil unions. More importantly, Múgica identified a new opponent for the state. For him, the worker's leaders, handicapped by corruption and alcohol,

> were used to preaching the religion of their rights, but now they do not know how to preach the religion of duty, which would be appropriate. . . . There is no doubt that one needs to take steps to centralize and discipline.

To centralize and discipline—this was no longer the pro-labor discourse from before the expropriation. Now, Mexican policy planners saw workers first and foremost as a critical factor that needed to be controlled and reorganized for the greater benefit of the state's development.

The new discourse also appeared, in May 1938, in a memorandum of the Mexican presidential study commission that advised Cárdenas on how to deal with the oil question and publicity after the expropriation. The memo stated that the oil expropriation

> is a national problem, not only of political, but essentially of economic nature. It affects every Mexican and the unity of nationality, demonstrated clearly by the united expression of interests and solidarity of all Mexican sectors. . . . The same leftist and rightists, catholics, protestants and atheists, capitalists as well as employees, all have one common interest in the economic independence of Mexico and in the development of the exploitation of its natural riches, because this will be to the benefit of everybody, improving the general living standard and releasing the consumptive capacity of every Mexican.[1]

In this memo, too, the state's economic needs have begun to supersede the needs of individual Mexican social sectors. The economic nationalism of the expropriation is used here to decree from above a national solidarity that overcomes all existing social cleavages. Mexican state representatives began to think, argue, and act like a patron who expected obedience from his workers.

By June 1938, Cárdenas's presidential study commission had developed the new approach more clearly. In a new economic policy proposal to the Presidential Palace, it proposed "coherent national planning" as the key to Mexico's future economic success. In reality, the economic proposal remained vague. Centralized planning was to solve everything: regional deficiencies, poor public administration, wasteful use of raw materials, poor income distribution, unjust levels of income, the lack of purchasing power, as well as the creation of consumptive power that would reenforce the state's efforts to increase national production.[2] The commission was much more precise, however, in recommending improvements in the economic attitude of the individual Mexican. Like Múgica, the commission prescribed "discipline and responsibility." In this context, even socialist education was supposed to be reorganized as a tool to increase the worker's "will to work"!

Within three months economic thinking by state planners had changed radically. Sociopolitical interpretations of economic activity from previous years were on their way out. The idea of national development was beginning to detach itself from its beneficiaries. National development was becoming an abstract goal for its own sake.

The first victims of this change were Mexican workers. Whereas the first Mexican Six-Year Plan and the early years of Cardenismo reverberated with sectoral classifications for Mexicans, such as peasant and worker, now bureaucrats in the ministries invented the image of a murky Mexican *homo economicus* who no longer belonged to any social sector. Mexican workers were no longer defined by whether they worked in the field or in the factory, but by abstract categories of living standard and consumptive capacity. The Mexican was reinvented as a consumer, regardless of real-life situations in Mexico's regions.

The relationship between Mexicans and national development was turned upside down. In early Cardenismo, social and economic changes in labor and agrarian sectors were to bring about national economic independence. Now national economic independence was to bring about improvements in labor and agricultural sectors. Here, we find the roots of the conservatism of Ávila Camacho's *sexeño*, which put the needs of the state above those of the individual. Mexican economic planners had abandoned their earlier sectorial economic-development strategy. Now, they reconfigured the state as one economic unit that, united by nationalism, was about to embark on a different developmental course. The question was which one?

The rest of 1938 and early 1939 was subsumed by the integration of the oil industry into the national economy. The export of Mexico's oil production had to be organized, and the economic foundations of the now more conservative Mexican state had to be repaired. By the time the petroleum industry functioned well and the export of Mexican oil was beginning to provide the state with new revenue for national economic development, it was clear that the stimulus for national economic development would come from the outside: the international war economy. Mexico's economic development resumed within the parameters of the approaching international conflict that, afterward, would be called World War II.

Mexican Minister of Agriculture Cedillo had been one of the first cabinet members to speculate about this scenario. Already in 1936, he had dreamed about how a European war would open up a big market for Mexican goods, especially petroleum.[3] In the same year, an anonymous planner for presidential adviser Luis I. Rodríguez had argued that during a war that involved the United States, Mexico could become the exclusive supplier of agricultural and industrial products for its northern neighbor.[4]

By May 1939, after the German attack on Czechoslovakia, Mexican Minister to Berlin Azcárate warned the Mexican Foreign Ministry "that in view of the imminent war all countries are liquidating their credits in Germany."[5] In addition, he urged the creation of a Mexican commission to prepare for the expected cessation of transatlantic trade.[6] The Mexicans knew that the war was coming. Finally, in August 1939, the German invasion of Poland triggered the expected large-scale war.

Right away, the Mexican presidential study commission went to work to study how national economic development and international war could benefit from each other. By December 1939, it urged Cárdenas

> that the opportunity to initiate the industrialization of the nation
> has not passed, quite the opposite. . . . The world war actually
> brings us great economic damage, but in return it gives us the possi-
> bility to industrialize, let us use it.[7]

In May 1940, Mexican presidential candidate Sánchez Tapia incorporated the opportunities engendered by the war into his electoral platform and declared that the war was the economic cure for Mexico's problems. He argued that cooperation with the United States was unavoidable and would provide Mexico with the desired stimuli for development in the areas of steel, mining, and livestock. It would guarantee the repair of railroads and streets that were of military importance and it would bring about the improvement and fortification of Mexican ports and airports. Most importantly, all of this would be realized with the "financial support of our allies and the investment of large capital."[8]

Other governmental voices joined Tapia and repeated his argument.

Cárdenas was urged to exploit the circumstances of the war more aggressively. The Mexican consul in Hamburg pointed to similar efforts by Peru, Colombia, Venezuela, Argentina, and Uruguay, writing that Mexico should be

> remembering that all the countries are assisting the war without realizing it, and especially the neutral, great producers of primary materials act as belligerents in the economic sector which the totalitarian war is creating.[9]

It was also during this time that the previously described conservative economic discourse fused with an analysis of the war that would become public rhetoric under Avilacamachismo.

In September 1939, the Mexican Ministry of Agriculture and Development suggested to the national palace that the central challenge of the emerging war be viewed as the need to "reestablish an equilibrium between production, consumption and exportation of Mexican products for which foreign demand decreases." The ministry identified a second key issue, the "internal rationalization of the centers of production with the goal that the goods reach the market cheaper." As a solution, the ministry recommended giving "financial support and investment preferably to groups that make or establish production centers which serve and strengthen the general economy of the country."[10] By now, human economic activity had been reduced to a mere structural challenge nearly void of social implications.

The unavoidable and serious socioeconomic inequities of war economies were addressed only as a problem that required "necessary modifications for those groups that make big profit from the war trade." In a veiled reference, the ministry warned about drastic social consequences only in macroeconomic terms, such as warnings about "price increases for imported goods" or the "increased emigration of valuable Mexican labor force to the United States." In a naive fashion, it was suggested that producers and "consumers" should create local associations that organized production, demand, and prices among themselves. While these organizations were to watch over "problems of distribution and prices," special emphasis was given to the fact that they should show "owners, directors and administrators how to promote the rationalization of centers of productions, save material and be careful with the enumeration of workers." These were code words for hoarding, speculation, black markets, hunger, lack of services, and the basic necessities of life. But in the new bureaucratic conservatism they were no longer recognized as political or social issues, merely as structural challenges that needed to be addressed.

The official patriotism previously described reenforced this trend. Within the context of the war, it was becoming almost an act of treason to voice social demands or to describe unsatisfactory living conditions. Only two years before, nationalism and patriotism had reenforced the bond between the Mexican state and Mexican citizens for the purpose of nationalizing the oil industry. Now, it was being changed into a tool that insulated the Mexican state from the justified economic demands of its citizenry.

For example, in March 1940, President Cárdenas and Minister Suárez used this new patriotic rhetoric in wage negotiations with the railroad syndicates, which had asked for a raise in order to combat wartime inflation and price increases. Like Múgica two years before, Cárdenas reacted by accusing the railroad union of a lack of discipline and of sabotaging goods that the state had entrusted to them.[11] He accused the railroad syndicate of displaying a lack of patriotism and an attitude that equaled treason.

Minister Suárez turned on the heat even more. He blamed the railroad workers for wartime inflation, which occurred, he argued, simply because of the "falling productivity of the workers,—if productivity increases, then also wages will increase." "Responsibility and patriotism"—that was what the wage question was really all about, he declared, repeating Cárdenas's charge of treason.[12] Suárez's words were extremely cynical, because Suárez understood better than anybody else in Mexico the macroeconomic origins of wartime inflation. Their cause did not involve the labor demands of railroad workers, but the disequilibrium created by the war itself.

At this point, we must remember that the Mexican administration had decided that the war itself posed no danger to Mexico until England was successfully defeated by Germany.[13] Thus, while the leadership insisted that the war was not yet a threat to the Mexican state, it did not hesitate to use fearful scenarios to intimidate workers and peasants and coerce them into obedience. Patriotism had become a key manipulative tool in the quest for national economic development.

By the summer of 1940, the Mexican cabinet no longer debated whether to use the war as a developmental stimulus; the question was now only how it would be used. Minister of Hacienda Suárez spearheaded the discussion.[14] Although he had decided that Mexican wartime cooperation with the United States was unavoidable, he insisted that Mexico's cooperation could be sold as expensively as possible to the United States. This unique chance, however, also required that workers and peasants once again postpone their struggle for social and economic justice for the greater good of the nation. He was backed by Mexican Minister of Gobernación García Téllez, who thought that the United States was in a real bind since it actually needed Mexican raw material to fight the Axis powers. For once, the United States would have to cooperate with Mexico and reciprocate on the economic level. This exchange was necessary for Mexico to be provided with the needed stimulus for industrialization.

But it was an opportunity that would not last long. Once the war ended, Suárez warned, the benevolent economic cooperation would vanish and the United States would again be a competitor for an industrializing Mexico. Clearly, socioeconomic aspects had no place in this scenario. During the last two years, Mexican bureaucratic planners and the emerging international war economy had joined forces and changed Mexican policies and political discourse in favor of the economic opportunity that the war offered. After the presidential elections in July 1940, the representatives of the Mexican military suggested to their U.S. counterparts for the first time that economic factors would be key to Mexico's defensive efforts. When the Mexicans thought about war they did not so much see guns and weapons, but a Mexican workforce that extracted the raw materials for U.S. armament and an increasing number of manufacturing sites in Mexico that produced manufactured and durable goods that the United States could no longer produce because it was becoming the arsenal of democracy.

The change in political direction and discourse and the preparations for exploiting international war would do little good, however, if the Cárdenas administration failed to install president-elect Ávila Camacho as the next Mexican president. If the considerable conservative opposition to Cárdenas succeeded in disrupting the transition of power, civil war could be the result. Then Mexico would miss the economic opportunity of the war, and perhaps it would disintegrate again in regional infighting and economic chaos. In the worst case, such a scenario of instability would offer itself as a unique opportunity for foreign fascist interests and provoke the feared preemptive invasion of Mexico by U.S. forces. In other words, before the Mexican leadership could benefit from the war it had to realize the transition of power from President Cárdenas to President Ávila Camacho in December 1940.

Speculations and anxieties about the July 6, 1940, Mexican presidential election had dominated the Mexican political climate from 1939 on.[15] Violent clashes between the opposing Almazanistas and Avilacamachistas occurred frequently and repeatedly, and it was hinted that President Cárdenas himself might cancel the elections. Also, the spectacular German advances in the European war during the first half of 1940 created an uncertain international context for events in Mexico that continued to cause concern among Mexican politicians in all political camps.

They were exploited by German Minister to Mexico Rüdt, who announced at diplomatic parties that a German attack and an easy victory over Great Britain was just a matter of time. Everybody who wanted to hear it learned from him that the war in Europe would be over soon. He reassured his superiors in Berlin that "the end of the fighting in France had improved the German position [in Mexico], since there exists little sympathy for England." He told Mexican officials that after the war a German-dominated Europe would be hungry for Mexico's natural resources and only too willing to resume trade relations.

Some Mexicans began to believe him. The *Boletín Financiero y Minero* mysteriously canceled the publication of daily British-pound quotations and replaced them with reichsmark quotations. Members of the Mexican administration, however, remained unconvinced that Great Britain would succumb to a German offensive soon. In any case, before Mexico could actively revive economic trade with Europe, Germany had to achieve the victory that Minister Rüdt was currently fantasizing about.

To play it safe, Mexican Minister of Hacienda Suárez tried to keep Minister Rüdt in a positive mood about possible future Mexican–German cooperation. In occasional conversations with Rüdt, Suárez assured Hitler's representative that Mexico would be eager to resume trade relations as soon as the war was over. In a talk with German economic attaché Burandt, Suárez thought aloud that now that "Germany was growing," its need for raw materials would also increase. Again, Suárez asserted that as soon as the war was over, President Cárdenas would do everything possible to guarantee a supply of Mexican raw materials for Germany. In addition, Suárez reassured Rüdt that German assets in Mexico were safe for the time being

> simply because of the Mexican people, who are overwhelmingly friendly toward Germany. No measures that would damage Germany could be expected, as long as this could be coordinated with the indispensable good relations with the United States.[16]

Suárez also indicated to German economic attaché Burandt that Mexico would not be opposed to giving Germany a major contract for the construction of an oil pipeline over the Isthmus. Only two "small" problems remained. First, the Roosevelt administration would have to keep U.S. suppliers from delivering pipes to Mexico, and second, the war would have to end.[17] At the end of August 1940, a German informant talked with Mexican Foreign Minister Hay. Afterward, he reported to Minister Rüdt that the Mexican administration would continue to wait for a decision in Great Britain and not automatically follow U.S. policy.[18]

By the early fall of 1940, Rüdt had become anxious. The German victory over Europe had not yet been achieved. The Mexican press had become almost entirely pro-Allies. Earlier, he had written to Berlin that "those who, until now, were our friends do not have the courage to act against the wishes of the president." In an even more desperate moment, he had tried to enlist the power of the German Foreign Ministry to intervene with Stalin to reverse Mexican labor leader Vicente Lombardo Toledano's recent resumption of anti-German propaganda.[19] The German Foreign Ministry replied that it had no influence over the labor leader through the Moscow channel. Rüdt simply had to wait until Great Britain would collapse.[20] Until then, the Mexicans would keep open the possibility of immediate trade resumption with Europe after the end of the war, while deepening their real cooperation with the United States.

Then the British Air Force stalled the German attack on Great Britain on September 15, 1940. Now, as Cárdenas had hoped in the summer, America's defense outpost would continue to exist. In addition, the destruction of a portion of the French fleet in Mers el Kebir further weakened the chance that Germany could amass a large enough fleet for an invasion of Latin America in the near future. Regardless, the Mexican constitution required that president-elect Ávila Camacho wait until December to assume the Mexican presidency. This offered three more months for the defeated Almazanista camp to prevent the installation of Ávila Camacho and derail the U.S.–Mexican rapprochement with foreign fascist help.

The Almazán opposition was a coalition of diverse Mexican conservative groups sharing the goal of reversing the policies of Cardenismo, but unable to agree on what should take place after July 1940. The U.S. informants in contact with Almazán reported a sense of confusion and indecision inside his camp. Almazán himself confided only in a few people. His postelection plans were unknown.

Already before the day of the presidential election, Almazán had established contact with U.S. supporters of a more conservative regime in Mexico. George Creel, former head of the U.S. Federal Committee on Public Information during World War I, an influential member of the Democratic party, and Commissioner of the Golden Gate International Exposition in San Francisco, had offered his services to the Almazán camp. Creel had impressed Almazán with his access to U.S. Secretary of State Cordell Hull. Also, former Callista labor leader Luis N. Morones had offered his ties to the American Federation of Labor. Together, these two men proposed to create a pro-Almazán propaganda campaign in the United States, gain backing from the U.S. State Department, and hopefully, gain the sympathy of the White House.[21] This strategy would lead Almazán on a five-month odyssey through the United States and its competing foreign-policy camps.

This odyssey began eleven days after the Mexican presidential election, on July 17, 1940, when Almazán surprisingly left Mexico for Cuba. His departure would make it impossible for Cárdenas to force Almazán into open rebellion early,[22] for Almazán had learned the lesson of the Cedillo rebellion two years earlier. Also, Cuba afforded him a safe place to await local uprisings in Mexico and to lobby for foreign support. As he had hoped, his departure generated international-press attention and bestowed on him the aura of a betrayed challenger who had gone abroad to make his case and prepare a counterattack. At the same time, the Pan-American Conference was meeting in Havana, providing Almazán with an opportunity to lobby U.S. Secretary of State Cordell Hull and other members of the U.S. delegation. Any meeting with such high-ranking U.S. officials would increase the legitimacy of Almazán's claim to power. Creel and his propagandists could interpret it as a growing U.S. interest in his cause.

After his arrival, however, high U.S. officials refused to meet Almazán in Havana. Only the low-ranking U.S. military attaché to Cuba received him for an unofficial audience. Almazán asked the attaché for special U.S. visas for his agents and demanded that the U.S. not obstruct their preparations in the United States.[23] On August 12, 1940, he announced in a radio transmission from Cuba that he would return to Mexico "when he deemed it to be opportune."[24] Almazán also used the opportunity to solicit the support of influential British individuals in Havana. He received letters of introduction for Lord Lothian, the British ambassador to the United States in Washington, which included the suggestion that the British should supply him with military hardware. Almazán's political adviser, Manuel Reachi, then left for Miami to launch the pro-Almazán propaganda campaign in the United States.[25] His military adviser went to Guatemala, probably to reenter Mexico illegally.[26] Almazán himself accepted the invitation of Associated Press reporter Edmund Chester to go to Panama, where his friend was the head of U.S. security forces of the Panama Canal.[27]

In the meantime, supporters in Mexico and the United States went to work. In Mexico City, Mexican conservative and Callista Montes de Oca inquired among U.S. representatives whether a revolt against Cárdenas could count, at least, on secret U.S. tolerance. He remarked in oracular fashion to the secretary of the U.S. embassy:

> Our problem is whether the United States will continue to support
> the Mexican government with arms and credits if a serious revolt
> occurs. If revolutionaries should control Nuevo Laredo and
> Monterrey, would that be a basis for recognizing their belligerency?

Then he asked the U.S. diplomat whether it "would be constructive . . . for the U.S. to have in Mexico a government which is imposed against the will of the great majority of the people?"[28]

In the United States, George Creel demanded that the State Department allow Almazán to proceed to any destination of his choice.[29] Almazán adviser Víctor Velázquez visited the U.S. State Department and claimed that Mexican labor was deserting the old union leaders and moving toward the Almazán camp. The Hearst representative, Arthur Constantine, advised the State Department that "it was up to the U.S. to pick the next Mexican president."[30] Creel and Almazán aide Manuel Reachi contacted the National Broadcasting Company, *Life Magazine,* and *Time Magazine* asking for support on August 23, 1940.[31] Later, the leader of Almazán's National Revolutionary Party of Unification (PRUN), Emilio Madero, tried to impress the U.S. embassy in Mexico by suggesting that an armed struggle against the Cárdenas government was unnecessary since so many people and the majority of the Mexican army were already backing Almazán. The White House and Undersecretary of State Sumner Welles only registered these advances without reacting to them.[32] So far Creel's hope for Secretary of State Cordell Hull's influence had not materialized.

Quite the opposite: U.S. Undersecretary Sumner Wells, who "feared Almazán like the devil feared holy water," ordered U.S. officials in Panama to avoid any official contact with Almazán. They must listen only to his demands.[33] At all costs, the impression must be avoided that the U.S. was intervening in Mexican domestic affairs. In Panama, Almazán journalist Edmund A. Chester acted as an intermediary to arrange a meeting with U.S. government representatives.[34] In a meeting with a low-level U.S. diplomat, Almazán repeated his demand for an unrestricted, confidential U.S. visa. He complained that the publicity his appearances were creating in Central America were detrimental to his plans. Therefore, he wanted to enter the United States incognito and hide in Arkansas under a false name until December 1.

The U.S. State Department did grant his wish. He received a standard U.S. visitor visa issued under his real name.[35] He left Panama and arrived in Mobile, Alabama, on August 26, 1940. To his complete surprise, the local INS office put him through a very thorough physical examination and questioned him about his future plans. This very public welcome in the United States troubled Almazán and he complained about this treatment through Creel to the U.S. State Department. Creel told him that the State Department and President Roosevelt's secretary had assured him continued sympathy for his cause.[36]

In the meantime in Mexico, the Cárdenas administration remained very afraid of a possible armed infiltration by Almazanistas from the Pacific Coast. Mexican navy gunboats patrolled the coastal waters with such diligence that their action created diplomatic tensions with the United States. On August 19, 1940, the Mexican gunboat G-22 stopped and boarded the S.S. Herman Frasch, owned by the Union Sulphur Company.[37] Five days later, Mexican forces ordered another U.S.-owned ship, the S.S. Hanna, to stop at gunpoint.[38] The next day, the U.S. steamer Endeavour was briefly detained.[39] All ships were searched and eventually released. The U.S. Department of State simply overlooked the bitter complaints by their U.S. owners. Mexican vigilance along the U.S.–Mexican border was equally determined.[40] The State Department faction around Sumner Welles supported Cárdenas's efforts to prevent the landing of individuals or arms at Mexico's southern and northern coasts.[41]

Next, the Almazán coalition tried to build political legitimacy for its rebellious candidate. An Almazanista campaign began that was designed to counter the Cárdenas administration's plans for the Mexican Congress to declare Avila Camacho the legitimate winner of the presidential election on September 15, 1940. On September 1, 1940, the day of Cárdenas's last official state of the union address to the Mexican Congress, the Almazanistas opened their own congress in the Mexican capital. Due to Almazán's absence from the country, General Héctor F. López, who was hiding in the mountains of Guerrero, was appointed provisional president of Mexico. He was to serve as interim president-elect until Almazán took over the presidency on December 1, 1940. On September 3, Creel distributed to the interested U.S. press an inflammatory accusation that charged the Cárdenas administration with the "illegal" act of forcing Ávila Camacho upon the presidential throne.[42] On September 11, 1940, in San Antonio a small group of Almazanistas[43] issued a manifesto in the San Antonio Evening News proclaiming that the secret congress of Almazanistas had impeached President Cárdenas.[44] On the same day, George Creel wrote a letter to President Roosevelt's private secretary, McIntyre. He assured the White House that Almazán was planning to cross the U.S.–Mexican border in the near future. He described Almazán and his campaign as antifascist and anticommunist. Roosevelt was promised that labor leader Vincente Lombardo Toledano would be exiled from Mexico or shot once Almazán entered office. He implied that all U.S. consuls and naval and military attachés shared this view. Also, U.S. Secretary of State Cordell Hull could be counted as somebody who preferred Almazán. In short, Roosevelt should cast his lot with Almazán and grant U.S. recognition to the rebels. In addition, Almazán aide Victor

Velazquez and Almazán's brother Leonides visited U.S. Lieut. Col. A. R. Harris, chief of the U.S. Intelligence Branch, Latin American Section, in Washington. They informed him that Mexico stood at the brink of an armed revolt.[45]

Now Roosevelt personally entered the struggle for recognition in Mexico. He confronted Secretary of State Hull in a short written note. Hull replied immediately, "I never thought to convey any definite conclusions."[46] Also, the U.S. military remained unimpressed by the presentation of the two Almazán supporters.[47] The Creel efforts were failing to win real political support.

On September 15, 1940, the Mexican Congress declared Ávila Camacho the official winner of the presidential election. On the same day, Ávila Camacho weakened Almazán's following further by stating that he was indeed a religious believer, a Catholic. These words sent a strong signal to Mexican Catholics and conservatives indicating that religious tolerance could be expected during the next *sexeño*. A more serious blow to the Almazán challenge came only twenty-four hours later. In Washington, Secretary of State Cordell Hull declared publicly, on September 16, that Ávila Camacho would be welcome in the United States. This was a critical public recognition of the Mexican president-elect by the outgoing Roosevelt administration. If Roosevelt were to be reelected in November, he expected to deal with Ávila Camacho. If not, a Republican administration's policy would be seriously limited by these acts of public recognition. Three days later, Undersecretary Welles told Mexican Ambassador Castillo Nájera officially that the Roosevelt administration was recognizing the result of the presidential election of 1940. The Almazán camp had lost the political part of its battle against the Ávila Camacho camp.

From now on, the only option that Almazán had left was to defeat the recognized Mexican president-elect in an armed uprising. Consequently, during the following months, the Almazán camp moved toward an armed insurrection. It would begin with smaller local rebellions and then hopefully spread throughout the nation. Foreign fascist forces would be asked to back the effort.

Several foreign individuals and political groups were willing to participate in a violent Almazán armed uprising. German Minister Rüdt reported that Almazán had promised the U.S. oil man Rous the return of his Mexican property in exchange for armed support after Republican presidential candidate Wilkie was elected.[48] The Mexican Policía Judicial Federal obtained information that Almazanistas were signing up petroleum workers and preparing sabotage acts in the northern and southern zones of PEMEX's oil fields.[49] Mexican intelligence reports predicted sabotage activities by Standard Oil of California in the ethylene plant at Atzcapotzalco. Standard Oil agents also allegedly attempted to sabotage ships in Cerro Azul and Tampico.[50] At least one U.S. mining company had links to the Almazán camp. On September 4, 1940, the American Smelting Company paid $20171.41 to the account of Augusto Flores y Cia, a firm affiliated with the Almazán movement.[51] Still, whether this was merely a business transaction, or, indeed, financial support for Almazán can only be answered when researchers gain access to company archives.

By then Almazán had moved from New Orleans to San Francisco, where he met with the former senator Hastings. From there, he went to the suburbs of Los Angeles, where he hid in the house of a Creel friend.[52] Most likely, he also met there exiled *jefe maximo* Plutarco Elías Calles.[53] There existed financial ties between Calles and Almazán. On September 7, 1940, a Raymond Eller had wired eight thousand U.S. dollars to P. Edward Calles in California and ten thousand U.S. dollars to a business office in San Antonio. A connection between Eller and the Almazanistas was made when Eller was seen leaving the New York hotel in which Manuel Reachi, Almazán's press attaché, was residing at that time.[54] Another possible Calles–Almazán financial link can be traced back to a series of sudden withdrawals of large sums of money from the bank account of Calles's son-in-law, F. Torre Blanca, in October 1940. Between 1937 and 1940, Torre Blanca had kept 150,000 U.S. dollars in a bank account in San Diego. During that period he never withdrew more than 300 U.S. dollars at one time. Suddenly, on October 15, 1940, he wrote six checks, each valued at 25,000 U.S. dollars.[55] Of course, this by itself does not establish a direct link with Almazán; it occurred, however, at the same time that a "prominent California business man" was acquiring arms worth 100,000 U.S. dollars for the Almazán camp.

Calles was also involved in contacts between the Spanish Falange and the Almazán group. The Falange had continued to be interested in the tensions in Mexico. On August 23, 1940, the Spanish Minister of the Interior had decided to send "several unassuming groups of Falangists to Mexico, in order to advise and support the followers of a totalitarian form of government." According to him, "the time seemed right for a fascist government to come to power in Mexico."[56] Then, two weeks later, Calles himself contacted a representative of the Falange, asking for a meeting to analyze the Mexican situation.[57] The Almazanista liaison, Melchor Ortega, who was in charge of organizing weaponry in the United States, was present at the second part of this meeting. At the gathering, a memorandum was prepared for Colonel Sane Agero, the main Spanish contact for Falange agents in

Latin America. The memo concluded that an uprising might be successful and urgently requested 50,000 dollars. The document shows that armaments valued at 100,000 dollars had been ordered by a California businessmen.[58] On October 10, 1940, a confidant of the Almazán movement approached the Spanish Ministry of the Interior.[59] First, he asked for financial support, arguing that the Almazanistas "did not want to accept support from the U.S., in order not to threaten the success of the national movement." However, he argued, it would strengthen the national movement if it could point to help from Spain. Second, the Almazanistas wanted the following goods delivered to a Mexican Pacific port: fifty light tanks, twenty thousand rifles, ten million cartridges of ammunition, and, if possible, some airplanes. This equipment, they assured Spain, could lead their movement to a final victory. The Franco regime agreed to help.

The Spaniards also inquired whether the Germans wanted to be involved. It was suggested that the Germans ship the Almazán supplies via Japan to a Mexican Pacific port. Several days later, the German Foreign Ministry rejected the Spanish offer, arguing that

> out of principle we do not like to interfere in domestic partisan struggles of Ibero American states. A deviation from this position would only be justified, when towering military or political interests would make it unavoidable. In the case of the Almazán movement this precondition does not exist. According to news here the movement lacks greater support, its leader is unimportant and a follower of the U.S. by whom he seems to have been bought. Our legation sees Camacho as more advantageous for us than his opponent. Please refrain from any sort of participation in these plans.[60]

In other words, when the Almazanistas tried to expand cooperation with the Germans, hoping to gain the active involvement of ministries in Berlin, their movement was declared not important enough for Germany.[61] The German policy toward Mexico was still dominated by the German Foreign Ministry's bureaucracy, which did not want to create disorder in Mexico and provide a pretext for the United States to enter the war. The Almazanista push for critical foreign support to transform small local uprisings into a national armed challenge was failing. An educated guess would suggest that the German refusal was a serious blow to the Almazanista efforts. At that time, the Franco administration probably did not have the requested weapons available as surplus material and also lacked shipping capacity. Unfortunately, available sources do not provide more information about other cooperation between fascist countries and the Almazán movement.

Then, finally, the Almazán group seemed to achieve a major breakthrough.

On September 19, aide Manuel Reachi had come to Los Angeles and informed Almazán that he had been able to gain the interest of President Roosevelt's son, Elliott. Elliott Roosevelt was willing to receive Almazán on September 25. The meeting took place on September 26, when the two men talked for ninety minutes. Almazán left with the impression that Elliott Roosevelt was quite interested in his cause. He had agreed with the Mexican rebel leader that a violent coup was likely to occur in Mexico, since the majority of the Mexican army seemed to be pro-Almazán. He reassured him that his father's current lack of public support for the Almazanistas was due to the ongoing presidential campaign. However, once the Almazanistas would enter Mexico, the United States would grant them belligerent rights. Once they controlled several Mexican states, the Almazanistas would receive U.S. recognition, he promised. Two days later, the U.S. State Department recognized the former governor of Nuevo León, Francisco A. Cárdenas, as spokesman for Almazán's National Revolutionary Party of Unification. Cárdenas announced the opening of party offices in San Antonio and in New York, and interpreted the State Department's action as a sign of official U.S. support for the Almazán rebellion.[62] Right away, President Roosevelt intervened personally and ordered Sumner Welles to act against Almazán's organization. By October 4, Sumner Welles had cancelled Governor Cárdenas's registration "on the ground that it contained an improper description of the agent's principal." He wrote to Roosevelt: "I believe that there will be no more trouble with regard to this incident—that is, in so far as the Government of Mexico is concerned."[63]

On October 5, Almazán flew to Atlantic City to wait for arms deliveries and the outcome of the U.S. presidential election on November 5, 1940. By then his Mexico City adviser, Luis Montes de Oca, had expressed serious doubts about the value of Elliott Roosevelt's promises. In addition, George Creel's vision for the success of the Almazán rebellion was called into question. Creel had the opportunity to discuss events with President Roosevelt on October 10, in a ten-minute-long audience.[64] Later in October, he joined a group of U.S. investors who toured Mexico and talked with president-elect Avila Camacho about investment opportunities for tourist resorts, automobile courts, and gasoline stations. After the trip, Creel wrote a letter to President Roosevelt suddenly stating, "we have close connections with the new administration and the chances are good for us to make money and at the same time help Mexico." A two-hour talk with Manuel Ávila Camacho and his brother Maximino had convinced him that Ávila Camacho was better for the United States. Even worse for Almazán, George Creel returned from Mexico as a messenger for president-elect Ávila Camacho, asking

Roosevelt to invite him to a visit of the U.S. capital in November. Suddenly, Creel could no longer see any sign of an Almazán rebellion inside Mexico.[65] When he informed Almazán that he should seek some kind of accommodation with the incoming Ávila Camacho administration, the rebellious presidential candidate became outraged and broke off all relations with the U.S. deal maker.[66]

The small number of uprisings inside Mexico that the Almazanistas had hoped to use as a springboard for a national rebellion had fizzled out by then. In Chihuahua, Taracena counted fourteen uprisings with a total of 450 participants.[67] Some of them were led by the defeated Almazanista candidate for governor, Cruz Villaba. In Huetamo, Michoacán, the defeated Almazán candidate for governor, Efrain Pineda, rebelled with 200 supporters. A minor anti-Cárdenas riot occurred in Monterrey, but the Mexican army had no difficulty dealing with them and the Monterrey incident was easily squashed by force. In Michoacán, 150 followers of Pineda put down their weapons accepting an amnesty offered by the federal government, with the remaining 50 fighters fleeing to Guerrero.[68] The Cruz Villaba followers, too, soon surrendered or fled across the U.S. border to Texas.[69] In general, northern regional support for Almazán from landowners and industrial entrepreneurs had remained half-hearted. Their preference for Almazán had been always more a vote against Cárdenas than a vote for Almazán. In the end, the business community of the north preferred accommodation with the Ávila Camacho camp, hoping to exploit the increasing number of concessions that the government was willing to make.[70] In Chilpancingo, Guerrero, where a possible attack was expected, Cárdenas stationed two hundred experienced Spanish republican soldiers, including Spanish aviators.[71] Federal forces squashed a strike at the refinery at Atzcapotzalco, an ideal opportunity to start pro-Almazán movements in the oil industry. Also, the federal army was called in during a strike at the lead tetraethylene factory Al Atoron.[72] To add insult to injury, on October 29, 1940, U.S. Undersecretary of State Sumner Welles invited president-elect Ávila Camacho for a visit to Washington. Now all that Almazán could hope for was Roosevelt's defeat in the election on November 5, and a Republican U.S. president who would be willing to reverse all the pro-Ávila Camacho decisions that the outgoing Roosevelt administration had undertaken so far.

But Roosevelt was reelected for a third term in November 1940. Immediately, Almazán tried to contact the Roosevelt camp one more time, trying to see whether the U.S. administration was willing to change its attitude toward the Ávila Camacho group. But when he tried to contact Elliott Roosevelt, he could not get in touch with him.[73] When it was announced that

U.S. vice president-elect Wallace would represent the United States at the inauguration in December 1940, Almazán was realistic enough to recognize his hopeless situation and prepared his return to Mexico. On November 26, 1940, he returned to Mexico City and accepted Ávila Camacho as the next legitimate president of Mexico.[74] His return proved once again that it was impossible to challenge successfully the official Mexican political nomenclature without U.S. tolerance, at the very least. Moreover, the political leaders of Mexico demonstrated self-confidence and flexibility when they allowed Almazán to reintegrate himself into the revolutionary family as a business man. Almazán's experience suggested that, from now on, regional caudillos would gain power and influence through entrepreneurial activity rather than violent challenges to the system.

The other side of the successful prevention of an Almazán rebellion were attempts by the Ávila Camacho camp to win U.S. support. Just as the Almazanistas had courted foreign support, so did the Ávila Camacho camp.

Pro–Ávila Camacho efforts began immediately after the presidential election. In the last week of July 1940, the Mexican chief of staff, General Bobodilla, promised to U.S. military intelligence officer Gibson that labor leader Vicente Lombardo Toledano would be dismissed as soon as Ávila Camacho took office.[75] Next, during the first week of August 1940, Ávila Camacho's campaign manager and future Minister of Gobernacion, Miguel Alemán, traveled all the way to Washington to meet U.S. Undersecretary Sumner Welles.[76] During the talks, he went to great lengths to create the impression that the future Mexican administration would be economically and socially more conservative. He told Welles that

> many excesses have taken place under the present Mexican administration, but that . . . excesses of any kind would not take place under an administration headed by General Ávila Camacho.

He promised that Ávila Camacho's policy goal would be

> to further in every way possible closer and better relations between Mexico and the United States . . . and . . . to solve in a friendly and equitable manner all of the pending controversies between the two countries.

Then Alemán informed the surprised U.S. secretary that president-elect Ávila Camacho wanted to pay a visit to Washington soon in order to "indicate to his own people and to the rest of the country his desire to promote good relations between the U.S. and Mexico."[77] It was an attempt to link himself publicly with Roosevelt before the U.S. president's second term expired. If the Roosevelt administration had received Ávila Camacho as Mexican president-elect in the U.S. capital, it would have bestowed a decisive degree of public recognition on the Mexican visitor and the hands of a possible Republican president after December 1 would have been tied. But in August, the Roosevelt administration hesitated and insisted that Ávila Camacho come after the U.S. presidential election in November. Nevertheless, Alemán left Washington with the explicit assurance that nothing would be done to support the Almazán opposition.[78]

By September the Roosevelt administration had changed its mind. Secretary of State Cordell Hull declared publicly that Ávila Camacho would be welcome in the United States. On September 19, 1940, Undersecretary Welles told Mexican Ambassador Castillo Nájera that the Roosevelt administration was recognizing the results of the presidential election of 1940. The Avilacamachistas had reached their first objective. With the support of the United States, they could now focus on the presidential inauguration scheduled for the first week of December 1940.

The inauguration was a delicate task. The United States needed to be reassured that Ávila Camacho's commitment to close bilateral cooperation was sincere. At the same time, the Mexican public had to be reassured that Mexico's national independence and sovereignty would not be compromised by such cooperation. The Mexican public was not ready for a close, open relationship with the United States. And finally, due to the unsettled situation in Europe and Asia, the Ávila Camacho administration also had to nurture the hopes of Axis countries that Mexico would revive trade with them as soon as the war ended.

The Mexicans proved to be masters of diplomacy. The U.S. State Department received the customary invitation for a special representative to the inauguration on October 24, 1990, before any European government received one.[79] The invitation was accompanied by a strong letter of support from U.S. Ambassador Daniels. He urged the U.S. State Department to use this inauguration as an opportunity to further strengthen the U.S.–Mexican relationship. Daniels reassured the U.S. State Department once more that Ávila Camacho was

> the choice of the majority of the voters in Mexico. He possesses the confidence of the great majority of the people, including most of those who supported his opponent in the election.

Mexicans had no desire for a revolution, he emphasized. The current mood in Mexico was "better a poor President than a good revolution."[80]

Four days later, president-elect Ávila Camacho sent a personal invitation for the inauguration to U.S. Undersecretary of State Sumner Welles. He emphasized that this personal invitation was not simply "a mere matter of form."[81] In case of Roosevelt's reelection, the U.S. administration's point man for Latin American policy could experience firsthand Ávila Camacho's commitment to the Mexican friendship with the United States. But the Mexican courting of members of the Roosevelt administration reached its peak after Roosevelt's reelection. Then, Mexican Ambassador Castillo Nájera and First Secretary of the Mexican Embassy in Washington Luis Quintanilla approached U.S. vice president-elect Wallace and invited him, too, to come to Mexico City for the festivities.[82] When the U.S. State Department supported the invitation, President Roosevelt ordered Wallace to cancel a planned vacation in Costa Rica and to proceed to Mexico City instead. For the first time in U.S.–Mexican relations, a U.S. vice president would travel south of the Rio Grande and participate in a Mexican presidential inauguration. Wallace was one of the most liberal members of the new Roosevelt administration and sincerely interested in Latin American agricultural affairs, and his presence in Mexico City would provide a more sympathetic image of the northern neighbor—not that of a hegemonic Yankee breathing down Mexico's neck—one hundred years after the two countries had fought a bitter war against each other.

The most important European representative at the inauguration would be German Minister Rüdt, due to the state of Mexican–British relations and the French defeat by the Germans. But Germany was accorded a lower representational status than the United States. Rüdt received the Mexican invitation after the United States, and then only from Foreign Minister Hay.[83] Also, Ávila Camacho abstained from sending any personal invitation to Berlin. Therefore, Rüdt himself had to lobby Berlin to impress the importance of the Mexican inauguration on his superiors. He saw it as a unique chance to demonstrate German pride and economic promise in the Mexican capital. For that purpose, he wanted to be appointed special representative, together with German military attaché to Washington von Boetticher.[84] He asked Berlin to promise Ávila Camacho large future purchases of Mexican silver. He also suggested the advertisement of Germany as a possible future European distributor of Mexican oil. Finally, he asked Berlin to inform him whether any German government ministry had plans for an increased participation in Mexico's future industrialization.[85] Such economic enticements, he hoped, could keep Mexican goodwill toward Germany alive. But for the German Foreign Ministry, Mexico was not important. For weeks, Rüdt's requests remained unanswered.

In the meantime, Rüdt tried to identify the future foreign policy of Ávila

Camacho and its significance for Germany. As usual, there existed no shortage of "insiders" who were willing to tell Rüdt what he wanted to hear. Columbian Ambassador to Mexico Pinzon N. became Rüdt's main source of information about Ávila Camacho's intentions.[86] Pinzon promised Rüdt that Ávila Camacho would maintain a

> prudent attitude toward Germany-Europe [sic] and Japan, since this is the only counterweight against U.S. imperialism. As long as this door [to the Axis] remained open the United States would continue its Good Neighbor policy out of fear that Mexico might side with totalitarian countries.

Rüdt was particularly pleased to hear that Ávila Camacho intended to continue Cárdenas's policy in the ongoing oil dispute. He was devastated when he learned that Wallace would represent the United States at the inauguration. His presence would dominate the event and upstage Rüdt's efforts to show the German flag. Rüdt also feared that Wallace was really coming to Mexico City to sign a defense treaty. Quite the contrary, Pinzon told Rüdt; Wallace would be forced to make a statement that no defense cooperation existed between the two countries. Pinzon told Rüdt in confidence that Ávila Camacho "could not express his favorable opinion about Germans publicly, because he had to avoid defamations by Mexico's neighbor which bordered on hysteria."[87] These consoling remarks allowed Rüdt to interpret the obvious Mexican–U.S. rapprochement during fall 1940 as a mere tactical concession by Ávila Camacho to prevent deeper, more "dramatic" cooperation with the colossus of the north.[88] Eventually, German foreign-policy bureaucrats appointed Rüdt as a special envoy to the inauguration. Military attaché von Boetticher, however, was ordered to remain in the U.S. capital. The overt demonstrative display of a German officer at the Mexican inauguration would have caused only misunderstandings. Also, Rüdt was not allowed to make economic promises to Ávila Camacho. Compared to the emerging U.S.–Mexican economic relationship, Germany had little to offer to the Ávila Camacho administration at the eve of the inauguration.

The inauguration of president-elect Ávila Camacho also marked the end of the last personal foreign-policy initiative of President Cárdenas. While Mexican bureaucrats were busy weaving tighter and tighter economic links between the United States and Mexico, and while U.S. and Mexican security forces prevented the Almazán rebellion from becoming reality, Cárdenas used his presidential office one more time to pursue a very personal initiative: the rescue of more than 100,000 Spanish refugees in France. Immedi-

ately after the signing of the German–French armistice, Cárdenas had ordered Mexican Ambassador to France Luis I. Rodríguez to negotiate with
the newly formed French Vichy administration about the fate of Republican
refugees in France. Ambassador Rodriguez saw Marshall Petain on July 8,
1940. At the end of the meeting, the two men created a French–Mexican
commission for the study of the issue. It convened for the first time on July
23, 1940.[89] Exactly one month later, on August 23, 1940, both sides signed
an accord that envisioned a comprehensive solution of the Spanish refugee
problem in France. Mexico agreed to grant all Spanish refugees immigrant
status, provide them with diplomatic protection, and give residence in Mexico
to those who were willing to come.[90] The execution of the terms of the
accord, however, encountered a serious obstacle early on. The Mexican government did not own ships to transport refugees from France to Mexico.
And the French merchant marine had come under German control. Therefore, German support for the Mexican–French accord was a prerequisite
for its realization.[91]

Mexican Minister to Germany Azcárate formally asked for German support on August 24, 1940. He tried to make the Mexican requests palatable
to the Germans by suggesting that the Mexican offer alleviate Vichy and its
German supporters from an unnecessary economic burden at a critical point
in time.[92] In addition, he promised that Mexico would use the French mer-
chant-marine ships "according to the limitations set by the German government."[93]

For the German Foreign Ministry, the Mexican request was not urgent.
Minister Azcárate waited six weeks for a German reply. Suddenly, he was
invited to a rare personal discussion with German Foreign Minister
Ribbentrop on October 15, 1940. In the privacy of Ribbentrop's office,
Azcárate repeated his government's request for the use of French ships to
evacuate ten thousand to fifteen thousand Spaniards. In return, the Cárdenas
administration was "willing to leave the selection of the . . . refugees from
lists to be submitted to the German government."[94] After Azcárate's presentation, the two men split without reaching any agreement.

Azcárate's concession to submit the Spanish refugee lists to the Germans
is surprising. It gave Nazi bureaucrats control over who could leave Europe.
Mexican sources do not show that Cárdenas had agreed to this concession.
An educated guess suggests that it seemed to have been a concession by
pragmatic Mexican bureaucrats who wanted to begin the evacuation of
Spanish refugees as soon as possible. It might also have been influenced by
Azcárate's tendency to defer to German officials to protect future Mexican–
German relations. Moreover, because of his own conservative political atti-

tude, Azcárate might have had little personal sympathy for radical Spanish socialists or communists.

After the meeting, Ribbentrop revealed his personal position on the issue in a memorandum. He did not care about the Spanish refugees per se. But he saw them as a possible source for the creation of instability in Mexico that could bind precious U.S. resources. The presence of "international agents, communists and other persons," he noted, "could create undesired surprises for Mexico." Communist agitation might shake the stability of the Mexican administration and, therefore, make life more difficult for President Roosevelt. In other words, Ribbentrop saw an opportunity to redirect German policy toward the United States, which currently was determined by the petroleum needs of the German Navy and Hitler's desire to keep the United States out of the war. Ribbentrop forwarded the Mexican request to the German army high command,[95] informed the Italian government, and asked the Spanish Franco government for comments.

The Franco administration gave its qualified approval. Most refugees were allowed to leave.[96] Only eight hundred Spaniards were selected to stay behind. These "particular implicated red-Spanish leaders . . . should not receive the opportunity to flee to Mexico," the Franco government wrote to Berlin.[97]

In the end, Cárdenas's heroic effort to guarantee the survival of Republican Spaniards before he lost the power of the presidency failed. In November 1940, the German army rejected the Mexican request based on an interpretation of Article 10 of the French–German armistice agreement. Right away, the embarkation of five hundred Spaniards to Mexico stopped. Then Vichy suspended all further activities until March 1941.[98] This temporary suspension became permanent in the summer of 1941. About 123,000 Spanish refugees remained stranded in France, easy prey for German and Vichy security forces. At about the same time, the deportation of Spanish refugees to German concentration camps began.

Finally, in December 1940, the inauguration of president-elect Ávila Camacho became the crowning foreign-policy event for the postrevolutionary Mexican political establishment. It was symbolic in several ways.

For the first time, it revealed to the Mexican public how close U.S.–Mexican relations had become during the last twelve months. At the inaugural ceremony, Ambassador Daniels and Vice President Wallace were received with a standing ovation. Later, Wallace placed a wreath at the monument of the Niños Héroes at Chapultepec, Mexico's heroes of the U.S.–Mexican war, a gesture intended to symbolize "the end of the era of the powerful

U.S.'s aggression upon its neighbor."[99] Two days later, on December 4, Wallace was allowed to address the Mexican Congress, trying to bring about a "meeting of men of good will, of which there cannot be too many."[100] Throughout his trip, his humble but sincere efforts to speak Spanish further impressed the Mexican public. Finally, he retreated to Pátzcuaro for a short vacation, and even there he charmed local farmers with private clinics in corn growing.

In contrast, German activities during the inauguration impressed with their negative nature. When Vice President Wallace arrived at the U.S. embassy building, it was suddenly surrounded by a group of antigovernment protesters, who yelled, "Down with the gringos who meddle in our affairs!" Wallace had to be shuffled to the side entrance of the embassy. The agitators had been financed by the German legation. Hours later, Gus Jones, the United States' FBI chief in Mexico, learned that the Germans also had recruited a member of the Mexican secret-service team that was protecting Wallace; his job was to inform the Germans about Wallace's itinerary.[101] These incidents convinced the Cárdenas administration to move the inauguration from the National Stadium to the enclosed and controlled space of the Chamber of Deputies.[102] Whereas the United States made an impression with Vice President Wallace, the German legation gained attention through mobs, agent provocateurs, and spies.[103] Compared to the German activities, U.S. Vice President Wallace looked like the benign, well-meaning neighbor from the north.

The inauguration was also symbolic of how much U.S. policy makers were interested in friendship and cooperation with the complex neighbor to the south. Wallace realized that Ávila Camacho had not been the choice of Mexico's urban electorate.[104] Only the organized vote of the countryside had produced Ávila Camacho's victory. Nevertheless, Wallace came to think of Ávila Camacho as a genuine friend of the United States. Wallace wrote to U.S. Secretary of State Hull:

> I am convinced from talking with Ávila Camacho that he is fully aware of the economic and political importance of the U.S. to Mexico and that he is anxious to move in our direction as fast as political necessities permit him to do so.[105]

Furthermore, he appreciated the delicate domestic political balancing act that Ávila Camacho had to perform in regard to future U.S.–Mexican relations. He explained:

> If he [Ávila Camacho] moves too rapidly and completely in the direction of the U.S., he allows the totalitarian powers operating in

Mexico to utilize the power which may exist among the Almazanistas and other disgruntled elements to our disadvantage.[106]

Wallace's visit demonstrated that cordial, even personally close U.S.–Mexican bilateral contacts now extended all the way to the executive level of both countries, and, equally important, they could be displayed publicly. The respectful yet distant approach by Cárdenas toward Roosevelt was replaced by a direct, personal, and open relationship between Ávila Camacho and the U.S. vice president and, later, Roosevelt himself. The first visit of a U.S. vice president to the Mexican revolutionary government was a bigger than expected success. It strengthened a most critical Mexican foreign relationship at a time when Europe continued to be unavailable to support Mexico's economic and political interests.

Finally, the inauguration also marked the time the conservative ideas and positions that had been developed during the last two years of Cardenismo became the official position of the Mexican administration. Contrary to the troubling reality of difficult living situations in the Mexican countryside and many urban areas, President Ávila Camacho had the audacity to proclaim in his inauguration speech:

> everybody will reach the conclusion that the Mexican Revolution has been a social movement guided by justice alone, which is now historical. It has achieved for a people the essentials of living.[107]

But it would take the Japanese attack on Pearl Harbor to admit publicly what had emerged in the bureaucratic documents in the immediate aftermath of the oil expropriation in May 1938. President Ávila Camacho explained in a speech following the attack of Pearl Harbor:

> Our industries and our agriculture must also intensify their labors. Since the circumstances do not obligate us to outright belligerent acts, our fight will not be in the trenches, but in the factories and in the furrows. We must develop the capacity of our economy and strengthen the productivity of our commerce so that all these efforts will be directed toward one end: to contribute to the security of the Americas with order and with work. . . .
>
> In the present condition of emergency, patriotism must be placed above everything else. America is in danger. Mexico is in danger, therefore, no effort is too small and no risk too great. Workers, peasants, professionals, the poor, both industrial and commercial classes, we must all rally ourselves around the glorious flag of the Republic.[108]

9

Conclusion

Two Themes in Mexican Foreign Relations between 1934 and 1940: Development and War

THE EVENTS ANALYZED IN THE PREVIOUS CHAPTERS SUGGEST A RETHINKING of Mexican foreign policy between World Wars I and II, in general and during the Cárdenas presidency, in particular. A multilateral research approach identified Mexico City as the hub of an expanding network of complex Mexican foreign relations. They symbolized an ongoing dialogue between a group of domestic policy planners who wanted to modernize the Mexican nation and an international economic, social, and political situation that was increasingly influenced by state-sanctioned international violence.

Mexico's most important economic and political relationship was with the United States. Mexico's most important cultural and social link abroad remained Spain, more precisely Republican Spain. To these two pivotal foreign relations, Mexican foreign-policy professionals added foreign links that systematically expanded policy options for Mexican postrevolutionary administrations, regardless of their own domestic political leanings. In other words, the essence of Mexican foreign relations during the 1930s was how to modernize Mexico economically through as many beneficial international foreign relations as possible, not the battle against U.S. or European economic and political hegemony. This quest was also influenced by a need for international political friendships that allowed Mexican administrations to point to external references as a justification for domestic social and political reforms. The modernization of Mexican society would be achieved only if its backward-oriented *hispanista* values could be unmasked as outdated, and if the depressed, self-defeating, negative image of Mexico's indigenous past could be reversed.

From that vantage point, foreign relations did not merely exist for their own sake, or because postrevolutionary Mexico could not remain in isolation in the international system, or simply because Mexico had to react to foreign pressures. Rather, foreign relations had gained a distinct value for the postrevolutionary elite. Every foreign relation that the Mexican state established, maintained, or usurped was a power asset for the emerging postrevolutionary state; and indirectly, it robbed domestic and foreign opponents of valuable support for the realization of alternative visions.

This explains why members of the Cárdenas administration intensified, concurrently, linkages with the United States, Republican Spain, Nazi Germany, and Mussolini's Italy. Also, it suggests an answer to the question of why so many Mexican foreign relations developed during the conservative *maximato* period were continued and expanded by the radical Cárdenas administration. Consequently, Mexican foreign relations during the 1930s remained pragmatic and unselective in regard to ideological implications, with some notable exceptions. Again, this Mexican pragmatism was not a reaction to Great Powers' political games or First World economic desires for Latin American markets. It was a self-confident, assertive approach by Mexicans who saw themselves as developers of their own state, not as victims of international capitalism. Their goal was to anchor Mexico in the international economy in such a way that it would receive maximum benefit for capitalist economic development. In this process, Mexican foreign-policy professionals proved themselves as independent actors. They were willing to engage in, and were successful in, the pursuit of constructive, proactive steps within the constantly changing opportunities and limits that the domestic–foreign interrelationship provided. Mexico and Mexican foreign policy makers were not mere victims of the international system of the 1930s. Neither traditional Great Powers diplomatic analysis in the tradition of geopolitics nor a dependency theory–oriented approach can accommodate this development of Mexican foreign relations during the 1930s. Both of them would deny an entire generation of Mexican politicians, policy makers, and professionals their determination and capacity to pursue genuine Mexican foreign relations.

The chief architects and actors in such a foreign-relations approach were the leaders and members of Mexico's growing state bureaucracy. After World War I, an evolving international economy and the implications of the world depression elevated national economic professionals and diplomats to positions of unprecedented influence and power within the postrevolutionary state. By the end of the 1930s, the power and foreign-policy preferences of Mexican presidents had been matched permanently by politically undesirable, but developmentally "necessary," visions of foreign-relations professionals.

Of course, there existed a wide gap between public official discourse and what went on in the inner circles of the Cárdenas state. Whereas Cardenista public discourses celebrated Porfirio Díaz's self-serving lament about a poor Mexico so far from God and so close to the United States, the interactions described in the previous chapters unmasked this sigh of frustration as a mirage for a school of thought that still has many faithful followers. If geography is destiny, then the Cárdenas administration's proximity to the Roosevelt administration was a blessing in disguise. Mexico's relationship with the pro-Mexico faction in the White House proved critical for many policy inspirations, provided it with the financial base to realize its radical politics, and repeatedly assured its survival against domestic and foreign foes alike. It was a good relationship.

Because the Cárdenas administration was close to the New Dealers in the U.S. administration, the Mexican postrevolutionary state gained unprecedented advantages. Silver policy and silver companies in the United States provided the Cárdenas government with critical funds for its domestic infrastructure projects throughout its entire *sexeño*. Financial support by the U.S. Treasury during the economic crisis of 1937 was decisive and came without any strings attached. Before, during, and after the oil expropriation, U.S. Ambassador Daniels shielded the Cárdenas administration against more serious punitive actions and coup attempts by U.S. private business. Secretly, after the oil expropriation U.S. financial support for the Cárdenas administration continued, allowing it to rebuild its economic base and, therefore, to finish its *sexeño*. Finally, behind the scenes President Roosevelt refused to become an agent for the multinational oil companies and pushed for a settlement of the oil conflict, which kept Mexico's oil industry under national control.

An often overlooked part of this complex U.S.–Mexican relationship was unspoken U.S. approval of Mexico's aggressive stance against British economic property in Mexico. U.S. Ambassador Daniels's refusal to create a united diplomatic and economic Anglo-Saxon front in the Mexican capital and his letters to President Roosevelt assured that such a potentially powerful alliance would not materialize in Washington D.C., as well. Therefore, the British were rendered impotent in the Mexican setting. The Mexican state could expropriate foreign petroleum holdings—the majority of which were British—and add a critical industrial sector to its national economic developmental structure. Great Britain was too far away and had no effective forces left to keep the Mexicans from acting against their interests and property. Indeed, in this case geography was destiny.

U.S. ideas and goods influenced the Cárdenas administration in other important ways. New Deal experiments served as examples for Mexican financial experts. U.S. commercial agricultural programs were invited to introduce new hybrid seeds and agricultural technology into Mexico to accelerate the commercialization of its agriculture. Mexican military aviators wanted U.S. fighter planes for Mexico's air force. The FBI strengthened the

power of the state by training Cárdenas's secret services in surveillance technology and technique. Finally, Roosevelt's repeated personal intervention
against the Almazán rebellion ensured Ávila Camacho succession of Cárdenas
as Mexican president. In short, the Mexican relationship with New Dealers
in the United States was critical in terms of support, resources, and ideas for
those in the postrevolutionary state who wanted to modernize Mexican society and economy. And only in the United States were there individuals,
organizations, and government representatives who were genuinely and sincerely interested in the economic and social modernization of Mexico.

In contrast, Mexico's relations with European countries during the same
period remained full of frustrations. Initially, German interests in Mexico
were limited to those of the German Navy and the trade activities of ethnic
Germans in Mexico. Then, the German Navy's silly and deceitful plan to
exploit Mexico's Tehuantepec region as a German oil-supply base only threat-
ened to convert Mexican soil into a Great Powers battlefield during the next
war. Immediately after the oil expropriation, German, Italian, and Japanese
governments were unwilling to endanger their long-term relationships with
the oil multinationals, and thus they refused to import expropriated Mexican oil. Only slowly, during late 1938 and early 1939, did the fascist powers
begin to support Cárdenas's government. Even then, their cooperation was
selfish and a one-way street. In spite of lofty plans developed during 1937
and 1938, Germany delivered little of the infrastructure technology that
Mexico bought for its oil deliveries. Also, Italy used Mexican oil without
delivering the oil tankers that would have increased Mexican economic independence through a national tanker fleet. At least, Japan paid cash for
Mexican oil deliveries. But the Mexican trade commission that traveled to
Japan in 1940 to explore future cooperation returned home with the impression that Japan was not interested in contributing to Mexico's national economic development. Japan continued to see Mexico only in relationship to
its proximity to the United States. Republican Spain disappointed as an economic partner when it delivered ships of poor quality to the Mexican Navy
and refused to help in the aftermath of the oil expropriation.

Even the close political relationship with Republican Spain was a disappointment. Already during the *maximato*, Mexican administrations had been
ecstatic about the creation of a Republican Spain. It promised Mexico's
postrevolutionary state the projection screen of a modern and developing
former motherland whose secular modernization would relegate the conservative dreams of many Mexican *hispanistas* to the history books. If Spain
became modern and capitalist, then contemporary Mexican yearnings for a

conservative, antirevolutionary Catholicism would be proven outdated and Mexican *hispanistas* would be forced to come to terms with Mexico's postrevolutionary state and its capitalist developmental projects. Also, those Mexicans who, for cultural reasons, could never develop a liking for Protestant and often racist Anglo-Saxon economic values would gain an important modernized Iberian point of reference. From that angle, Cárdenas's deeply personal advocacy of the Spanish Republican cause was merely an intensified expression of attitudes that had already existed before 1934. It is no surprise, then, that the Spanish Civil War became Mexico's key political foreign-policy event of the 1930s.

But the victory of Franco and his fascist vision in Spain only reinvigorated *hispanista* dreams in Mexico and strengthened the most organized social mass movement against Cardenismo and the postrevolutionary state. In addition, Franco's Spain sent secret services and agents provocateurs to damage Mexico. Through the Falange and with German money, they intensified Mexican social tensions. Mexican conservative and Catholic circles contemplated fascist solutions to Mexico's economic, social, and political problems as never before. Only the ideological nightmare of the Hitler-Stalin pact effectively paralyzed the Mexican right. It provided the Cárdenas administration with a much-needed reprieve in the midst of the polarized presidential election campaign of 1939 and 1940. Without it, the course of the elections would have been influenced by a stronger, better-organized, foreign-supported conservative—sometimes fascist—Mexican social and political movement. Perhaps it would have provided the Almazán camp with enough domestic disturbance to plunge the Cárdenas administration into a serious domestic military engagement at a time when U.S. military planners were already seriously worried about the state of Mexico's national security. It could have initiated another U.S. invasion, this time as a preemptive occupation of Mexico to keep out Spanish and German fascist subversive forces.

Clearly, Mexican foreign relations during this time grew out of elite politics, not from the consideration or expression of the popular will. Mexican rural populations, urban dwellers, industrial workers, members of the federal bureaucracy, private business owners, and the political leadership all favored different linkages when it came to foreign affairs. A national consensus toward foreign relations did not exist in the 1930s. And yet, in 1934, many of Mexico's cultural, social, and political links abroad were conducted outside of government control. Century-old conservative, historical, and cultural ties with Spain and more recent influences from foreign anarchist and communist interests were affecting Mexican politics in a way that was threatening to the postrevolutionary state. To a certain degree, this problem had been addressed by the *cristiada* religious war in the late 1920s, which eliminated the influence of the Vatican in Mexico. Also, President Portes Gil's diplomatic break with the Soviet Union demonstrated the determination of the Mexican state to prevent foreign ideologies from shaping the meaning of its revolutionary path. Still, by the time Cárdenas came to power a significant and increasing number of foreign political groups were systematically advertising their ideas as solutions to Mexico's domestic problems. Catholics and Protestants in the United States, European and U.S. trade unionists, Spanish *hispanistas*, German National Socialists, Soviet Popular Front Internationalists, Trotskyists, and admirers of Mussolini all offered their political remedies for Mexico's continuously polarized society.

The postrevolutionary state reacted by endorsing a strong nationalist and indigenous political stance that offered a Mexican counter-discourse to the attractive foreign voices. In addition, the power of Mexican political groups who were actively and independently communicating abroad were systematically weakened during the 1930s. The internationalist union movement and Mexico's political left was split through Vincente Lombardo Toledano's growth to prominence, Trotsky's asylum in Mexico, and the reorganization of Mexican mass party politics in 1938. The anger of the political right was appeased with a modus vivendi in the church question, and its extreme fringes were suppressed by Mexican secret services. Efforts by the Falange and German Nazi organizations to instrumentalize these battles were weakened through Cárdenas's support for European and Mexican antifascist organizations and their propaganda in Mexico. The expanding democratic propaganda support from Czechoslovakia and France before 1939 helped Cárdenas counterbalance similar German and Spanish activities. The Allied propaganda campaign beginning in 1939 virtually established a state monopoly over foreign images and ideas in all Mexican media. Not least of all, it helped Cárdenas reduce the attractiveness of a fascist Spain under General Franco. Public paranoia in the United States about an alliance of communists and Nazis in Mexico, as a consequence of the Hitler-Stalin pact, further intimidated Cárdenas's conservative opponents at home. Diego Rivera's accusations against Stalinists in Mexico during 1939 and 1940 and Trotsky's agitation helped to maintain the international image of the Cárdenas government as a reasonable centrist force within this whirlwind of ideological competition in Mexico.

The Mexican state did not stop at neutralizing the foreign relations of opposition groups. It also augmented its capacity to react to international events and to exploit them for the benefit of existing political and economic arrangements. Through its professionalized diplomatic reporting system, it learned about the meaning of foreign developments early, considered their implications for Mexico's development, and prepared their exploitation for the states' gain. In contrast to 1934, the Mexican state had penetrated most Mexican linkages abroad by the time Cárdenas left office. In other words, between 1934 and 1940, control of foreign relations had become a critical resource for the Mexican state and postrevolutionary elite against domestic political opposition groups and mass organizations that championed alternative social and economic visions. The Mexican government's increasing expansion, manipulation and public reinterpretation of Mexico's links abroad had become a critical aspect of postrevolutionary-regime maintenance. Foreign relations had a clear and distinct value for Mexico's political elite and could no longer be left to chance or to the conduct of amateurs. Finally, the emergency of the Second World War would give the state the reason to establish itself at the center of all Mexican foreign relations. By 1941 the monopolization of foreign relations by the state would be achieved. Once the real threat of the war subsided, the Mexican state would refuse to relinquish its supremacy in foreign affairs.

This interpretation emphasizes the deep interrelationship between domestic Mexican domestic postrevolutionary politics and developments in the international environment between 1934 and 1940. Mexican events during the Cárdenas *sexeño* were directly and indirectly linked to an international environment that increasingly sought to solve economic, political, and social problems through state-supported violence, although most Mexican contemporaries did not realize it. Nevertheless, Mexico's domestic political discourses, social changes, state finances, ideological debates, and elite interests were linked to forces outside Mexico's borders, whether one likes it or not. The possibility and implications of international war moved through the Cárdenas *sexeño* like a red thread. A few Mexicans pondered such thoughts early on. Mexican military planners discussed the negative consequences of a U.S.–Japanese war in 1932. By 1934 other Mexican military planners had discovered a positive aspect of this process, using its appearance as a reason for the technological modernization of the Mexican armed forces. At the same time, a few Mexican diplomats were busy keeping international war away from Latin America through their mediation efforts in the Chaco War. Soon thereafter, Mexicans argued in the League of Nations against Italy's conquest of Ethiopia. These actions continued when Germany invaded the French-occupied areas and Japan attacked China. By then, early tremors of World War II were reaching Mexico in the form of the Popular Front movement. Mexico actively entered the preparations for World War

II when it supplied Republican Spain with weapons against the Franco uprising. Cárdenas hoped that a defeat of Franco would keep European fascism from entering Latin America. By 1938 Cárdenas publicly used the theme of the emerging war as a reference point in speeches to Mexican workers and peasants. At the same time, he sincerely offered his diplomatic skills to Roosevelt, hoping that a Mexican–U.S. peace-conference process would settle the European tensions. On the other side of the Rio Bravo, fear about Nazi inroads in Latin America encouraged the U.S. Secretary of the Treasury to block the revengeful politics of the U.S. State Department against Cárdenas.

Other Mexicans, however, began to see war in a new light. Whereas in 1932 it had been a threat, by 1937 it was becoming a reality beginning to impact Mexico. However, if there was a crisis, there also existed an opportunity. By 1938 some Mexicans began to ponder international war as an economic promise. Little by little, it was recognized as an innovative solution to Mexico's quest for national economic development. Ironically, Hitler's annexation of Austria provided Cárdenas with a perfect detraction for Great Powers diplomats, which made the Mexican oil nationalization easier to pull off. Thereafter, fear about war hurt Mexico when all European powers refused to endanger long-term—that is, wartime—delivery arrangements with Shell and Standard Oil. Consequently, Mexican petroleum products were kept out of European military depots. Only the supply politics of Shell Oil, during the German attack on the Czech Sudeten area, convinced the Germans to disregard British threats and finally allow the importation of Mexican oil products. In 1939, Italian and Japanese war preparations stabilized Mexican oil sales and allowed Cárdenas to remain tough vis-à-vis pressure from the oil companies and President Roosevelt, who tried to bring about a Mexican oil settlement advantageous to his presidential campaign. In 1939, the Hitler-Stalin pact shook up Mexico's internal political debates. The Soviet invasion of Poland and Finland generated much popular sympathy among Mexicans for the small neighbors of Soviet imperial power. The loss of the European market in 1940 hurried the Mexican technocrats into deeper and deeper economic cooperation with the United States. And the presidential campaign of Andreu Almazán suffered severely from the allegations that he was a merely a front for more dangerous Nazi fifth-column plans in Mexico. By then war also meant danger to Mexico's territorial sovereignty, as Cárdenas learned when U.S. military planners wanted to take over the defense of Mexico's borders against possible Axis invasion armies. At the same time, Mexican diplomats and politicians committed heroic acts when they rescued many of Europe's antifascists, Jews, and Republican Spaniards from an increasingly German-occupied Europe.

By then Mexican developmentalists expected U.S. war preparations to provide new energy for Mexico's continuing dilemma of national development. The external stimulus of the war was to produce what could not be achieved through a domestic economic takeoff. Finally, the war also brought foreign support for the security of the Mexican state. British, French, and other international antifascists and the United States' FBI informed the Mexican administration of foreign fascist subversive plots and domestic anti-Cárdenas organizations. Also, these foreign observers reassured policy makers in Washington and London that the Zimmermann affair of 1917 was not about to be repeated in Mexico. The secret service and military support of the United States was also critical in robbing the Almazán rebellion of its possibly friendly staging ground along the U.S.–Mexican border, thus defeating its confused, yet very real plans for violence. Ávila Camacho, the candidate of the postrevolutionary establishment, was brought into office with the combined efforts of the United States and Mexico. It was the first successful Mexican–U.S. wartime military cooperation, long before either side ever declared war.

The Cárdenas presidency had begun with the recognition that international war was possible. During the middle of the *sexeño*, Mexican policy professionals adjusted Mexican foreign policy to the increasing presence of war and began to exploit its contradictions. By the time Cárdenas left office, many Mexican technocrats and policy professionals had embraced war as an international context that in many ways would provide solutions to the needs of the postrevolutionary Mexican state. The theme of war and its manifold implications influenced the development of the Cárdenas state as much as the postrevolutionary quest for national economic development. As far as Mexican foreign relations were concerned, Mexican history between 1934 and 1940 was a grand dialogue between the domestic push for capitalist economic development and the reverberations of international war.

꙳

Notes

Chapter 2

1. Hereafter cited as AHSRE.

2. Alberto J. Pani, *Apuntes Autobiographicos* (México: Editorial Stylo, 1945), chap. 3.

3. Linda B. Hall, *Oil, Banks and Politics: The U.S. and Postrevolutionary Mexico 1917–1924* (Austin: University of Texas Press, 1995).

4. Samuel Guy Inman, *Inter-American Conferences 1826–1954: History and Problems* (Washington: The University Press of Washington, D.C., 1965), 101.

5. Ibid., 112.

6. Ibid., 130.

7. Emilio Portes Gil, *Autobiografía de la Revolución Mexicana* (México, D.F.: Instituto Mexicano de Cultura, 1964), 666.

8. Eduardo Villaseñor, *Memorias-Testimonio* (México: Fondo de Cultura Económica, 1974), 98.

9. League of Nations. League of Nations Documents 1919–1946 (hereafter cited as LON), Reel VII–16, Section: Political Questions, Doc. No. A 43.1931 [VII], "Invitation to Mexico to join the League of Nations," September 7, 1931; and Doc. No. A.50.1931 [VII], Mexican Foreign Minister Genaro Estrada, "Telegram to Secretary General League of Nations," Sept. 11, 1931.

10. Ibid.

11. Great Britain, Public Record Office, Foreign Office 371 (hereafter cited as PRO, F.O. 371), File 15846, A 337/337/26, Forbes, "Mexico Annual Report 1931," Dec. 29, 1931, 8.

12. United States, National Archive of the United States (hereafter cited as NAUS), Record Group (hereafter cited as RG) 165, Military Attaché Cummings, "G-2 Report No. 4329," Dec. 29, 1932. LON, Reel VII–21, Doc. No. C840.M390.1932 [VII], Manuel C. Téllez, "Letter to Secretary General" Dec. 15, 1932.

13. The rumor was that he had to resign because President Calles had received U.S. complaints that Estrada was too active internationally.

14. NAUS, RG 165, U.S. Military Attaché Cummings, "G-2 Report No. 4543," Apr. 25, 1933. The U.S. military attaché sent this source to Washington after its publication in a Mexican newspaper.

15. Mexico, Mexico City, Archivo Histórico de la Secretaria de las Relaciones Exteriores (hereafter cited as AHSRE), Circular IV–9–26, Apr. 14, 1932.

16. For a general impression of early Mexican reporting style and quality, consult the Official Mayor series in AHSRE.

17. AHSRE, Exp. 34–5–3, Leopoldo Ortiz, "Letter to Foreign Minister Hay," Jan. 10, 1935.

18. Ibid.

19. For example, see ibid., Exp. III–536–6, Portes Gil, "Letter to Leopoldo Ortiz," Jan. 29, 1935.

20. NAUS, RG 169, Pattin, "G-2 Report No. 5297," May 11, 1934.

21. AHSRE, Exp. III–2340–23, Hay, "Letter to Jefe del Departamento Diplomático," Oct. 10, 1938.

22. Ibid., "Proyecto de Repuesta al Acuerdo del C. Secretario sobre el Reglamiento Interiór de lo SRE. Distribución de los Asuntos entre los Secciones"; this reorganization of the SRE was confirmed by Lic. Anselmo Mena, Jefe del Departamento, Jan. 31, 1939.

23. Ibid.

24. Ibid., Exp. III–2340–23, "Proyecto de Reglamento Interiór de la Secretaría," initiated by Cenisceros and signed by Hay on Dec. 31, 1935.

25. Ibid., Exp. 30–23–1, Anselmo Mena, Jefe del Departamento, "Letter to Villa Michel," Jan. 23, 1938.

26. Ibid.; for example, see Circular, IV–43–129, Oct. 10, 1938, which requested a study of the use of water for the generation of electricity. Also, consult Circular III–2–47 and Exp. 30–3–9–(I), Castillo Nájera, "Estudios Para Encontrar Nuevos Usos Del Metál y Sus Compuestos," Mar. 31, 1931.

27. Examples of the new communication between SRE and the diplomats in the field are Exp. 27–27–3, Hay, "Letter to Encargado Interim," Dec. 16, 1936; ibid., Oficio de Mayor Hidalgo, "Restricted Letter to Azcárate," Nov. 19, 1936; Exp. 30–23–3, J. T. Bodet, "Note to Mexican Legation in Berlin," Mar. 25, 1937; ibid., J. T. Bodet, "Letter to Mexican Legation in Berlin," May 19, 1937; ibid., Exp. 30–23–4, Beteta, "Cover letter on Economic Report July 1937."

28. Ibid., Circular V–22–65, May 3, 1938.

29. Ibid.,"Informe November 1936," Signature by Jaime Torres Bodet.

30. Ibid., Exp. 30–23–3, J. T. Bodet, "Letter to Mexican Legation in Berlin," June 5, 1937.

31. Hall, *Oil, Banks and Politics*, 84–104.

32. José Ituriaga de la Fuente, *La Revolución Hacienda* (México: Secretaría de la Educación Pública, 1976), 126.

33. Enrique Krauze, Jean Meyer, y Cayetano Reyes, *La Reconstrucción Económica* (México: El Colegio de México, 1977), 9.

34. NAUS, RG 165, Military Attache Mashburn, "G-2 Report No. 6224," June 18, 1935.

35. Eduardo Suárez, "El Problema Supremo de México," Excélsior, May 3, 1955, in Suárez, Comentarios y Recuerdos (México: Editorial Porrúa, 1977), 407.

36. Suárez, Comentarios y Recuerdos, 164–65.

37. Ibid., 306.

38. NAUS, Microfilm Collection of Captured German Records, T-120: Records of the German Foreign Ministry (hereafter cited as T-120), Roll 2725, Fr. 416337–416338, Rüdt, "Memo from Engineer Viscaya", Oct. 20, 1937.

39. Suárez, Comentarios y Recuerdos, 182–85.

40. NAUS, Record Group 59, Records of the U.S. Department of State Relating to Internal Affairs of Mexico, 1930–1944 (hereafter cited as RG 59), 812.00/30559, Josephus Daniels, "Resume of Conditions in Mexico during March 1938," Apr. 15, 1938.

41. Frank Brandenburg, The Making of Modern Mexico (Englewood Cliffs, N.J.: Prentice Hall, 1964), 318–40.

42. Suárez, Comentarios y Recuerdos, 104.

43. Ibid., 132.

44. Raymond Vernon, The Dilemma of Mexico's Development (Cambridge: Harvard University Press, 1965), 84–85.

45. Irwin F. Gellman, Secret Affairs: Franklin Roosevelt, Cordell Hull, and Sumner Welles (Baltimore and London: The Johns Hopkins University Press, 1995), 66.

46. "Statement by Cárdenas in Villahermosa, Tabasco State," March 28, 1934, in Gilberto Bosques, The National Revolutionary Party of Mexico and the Six Year Plan (Mexico: Bureau of Foreign Information, 1937), 132.

47. Mexico, Michoacán, Jiquilpan, Archivo de la Revolución Mexicana Lázaro Cárdenas (hereafter cited as ARMLC), Fondo Múgica (hereafter cited as FJM), Vol. 29, Doc. 1: "Memorandum: Un Concepto Mexicano de Economía Dirigida," 1935.

48. Bosques, National Revolutionary Party, 66.

49. Ibid., 149.

50. Ibid.

51. Bosques, National Revolutionary Party, 62–63.

52. Ibid.

53. Ramon Beteta, "Economic Aspects of the Six Year Plan," in The Economic and Social Program of Mexico (Mexico: DAPP, 1935), 45.

54. NAUS, T-120, Roll 3190, Fr. E527051-E527060, Burandt, "Letter to Goering, copy to German Foreign Ministry (hereafter cited as AA), German Economic Ministry (hereafter cited as RWM) and Chancellery, Aufzeichnung über meine gestrige Audienz beim Staatspräsidenten General Lázaro Cárdenas," Jan. 20, 1937.

55. Suárez, Comentarios y Recuerdos, 105–7.

56. NAUS, T-120, Roll 3185, Fr. E526960, Rüdt, "Letter to AA," Sept.

28, 1935.

57. Ibid.

58. AHSRE, Exp. 30–23–3, Sanchez Mejorada, "Informe to SRE," Mar. 10, 1933.

59. Ibid., Exp. 34–5–3, Juan B. Saldana, "Informe Políticos Económicos," Mar. 29, 1934. Also, see Ortiz's interview with the *Nürnberger Zeitung,* Apr. 14, 1934.

60. Examples of the role of Guerra can be found in ibid., Exp. IV–733–7, IV–733–9, IV–733–20, L-E-588. After the Second World War, Guerra became Undersecretary of Foreign Relations and the key figure in German–Mexican relations after the war. From 1953 until 1964, he was Mexican Ambassador to Germany. See Roderic Ai Camp, *Mexican Political Biographies* (Tucson: University of Arizona Press, 1978), 151.

61. Mexico, Mexico City, Archivo General de la Nación (hereafter cited as AGN), Fondo Lázaro Cárdenas (hereafter cited as Fo.LC.), Exp. 432.2./253–8, E. Calderón, Presidencia de la República, Comisión de Estudios, "Memorandum Sobre El Tratramiento Diplomático Y La Publicidad En El Caso Petrolero," May 18, 1938, 21.

62. Ibid., Exp. 545.3/236, Dr. Jesus Díaz Barriga, Presidencia de la República, Comisión de Estudios, July 26, 1938.

63. Ibid., Exp. 564.1/2016/leg 1, Dr. Jesus Díaz Barriga, "Memo: La Actual Guerra Europea Y Su Influencia En La Economía Nacional," Dec. 16, 1939.

64. Ibid., Exp. 550/46–4, Rafael Sánchez Tapia, "Memorandum al Presidente Cárdenas," May 16, 1940.

65. AHSRE, Exp. 31–1–5, Alfonso Guerra, Mexican General Consulate Hamburg, "Informes Comercial Num. 76, Reservado," May 1940, Tomo II.

66. AGN, Fo.LC., Exp. 550/46–6, "Junta Celebrada en El Palacio Nacional, con Asistencia de los CC. Secretarios de Gobernación, Relaciones Exteriores, Defensa Nacional, Subsecretarios de Hacienda, Relaciones, Economia Nacional y Lic. Isidro Fabela," June 21, 1940.

67. Ibid., Exp. 707.1/2, Cárdenas, "Memorandum," Oct. 19, 1939.

68. Ibid., Exp. 513/2, Memorandum, "Junta Celebrado En El Palacio Nacional Con El Secretario General Del Syndicato De Trabajadores Ferrocarrileros d.l.Rep. Mexico," July 11, 1940.

69. Ibid., Exp. 513/2, "Junta Celebrada Con El Elemento Ferrocarrillero En El Palacio Nacional," July 16, 1940.

70. Ibid., Exp. 564.1/2016/3, Sria. de Agricultura y Fomento, "Ponencia: Esbozo de Programa Para Neutralizar o Utilizar En Beneficio Del País Las Repercussiones De La Guerra Europea," Sept. 19, 1939.

71. NAUS, RG 59, Box 3974, 812.001 Ávila Camacho, President Ávila Camacho, "Translation of Inauguration Speech," December 1940.

Chapter 3

1. Mexican trade with Central America was slightly better.

2. ARMLC, FJM, Caja 1, Exp. 70, Doc. 19, Ing. Rafael C. Betancourt Perez, "El Comercio de México con la America Latina entre 1931 y 1936," June 30, 1937.

3. See also Thomas Schoonover's examination of Porfirio Díaz's efforts to use the Pan-American conference system against U.S. hegemonic intentions. Thomas David Schoonover, *The U.S. in Central America, 1860–1911: Episodes of Social Imperialism and Imperial Rivalry in the World System* (Durham: Duke University Press, 1991).

4. Juan Ortiz Escamilla, "Visión Latinoamericanista del General Múgica," *Desdeldiez* Boletín del Centro de Estudios de la Revolución Mexicana "Lázaro Cárdenas", (México: Michoacán, Jiquilpan, July 1985), 82.

5. PRO, FO 371, File 18710, A 2782/2782/26, Monson, "Annual Report 1934," Dec. 31, 1934, 9.

6. Ibid.

7. The exile of Sandino in Mexico is perhaps the most famous example of Mexican support for Latin American political movements.

8. The following vignettes are taken from the British PRO, FO 371, A 1976/1976/26, "Reports on Heads of Foreign Missions in Mexico City," Mar. 15, 1938.

9. The following descriptions are taken from PRO, FO 371, File 19794, A 1332/1041/26, "Report on Heads of Foreign Missions in Mexico City for 1935, Dec. 31, 1935, and FO 371, File 18709, A/2783/928/26, "Report on Heads of Foreign Missions in Mexico City for 1934," Dec. 31, 1934.

10. Ibid., File 19794, A1331/1331/26, Murray, "Mexican Annual Report 1935, Dec. 31, 1935, 21.

11. Ibid., A 1331/1331/26, Murray, "Mexico Annual Report 1935," Dec. 31, 1935, 11.

12. Mexico, AGN, FO.LC., Exp. 523.60, Juan F. Azcárate to Secretaria de Guerra y Marina, "Informe No. 78," June 11, 1935.

13. Ibid., Exp. 573.1/15, Eduardo Villaseñor, "Letter to Cárdenas", Apr. 24, 1936.

14. Randall Bennett Woods, *The Roosevelt Foreign-Policy Establishment and the "Good Neighbor": The U.S. and Argentina 1941-1945* (Lawrence: The Regents Press of Kansas, 1979), 23.

15. Ibid.

16. Ibid.

17. Ibid., 25.

18. Ibid., 22.

19. David Edmund Cronon, *Josephus Daniels in Mexico* (Madison: University of Wisconsin Press, 1960).

20. New York, Hyde Park, Franklin Delanor Roosevelt Presidential Library (hereafter cited as FDR), President's Secret Files (hereafter cited as PSF) 43, Mexico 1936–1937, Josephus Daniels, "Letter to Roosevelt," Aug. 15, 1933.

21. Ibid., PSF 43, Mexico 1936–1937, Daniels, "Letter to Roosevelt," Nov. 6, 1934.

22. Ibid., President's Personal Files (hereafter cited as PPF) 86, Daniels, "Letter to Roosevelt," June 18, 1935.

23. Ibid., PSF 43, Mexico 1936–1937, Daniels, "Letter to Roosevelt," June 20, 1935.

24. Ibid.

25. Ibid., PPF 86, Daniels, "Letter to Roosevelt," June 25, 1935.

26. Ibid., PPF 86, Daniels, "Letter to Hull and copy to Roosevelt," June 18, 1935.

27. U.S. Congressional Record, U.S. Senate, May 6, 1940, "Discussion of the History of Silver and Silver Legislation," 5542–5551.

28. FDR, Morgenthau Diaries (hereafter cited as MD), Josephus Daniels, "Letter to Department of State (hereafter cited as DOS)," July 12, 1935, 98–99, also found in NAUS, RG 59, 851.5/2722. Suárez tried to increase the international use of Mexican silver by suggesting the creation of a conference of American Central Banks, "through which at least the principal Central Banks of America would set up their reserves with an important ratio of silver . . ." Ibid.

29. The U.S. government agreed to buy up to five million ounces of newly mined silver on the daily price, allowing thirty days for delivery. The arrangement could be cancelled monthly and both administrations could choose to go back to the free market after a notice on the fifteenth of each month.

30. FDR, MD, Roll 5, Book 15–18, Jan. 2, 1936.

31. FDR, MD, Reel 5, Jan. 6, 1936, 43–44.

32. PRO, FO 371, File 18710, A 2782/2782/26, Monson, "Annual Report 1934," Mar. 25, 1935.

33. See the excellent examination by Lorenzo Meyer, *Su Majestád Británica* (México: El Colegio de México, 1992), 432–57.

34. A small part of El Águila was owned by Dutch capital; however, it followed British leadership.

35. PRO, FO 371, File 19794, A 1331/1331/26, "Annual Report 1935," 4.

36. Ibid., 3.

37. AHSRE, Exp. III–1317–14, Luis Quintanilla, "Report to SRE," Jan. 11, 1933.

38. Ibid., Exp. 30–23–1, Primo Villa Michel, "Report to SRE," June 14, 1937.

39. Ibid., 8.

40. PRO, FO 371, 19794, A 1331/1331/26, Murray, "Annual Report,

1935," Dec. 31, 1935.

41. Ibid., 8–9.

42. Department of Overseas Trade, Report No. 642, *Economic Conditions in Mexico* (London: His Majesty's Stationary Office, 1936), 25.

43. John Knappe, "British Foreign Policy in the Carribean Basin, 1938–1945: Oil, Nationalism and Relations with the United States," *Journal of Latin American Studies* 19 (November 1987), 279–94.

44. See the excellent book by Brígida von Mentz et al., *Los Empresarios Alemanes: El Tercer Reich y La Oposición de Derecha a Cárdenas*, 2 vols. (Mexico: Ciecas, Ediciones de la Casa Chata, 1988).

45. NAUS, T-120, Roll 357, Fr. 264894–265003, Rüdt, "The Founding of the DVM," Jan. 23, 1935. The reorganization of the German community in Guadalajara was fueled by similar developments in the French community. See ibid., Roll 27, Fr. 24381, Keil/Guadalajara, "Letter to the DAI," Nov. 15, 1933.

46. SRE, Exp. 34–2–4, J. Sánchez Mejorada, "Informe Supplementario to SRE," Mar. 10, 1933.

47. Ibid., Exp. III–134–8, German Minister Zechlin, "Protest Note to Casauranc," Apr. 10, 1933. During 1933 the German legation was flooded with anti-Nazi protest letters and petitions; see Exp. III–134–III, Rüdt, "Note to Casauranc," Aug. 5, 1934.

48. Ibid., Exp. III–134–20, Zechlin, "Note to Casauranc," Mar. 31, 1933.

49. Ibid., Exp. III–222–1, Vasconselos/Sec. de Gobernación, "Letter to State Governors," Jan. 5, 1934. Later, Vasconselos had to compromise and allow the showing of a cut version of the film.

50. Hans Adolf Jacobsen, *Nationalsozialistische Aussenpolitik (1933-1938)* (Frankfurt am Main, Berlin: Alfred Metzler Verlag, 1968), 36.

51. Germany, Berlin-Dahlem, *Documentcenter*, Document No. 3020394, Rüdt von Collenberg, "Letter Gauschatzmeister to Reichsleitung NSDAP," Apr. 19, 1944.

52. Hereafter cited as AO.

53. Rüdt's highest contact was Foreign Minister Ribbentrop, with whom he talked for the first time at the Diplomaten Conference Berlin in the fall of 1939.

54. Hans Jürgen Schroeder, "Die Neue Deutsche Südamerika Politik," *Jahrbuch für Geschichte von Staat, Wirtschaft und Gesellschaft Lateinamerikas* 6 (Cologne: Boehlau Verlag, 1969), 337–46.

55. Ibid., 337.

56. NAUS, T-120, Roll 2725, Fr. E416088–E416088, Hans Burandt, "Telegram to AA," Dec. 14, 1936.

57. AHSRE, Exp. 34–5–32, Leopoldo Ortiz, "Informe Político to SRE," Jan. 17, 1935.

58. Ibid.

59. Germany, *Nürnberger Zeitung*, "Deutschland und Mexico," Apr. 14,

1934. In this interview, Ortiz suggested that both Mexico and Germany were dependent on the world market and the United States.

60. AHSRE, Exp. IV–733–92, Consulado General de Hamburgo, Alfonso Guerra, "Informe Comercial por Junio de 1935," June 1935.

61. NAUS, T-120, Reel 3185, Fr. E526967–E526968, Ahrens, "Report to AA," Sept. 9, 1935. Also, see the note of the German minister in SRE, Exp. III–670–4, Sept. 2, 1935.

62. Ibid., Fr. 526960–526961, Rüdt, "Report to AA"; the document arrived in Berlin on Sept. 28, 1935.

63. AHSRE, Exp. L-E-1054, Dr. Leonides Almazán, "Letter to SRE: Asunto Presentación de Credenciales," Feb. 28, 1936.

64. Klaus Volland, *Das Dritte Reich und Mexico* (Frankfurt/Bern: Lang, 1976).

65. Donald M. McKale, *The Swastika outside Germany*, (Kent, Ohio: Kent University Press, 1977), 64.

66. Dennis Rolland, *Vichy et la France Libre au Mexique* (Paris: Harmattan, 1990), 37–43.

67. PRO, FO 371, File 18710, A 2782/2782/26, "Annual Report 1934," Dec. 31, 1934, 11.

68. Mexican Foreign Minister Hay, Mexican Ambassador to Washington Castillo Nájera and Mexican Ambassador to the League of Nations Isidro Fabela had all served with the Mexican diplomatic corps, either in Japan or in China.

69. Joseph Pyke, "Economic Conditions in Mexico," *Department of Overseas Trade Report* No. 642 (London: H. M. Stationery's Office, 1936), 11.

70. Sometimes his name was also spelled Tsuru or Tzuru.

71. The British were best informed about the Japanese activities; see PRO, FO 371, File 24215, A/2353/57/26, Consul General Rees, "Memorandum to Foreign Office," Mar. 12, 1940.

72. ARMLC, FJM, Caja 5, Exp. 203, Doc. 3, Joublanc, "Informe Mensual," June 1936.

73. Ibid., Caja 16, Carpa 380, Doc. 5100, F. Mújica, "Inquiry for Material about Soviet Industrial Organization," June 4, 1935.

74. The best in-depth examination of Hispanismo is Frederick B. Pike, *Hispanismo*, (Notre Dame: Notre Dame University Press, 1971).

75. Ricardo Pérez Montfort, "El Hispanismo, Bandera Ideológica de la Derecha," *Revolucíon y Contrarevolución en México: IX Jornadas de Historia de Occidente* (Jiquilpan, Michoacán, México: Centro de Estudios de la Revolución Mexicana "Lázaro Cárdenas," 1986), 163. Also, see Ricardo Pérez Montfort, "Hispanismo y Falange: Los Sueños Imperiales de la Derecha Española y México" (México: Unpublished manuscript, 1988), 243.

76. Joe Ashby, *Organized Labor and the Mexican Revolution under Cardenas* (Chapel Hill: University of North Carolina Press, 1967), 72–97.

77. Luis Gonzáles, *Los Días del Presidente Cárdenas* (México: El Colegio de México, 1981).

78. Hans Werner Tobler, *Die Mexikanische Revolution* (Frankfurt: Suhrkamp Verlag, 1984), 580.

79. In 1937, a Mexican diplomat warned Cárdenas about growing considerations by forces inside the Japanese military to grant diplomatic recognition to the Franco group; see AGN, Fo.LC., Microfilm No. 13, Alcaraz T., "Letter to Cárdenas," Apr. 20, 1937.

80. T. G. Powell, *Mexico and the Spanish Civil War* (Albuquerque: University of New Mexico Press, 1981).

81. AGN, FO.LC., Microfilm No. 5, Fabela, "Letter to Cárdenas, May 17, 1939.

82. Ibid., Microfilm No.5, Cárdenas, "Letter to Fabela," Sept. 11, 1937.

83. PRO, FO 371, File 19794, A 1331/1331/26, Murray, "Annual Report, 1935," Dec. 31, 1935, 10.

84. ARMLC, FJM, Ambassador C. Águilar, Suelta Caja 17, Carp. 385, Doc. 5397, "Letter to Múgica," July 29, 1935.

85. AHSRE, Exp. III–164–6, Ambassador C. Águilar, "Report to SRE: Tratado Alemania—Japón Contra el Communismo," Dec. 12, 1936.

86. NAUS, RG 165, Military Attache Marshburn, "G-2 Report No. 5613," Oct. 5, 1934.

87. AGN, Fo.LC., Exp. 120/1482, Union of Veterans, "Letter to Villaseñor," Sept. 14, 1936.

88. Ricardo Pérez Montfort, "Por la Patria y la Raza: Tres Movimientos Nacionalistas de Clase Media," in von Mentz et al., *Los Empresarios Alemanes*, 290.

89. NAUS, RG 59, 812.00/31396, U.S. Consul Waterman, "Report to Secretary of State," June 16, 1942.

90. Ibid., RG 165, Military Attache Marshburn, "G-2 Report No. 7365," 1936.

91. See the letter of the Confederation of the Middle Class to Franco, in Pérez Montfort, "Hispanismo y Falange," 256.

92. AGN, Fo.LC. Microfilm 5, "Circular to SRE," Mar. 22, 1937.

93. John W. F. Dulles, *Ayer en Mexico* (México: Fondo de Cultura Económica, 1977), 440.

94. PRO, FO 371, File 18710, A 2782/2782/26, Monson, "Annual Report 1934," Dec. 31, 1934, 9.

95. Donald L. Herman, *The Comintern in Mexico* (Washington, D.C.: Public Affairs Press, 1974), 103.

96. Ibid., 105.

97. Herman, *Comintern in Mexico*, 107.

98. Robert E. Scott, *Mexican Government in Transition* (Urbana: University of Illinois, 1959), 30.

99. Ibid., 130–31.

100. Ibid., 126.

101. Manuel Caballero, *Latin America and the Comintern, 1919–1943* (Cambridge and New York: Cambridge University Press, 1986), 149 ff., and Barry Carr, *Marxism and Communism in Twentieth-Century Mexico*, Lincoln: University of Nebraska Press, 1992.

Chapter 4

1. NAUS, RG 59, 812.00/30435, Josephus Daniels, "Monthly Report for February 1937." March 1937.

2. The Mexican government paid monthly about 8 million pesos to 200,000 workers employed in the construction of highways, railroads, and drainage and irrigation systems; 5.2 million pesos to the 58.000 members of the military; as well as 15 million pesos to government employees.

3. FDR, MD, Roll 17, Book 62, Sumner Welles, "Personal Memo to Morgenthau", Apr. 2, 1937, 186–95.

4. PRO, FO 371, File 20634, A 4686/132/26, Godber to Mr. Troutbeck, "Memorandum: Poza Rica Negotiations, June 29, 1937," June 30, 1937.

5. NAUS, T-120, Roll 3190, Fr E527051-E527060, Hans Burandt, "Aufzeichnung über meine gestrige Audienz beim Staatspräsidenten General Lázaro Cárdenas," Jan. 20, 1937.

6. Ibid., Roll 3018, Fr. E491452, Hans Burandt, "Report to AA: Vertrauliches Memo über zukünftige Deutsch-Mexikanische Zusammenarbeit," Jan. 28, 1937.

7. ARMLC, FJM, Vol. 179, Doc. 42, Strictly Confidential Memo to Cárdenas, "Memorandum Sobre Una Colaboración Económica Mas Estrecha Entre México y Alemania," Feb. 9, 1937. Although the document is unsigned, the manner of argumentation, the style, and the choice of words clearly identify Mújica as the author.

8. Ibid.

9. NAUS, T-120, Roll 3018, Minister Rüdt, Frame E491388 ff., "Kompensationsgeschäfte der Siemens Mexico SA," Nov. 26, 1936.

10. Ibid., Fr. E491390, Rüdt to AA, "Regierungsauftrag von Eisenbahnmaterial der Firma Orenstein und Koppel," Nov. 17, 1936.

11. Ibid., Fr. E491614-E491616, Siemens Mexico SA, "Telegram to Siemens Berlin," Apr. 28, 1937.

12. Ibid., Fr.E491610, Minister Rüdt, "Letter to AA," May 28, 1937.

13. Ibid., Roll 3190, Fr. 527072 ff., Minister Rüdt, "Telegram to AA," Jan. 14, 1937.

14. Ibid., Roll 3018, Fr. E491500 ff., Minister Rüdt,"Telegram to AA," Jan. 29, 1937.

15. Ibid., Fr. E491565-E491566, Beier, Beauftragter der Wirtschaftsgruppe

Luftfahrt Industrie für Nordamerika und Mexico, "Memo about meeting with Azcárate," Apr. 12, 1937. Also, Dr. Gilberto Bosques emphasized Azcárate's expertise in aircrafts as one reason for his selection as Mexican Minister to Germany; Interview with the author, Mexico City, January 1989.

16. Mexicans also considered barter trade with Japan at that time. The administration considered a Japanese barter proposal to exchange Mexican raw materials and scrap metal for Japanese rayon and chemical products. Another Japanese business group, backed by the Japanese government, inquired about the import of Mexican oil. The Mexican government had to decline because it did not have enough oil to export at that time.

17. See Lorenzo Meyer, *Mexico and the United States in the Oil Controversy* (Austin: University of Texas, 1977).

18. NAUS, RG 59, 812.00/30455, Boal to DOS, "Monthly Report, June 1937," June 12, 1937.

19. PRO, FO371, File 20635, A 6307–132–26, Gallop, "Mexico to F.O.", Aug. 28, 1937.

20. Ibid., A 7415/132/26, Department of Overseas Trade, "Cover Letter", Oct. 13, 1937.

21. Ibid., File 20635, A 6307/132/26, Gallop, "Mexico to FO", Aug. 28, 1937.

22. Ibid., A 6644/132/26, Pyke, "Confid. Letter to FO," Aug. 30, 1937.

23. Ibid., File 20636, A 7788/132/26, Pyke, Mexico, "Cable to FO," Oct. 4, 1937.

24. By the end of October 1937, Mexico's financial negotiators finally located some private capital in England. John Harrison of the Harrison Shipping line provided eighty thousand pounds, enough to incorporate the company but not enough to finance the whole deal; ibid., File 20636, A 8114/132/26, Department of Overseas Trade, "Letter to Mr. Allen," Nov. 9, 1937.

25. Rüdt, Strictly Confidential, "Letter to Manuel Santillan," Director General de la Administración General del Petroleo Nacional, Aug. 27, 1937; copy in ibid., A 6644/132/26, Pyke, "Confid. Letter to FO," Aug. 30, 1937.

26. In the summer of 1937, the pro-German head of the Mexican Petroleum Administration, Santillan, had offered the Germans 100,000 barrels of Panuco-region oil in exchange for artificial German barter currency that could buy German machinery or technology for Mexico's infrastructure projects.

27. NAUS, RG 59, 812.00/30468, Boal to DOS, "Monthly Report July," July 13, 1937.

28. Ibid., Blocker to DOS, "Monthly Report for August, 1937," Aug. 18, 1937.

29. Ibid., 812.00/30499, Daniels to DOS, "Monthly Report for August 1937," Sept. 14, 1937.

30. Lorenzo Meyer suggests that it was a move designed to squeeze the

Cárdenas administration politically; see Meyer, *Mexico and the United States*, 160–62.

31. NAUS, RG 59, 812.00/30499, Daniels to DOS, "Monthly Report for August 1937," Sept. 14, 1937.

32. PRO, FO 371, A 7902/132/26, Gallop, "Letter to Troutbeck," Oct. 19, 1937.

33. Ibid.

34. Hereafter cited as Sinarquistas.

35. Anne-Marie de la Vega-Leinert, "El Sinarquismo en México: Possibilidades de un Régimen Fascista en 1940," *Comercio Exterior* 26/9 (México: Septiembre 1976), 1090; Leinert argues that the Sinarquista's ideology aimed at destroying "the government of the great bourgeoisie, push aside the disorder created by the class struggle and finally create a government of order and for the small bourgeoisie," ibid., 1077–78.

36. Initially, Schreiter had come to Mexico from Guatemala trying to avoid charges of fraud. The German legation learned about him for the first time in 1927, when Mexican police arrested him for polygamy. Until 1930, he continued his career as a petty criminal in Mexico City. Then he moved to Coahuila and Celaya. See his file in Germany, Berlin-Dahlem, Geheimes Preussisches Staatsarchiv, Rep. 218/212, "Memorandum about Helmuth O. Schreiter," part of report from July 8, 1935, 43–45.

37. NAUS, T-120, Roll 3006, Fr. 484630–484638, Rüdt, "Report to AA," Feb. 27, 1937.

38. AHSRE, C-6–2–4 (1–5), Diary Rüdt, Aug. 1, 1937, 52.

39. ARMLC, FJM, Vol. 106–107; see the entire collection of security reports in Asuntos Confidenciales, "Levantamiento de Cedillo."

40. United States, Washington, Library of Congress (hereafter cited as LOC), Josephus Daniels Papers (hereafter cited as JDP), Box 657, Folder: Oil Expropriation, Bobby Mac Veagh, "Bobby Mac Veagh's Mexican Memories," Mar. 12, 1946.

41. See, for example, NAUS, RG 59, 812.00/30342, U.S. Consul Mexico City Bowmen, "Confidential Memorandum for the Embassy."

42. Ibid., RG 165, U.S. Military Attaché Freehoff, "Confidential G-2 Report No. 8216," Dec. 27, 1937.

43. PRO, FO 371, File 21488, A3404/10/26, Foreign Office, "Letter to Lindsay, Washington," Apr. 30, 1938.

44. See the extensive surveillance notes by Múgica himself on Cedillo, in ARMLC, Múgica Files, listed in *Boletín Desdeldiez,* Centro de Estudios de la Revolución Mexicana, Lázaro Cárdenas, A.C. (México, Jiquilpan: 1988), 468–91.

45. NAUS, RG 59, 812.00/30487, Pierre de L. Boal, "Strictly Confidential Letter to DOS," Aug. 20, 1937.

46. Ibid., 812.00/30472, Blocker, "Letter to Secretary of State," (hereafter cited as SOS), July 19, 1937.

47. PRO, FO 371, A1205/1205/26, Murray, "Annual Report to Foreign Office," Dec. 31, 1936.

48. NAUS, T-120, Roll 3018, Fr. E491289, Clodius, handwritten notice on correspondence, Aug. 3, 1936. Calles, however, did maintain relations with the German legation, after his return to Mexico in 1941, through the businessman Alexander Holste.

49. Ibid., RG 165, Military Attaché Mexico, "G-2 Report No. 8023," July 15, 1937.

50. Ibid., T-120, Roll 3006, Fr. 484665–484669, Rüdt, "Report to AA," Sept. 4, 1937.

51. Pérez Montfort, "Tres Movimientos de la Clase Media," in von Mentz et al., *Los Empresarios Alemanes,* 262.

52. Ibid., 263.

53. Hereafter cited as Falange and JONS.

54. Pérez Montfort, "Tres Movimientos de la Clase Media," 265.

55. Ibid., 267.

56. Ibid., 266.

57. Ibid., 265.

58. Allan Chase, *Falange: El Ejército Secreto del Eje en América,* traducción Felix Mantiel (La Habana: Edición Caribe, 1943).

59. Hereafter cited as CCM. For an excellent review of the history and literature about the group, consult Pérez Montfort, "Tres Movimientos de la Clase Media," pp. 299 ff.

60. NAUS, RG 165, Military Attaché Marshburn, "G-2 Report No. 7239," June 23, 1936.

61. Hereafter cited as PNSM.

62. NAUS, RG 165, U.S. Military Attaché Mexico, "G-2 Report No. 9898," June 13, 1941.

63. Ibid., T-120, Roll 3006, Fr. E484630-E484638, Rüdt, "Report to AA," Jan. 29, 1937.

64. Alicia Gojman de Backal, "El Fascismo en México," in *Jahrbuch für Geschichte von Staat, Wirtschaft und Gesellschaft Lateinamerikas* (hereafter cited as *JbLA*) 25 (1988), 297. Unfortunately, she fails to back this allegation with a source citation.

65. Perhaps more interesting is the fact that Rodríguez persistently offered Cedillo his services. When Cedillo began his term as Mexico's agrarian minister, Rodriguez offered him an honor guard of Doradas. He also asked him for financial support to buy arms and uniforms. Ricardo Pérez Montfort showed how, during 1936, the relationship between Cedillo and Rodríguez became more distant, mainly because of possible negative implications for Cedillo's position within the Mexican cabinet. In 1937, when Cedillo resigned from the cabinet, Rodríguez published a manifest that indicated that everything would be ready for a revolt of the right. See Ricardo Pérez Montfort, "Los Camisas Doradas" in *Sequencia* 4 (México: Enero/Abril

1986), 64–78.

66. Ibid.

67. NAUS, T-120, Roll 218, Fr. 168766–168775, Rüdt, "Report to AA," Apr. 14, 1938.

68. Ibid., Roll 1903, Fr. 054306, Bohle, "Telegram to Legations in Latin America," May 18, 1938.

69. Ibid.

70. AHSRE, C-6-2–4 (1–5), Diary Rüdt, Apr. 28, 1937, 44.

71. Ibid., Aug. 7, 1937, 62.

72. NAUS, RG 165, Military Attaché Report, "G-2 Report No. 7933," Apr. 29, 1937.

73. FDR, Morgenthau Papers (hereafter cited as MP), Book 104, Roll 27, Suárez, Confidential Memo Mexican Budgetary Situation, Dec. 1937, 175–81.

74. Meyer, *Mexico and the United States*, 160–62.

75. FDR, MP, Film No. 26, Book 101, Lockett, "Letter to Ambassador Daniels," Nov. 15, 1937, 55–57.

76. Ibid., Morgenthau to Daniels, "Letter Copy," stamped Dec. 7, 1937, 52.

77. PRO, FO 371, A 9433/132/26, Campbell, Chancery Washington to FO American Department, "Financial Situation in Mexico," Dec. 17, 1937.

78. FDR, MP; the development can be followed in detail in book 101–3.

79. Ibid., Roll 27, Book 102, Meeting Protocol, Present: Nájera, Suárez, Feis, Taylor, Lochhead, White, Oliphant and Opper, Dec. 14, 1937, 46–50.

80. Ibid., Roll 27, Book 104, "Meeting Protocoll," Dec. 28, 1937.

81. Ibid., Book 104, Roll Nr. 27, "Memorandum of Meeting," Dec. 28, 1937. Morgenthau: "I think that if the Mexican government could present, not only to our own people, but to the world, a strong budget picture, that you are going to get your revenue and you gradually—are going to come closer, when you have a balanced budget, I think that you would be surprised how quickly the financial people would begin to have confidence and would leave their money in Mexico."

82. Ibid., Book 101, Roll 26, Mr. White to Mrs. Klotz, "Inter Office Communication: Subject: Secretary's Proposal for the Record," Dec. 11, 1937, 266.

83. Ibid., Book 102, Roll 27, "Note," Dec. 15, 1937, 96.

84. Ibid., Diaries Book 104, Roll 27, Dec. 22, 1937, 32.

85. Ibid., Book 104, Roll 27, Castillo Nájera, "Letter to Sumner Welles," Dec. 25, 1937.

86. Ibid., Book 104, Roll 27, Group Meeting, Dec. 23, 1937.

87. Ibid., Book 104, Roll 27, Diary, Dec. 29, 1937, 2.

88. Ibid., Roll 27, Book 104, "Memorandum of Conversation," present: Morgenthau, Nájera, Suárez, Welles, Dec. 31, 1937, 297–304.

89. On the silver purchased the Bank of Mexico and the Mexican govern-

ment made an average profit of 0.009 cents per ounce; see NAUS, RG 59, 812.00/30528, Josephus Daniels, "Transmission of Resume of Conditions in Mexico during December, 1937," Jan. 12, 1937.

90. FDR, MP, Roll 27, Book 104, "Meeting Protocol," Dec. 31, 1937, 306–17.

91. Ibid., Roll 27, Book 104, "Record of Group Meeting," Dec. 31, 1937.

92. *New York Times*, Jan. 8, 1937.

93. FDR, MP, Roll 26, Book 101, Bank of Mexico, "Memo to U.S. Treasury," 91–93.

Chapter 5

1. FDR, Henry Morgenthau Jr. Papers (hereafter cited as HMjr.), Roll 31, Book 118, Mr. White, "Inter Office Communication to Secretary Morgenthau," Apr. 1, 1938, 27–31.

2. Initially, in Washington, D.C., Morgenthau and Roosevelt were willing to help Suárez and the Cárdenas administration. When, by the end of March 1938, it appeared that the Bank of Mexico's silver holdings were depleted, it was the U.S. president and the U.S. Secretary of Treasury who, once again, tried to keep the Mexican government and the Bank of Mexico afloat. In early May, Morgenthau proposed to Roosevelt that Mexico be loaned 200 million ounces of silver at a reasonable rate of interest. In order to make it palatable to Cordell Hull, Morgenthau suggested that the Mexicans be asked to sign a trade treaty and "straighten out the oil situation," without becoming more specific. With classic Morgenthau pragmatism, he told Roosevelt:

> After all in the room we can admit it isn't worth much sitting in our vaults and Key Pittman would be for it because it would mean that we got rid of that much silver and would have to buy that much more additional . . .

If the Mexicans agreed, Cárdenas would be invited up to Washington to sign the agreement. Roosevelt personally supported the plan.

Only the U.S. State Department rejected the initiative. In an internal State Department memo, Mexicans were disqualified as "completely irresponsible and could not be depended upon to carry through any such agreement." Furthermore, it was expected that soon the Mexican oil industry would collapse since the "Mexican people are completely incapable of operating any large scale industry let alone so complicated a matter as oil production." Soon the State Department expected Mexican oil production to cease through technical incompetency, graft, dishonesty, and irresponsibility.

3. NAUS, RG 151, Box 2800, File 265, Commercial Attaché Edward D. McLaughlin, "Sp.R.No.256: Financial Report for Last Two Weeks of March

1938," Apr. 1, 1938.

4. Ibid., Lockett, "Financial Report for two weeks ending December 1938," Dec. 19, 1938.

5. Ibid., Box 2800, File 265, Commercial Attache Thomas H. Lockett, "Sp.R.No.271: Financial Report," Apr. 25, 1938.

6. Ibid., Lockett, "Financial Report for two weeks ending July 23, 1938," July 27, 1938.

7. By then, the sale of oil from the Davis group added every month 600 thousand dollars in U.S. currency to Mexico's national income; see ibid., Lockett, "Financial Report for two weeks ending October 1938," Oct. 1, 1938.

8. Excellent studies that explore this event are Jonathan C. Brown, *Oil and Revolution in Mexico* (Berkeley: University of California Press, 1993), and Jonathan C. Brown and Alan Knight, *The Mexican Petroleum Industry in the Twentieth Century* (Austin: University of Texas Press, 1992).

9. Later, in 1936, when Japan joined the anticommunist pact with Germany, Cárdenas was warned that a coming world conflict could reproduce itself inside Mexico. SRE, Exp. III–164–6, Report Águilar to SRE, "Tratado Alemania-Japón contra el Comunismo", Dec. 12, 1936.

10. Cárdenas reacted by suggesting to Roosevelt the organization of a peace conference in which the nations of the Western Hemisphere would attempt to solve the problems of maintaining peace in the world system. But Roosevelt did not follow Cárdenas's advice. AGN, Fo.LC., Microfilm, Cárdenas, "Letter to Roosevelt," Feb. 19, 1936.

11. AHSRE, Exp. 34–8–11, Mexican Consul Berlin, "Report to SRE," November 1937.

12. Ibid., Almazán, "Informe Político Reglementario: Septiembre," September 1936.

13. AGN, Fo.LC. Microfilm No. 13, Ramón P. de Negri, "Letter to Cárdenas," Aug. 10, 1937.

14. Ibid., Microfilm No. 13, Cárdenas, "Letter to Fabela," Sept. 29, 1937.

15. Lázaro Cárdenas, "10 de Marzo," *Apuntes* (México: Universidad Nacional Autónoma de México, 1972), 389.

16. AGN, Fo.LC., Exp. 527/25, Nájera, "Report to Cárdenas," Aug. 29, 1937.

17. AHSRE, Exp. 30–3–10(I), Castillo Nájera, "Informe to SRE," Mar. 11, 1938.

18. Sir Owen O'Malley, K.C.M.G., *The Phantom Caravan* (London: John Murray, Albermarle Street, 1954), 170 ff.

19. PRO, FO 371, A 1975/1975/26, O'Malley, "Report to Eden", Paragraph 51, Jan. 19, 1938.

20. Ibid., A1975/1975/26, O'Malley, "Report to Eden," Jan. 19, 1938.

21. PRO, FO 371, File 21463O, A1899/10/26, O'Malley, "Telegram to London," Mar. 10, 1938.

22. Stephen J. Randall, *United States Foreign Oil Policy, 1919–1948: For Profits and Security* (Kingston and Montreal: McGill-Queen's University Press, 1985), 91.

23. Ibid.

24. *Wall Street Journal*, Sept. 20, 1937, 3.

25. FDR, HMjr., Roll 31, Book 118, Fr. 27–31, Mr. White, "Treasury Department Inter Office Communication," Apr. 1, 1938.

26. Ibid., Roll 34, Book 128, Treasury Department, Mr. White to Secretary Morgenthau, Inter-Office Memorandum, June 14, 1938, 408–14.

27. Suárez, *Comentarios y Recuerdos*, 213.

28. Meyer, *Mexico and the United States*, 201.

29. Ibid.

30. NAUS, T-120, Roll 2726, Fr. E417110-E417113, Rüdt, "Report to AA," Apr. 6, 1938.

31. Ibid., Fr. E417090, Rüdt, "Telegram to AA," Apr. 8, 1938, also see ibid., Fr. E417116-E417117, Rüdt, "Report to AA," Apr. 26, 1938.

32. Ibid., Fr. E417004, Müller/New York, "Telegram to AA," Apr. 7, 1938.

33. Ibid., Roll 2727, Fr. E417218-E417221, Rüdt, "Report to AA," Apr. 30, 1938. His main motive was to eliminate costly markups through middlemen.

34. Ibid., Fr.E417287, Dresdner Bank, "Letter to Davidsen," May 19, 1938; also, see ibid., Fr. E417160, Rüdt, "Telegram to AA," May 4, 1938.

35. Ibid., Roll 2726, Fr. 417107–417109, Rüdt, "Report to AA," Apr. 5, 1938.

36. Germany, Staatsarchiv Nürnberg, KV Anklage, PS-984, "OKM Report: Oil Supply of German Navy [probably written by Fetzer]," Apr. 29, 1940, 5.

37. Ibid.

38. NAUS, T-120, Roll 2727, Fr. E417364-E417366, Davidsen, "Discussion Protocol," May 28, 1938.

39. Until 1938, Japanese imports of Mexican oil averaged only five hundred tons yearly and then jumped to fifteen thousand tons, still a negligible amount; see PRO, FO 371, 24214, A/1749/57/26, Petroleum Department, "Letter to Balfour," Mar. 5, 1940.

40. NAUS, T-120, Roll 2727, Fr. 417247, Rüdt, "Report to AA," May 6, 1938.

41. Meyer, *Mexico and the United States*, 194.

42. Suárez, *Comentarios y Recuerdos*, 213.

43. Ibid., 211.

44. Ibid., 214-216.

45. NAUS, T-120, Roll 2727, Fr. E417437, Koppelmann/RWM, "Letter to Wiehl," June 28, 1938.

46. Ibid., Fr. E417352-E417358, Davidsen, "Protocol Discussion Mexican

Oil," June 7, 1938.

47. Ibid., Fr. E417465-E417467, Koppelmann/RWM, "Letter to AA," July 13, 1938.

48. Ibid., Fr. E417363-E417366, Davidsen, "Discussion Protocol," May 28, 1938.

49. AHSRE, Exp. L-E-588, A. Guerra, "Informe Especial por Mayo de 1938: El Petróleo en el Mercado Alemán," May 1938.

50. Germany, Staatsarchiv Nürnberg, PS-984, "OKM Report: Oil Supply of German Navy [probably written by Fetzer]," Apr. 29, 1940.

51. NAUS, T-120, Roll 2727, Fr. E417720, Davidsen, "Confidential Letter to Wiehl," Dec. 14, 1938.

52. Ibid., Roll 2728, Fr. E418113-E418116, Rüdt, "Statistic of German Petroleum Imports from Mexico 1937–1938," May 17, 1939.

53. Ibid., 812.6363/5878, Josephus Daniels, "Proposed Construction by Federal Government of Two Rayon Yarn Factories," June 19, 1939.

54. Ibid., 812.6363/5389, Josephus Daniels, "Progress of Barter Operations of Mexican Oil," Jan. 24, 1939.

55. Ibid., 812.6363/5845, Josephus Daniels, "Conversation with Minister Suárez," June 19, 1939. Also see PRO, FO 371, File 24214, A/1894/57/26, Godber, "Letter to Balfour," Mar. 11, 1940.

56. PRO, F0 371, File 24214, A/1749/57/26, John Balfour, "F.O. Minute," Feb. 28, 1940.

57. Ibid., 812.6363/6009, Bullitt/Paris, "Confidential Telegram to Secretary of State," Aug. 9, 1939. PRO, FO 371, File 24214, A/1894/57/26, Godber, Letter to Balfour," Mar. 11, 1940.

58. Ibid.

59. NAUS, T-120, Reel 2677, Fr. E402605, Mackensen/Rome, "Telegram to AA," Sept. 28, 1939.

60. After the expropriation, the Japanese Navy had joined private Japanese oil interests in Mexico through the Taiheiyi Sekiyu Kabushiki Kaisha, or Pacific Petroleum Company; see NAUS, RG 59, 812.6363/6256, Josephus Daniels, "Letter to Hull," Oct. 25, 1939. Pacific invested in the privately Japanese-owned Laguna oil exploration company in Mexico. The company's prospectus stated as its goals the "investment in overseas petroleum business, the purchase and sale of foreign crude and refined oils, the exploitation of overseas fields and investment therein and the prospecting and operation of overseas oil fields"; see NAUS, RG 59, 812.6363/5660, Standard Manager Tokyo, "Letter to Standard New York," March 9, 1939. The situation was complicated further when a private Japanese company, the Nippon Soda Company of Tokyo, appeared on the Mexican market with the hope of dislodging the Veracruzana from its preferred positions in Mexico and gaining access to oil for its newly built refinery in Japan. On June 1, 1939, the group signed with the Mexican government a barter of seven thousand tons of Manchurian soy beans for sixty-five hundred tons of gasoline. This was

organized by Yokio Nagamatsu, a former business partner of Tsuru; see NAUS, RG 165, Gordon H. McCoy, Mil. Attaché, "G-2 Report No. 9216," Oct. 27, 1939.

61. PRO, FO 371, File 24215, A/2353/57/26, Consul-General Rees, "Report to Balfour," Mar. 12, 1940.

62. NAUS, RG 59, 812.6363/6330, Josephus Daniels, "Letter to Hull," Nov. 27, 1939.

63. PRO, FO 371, File 24215, A/2353/57/26, Consul General Rees, "Memorandum to Foreign Office," Mar. 12, 1940.

64. NAUS, RG 165, 812.6363/5845, Josephus Daniels, "Letter to Hull," June 19, 1939. One year later, the project had not yet moved out of the planning stage; see PRO, FO 371, FO 24215, A/2353/57/26, Consul-General Rees, "Report to Balfour," Mar. 12, 1940.

65. AGN, Fo.LC., Microfilm, Roosevelt, "Letter to Cárdenas," Aug. 31, 1939.

66. This remark was also aimed at the flow of oil to Germany through dealings with Davis; see SRE, Exp. 39–10–2(II), Nájera, "Letter to Cárdenas," Oct. 19, 1939.

67. Cárdenas used the Soviet aggression against Finland to suggest to Roosevelt once more that the United States, together with Latin American countries, should stop the wildfire of European violence and mediate an armistice under the supervision of Pan-American presidents. But Roosevelt made no efforts to follow this Pan-American peace initiative; see AGN, Fo.LC., Exp. 550/46, Cárdenas, "Letter to Roosevelt," Jan. 6, 1940.

68. PRO, FO 371, File 24215, A/3195/57/26, General Consul Rees, "Report to Foreign Office," Apr. 4, 1940.

69. SRE, Exp. 39–10–2(II), Suárez, "Letter to Cárdenas," Mar. 26, 1940; Luis I. Rodríguez, "Telegram No. 60 to Cárdenas," Apr. 8, 1940; AGN, Fo.LC., Exp. 550/39660, Luis I. Rodríguez/Paris, "Telegram to Cárdenas," Apr. 8, 1940.

70. Ibid., Luis I. Rodríguez/Paris, "Telegram No. 103 to SRE," May 24, 1940. On May 25, 1940, Rodríguez cabled that the French had opened the economic blockade of the Atlantic and would allow the shipment of forty thousand tons of goods from Genoa to Mexico at the end of May; see AGN, Fo.LC., Exp. 550/46–11, Luis I. Rodríguez, "Letter to Cárdenas," May 25, 1940.

71. NAUS, RG 151, Box 359, Folder 266, Thomas H. Lockett, "Conversation with Minister Suárez," Feb. 3, 1939.

72. In contrast, German ministries were enthusiastic about the increased flow of oil into its storage tanks, which created opportunities for new German–Mexican economic exchange. Soon plans emerged that imagined the oil barters as part of a long-term German–Mexican bilateral trade agreement. Immediately, Minister of Hacienda Suárez refused to enter into any deeper involvement with the German Third Reich. Mexican business with Germany

would not expand beyond the short-term deals with Davis; see NAUS, T-120, Roll 2728, Fr. E418157-E418178, Wolfgang Budczies, "Report about Trip to Mexico," May 22, 1939.

73. NAUS, T-120, Roll 2677, Fr. E402599-E402600, Davis, "Telegram to Fetzer OKM," Sept. 4, 1939. Mexican credit in Germany was 4,685 million reichsmarks, of which 3,694 million reichsmarks had been spent on orders, leaving about 990,413 reichsmarks for future purchases. See ibid., Roll 2729, Fr. E418408, Dr. Schomaker, "Letter to AA," Nov. 29, 1939.

74. Ibid., Roll 2677, Fr. E402623, Davidsen, "Discussion Protocol," Oct. 11, 1939.

75. Ibid., Fr. E402608, Fetzer, "Telegram to Rüdt," Sept. 22, 1939.

76. Ibid., Roll 2729, Fr. E418343, Rüdt, "Telegram to AA," Sept. 25, 1939.

77. Ibid., Roll 2677, Fr. E402601, Rüdt, "Telegram to AA," Sept. 18, 1939. Undersecretary of Foreign Relations Von Weizaecker backed this argument; see ibid., Roll 2766, Fr. E402621-E402622, Davidsen, "Letter to Undersecretary Landfried/RWM," Oct. 27, 1939.

78. Ibid., Roll 2729, Fr. E418380, Rüdt, "Telegram to AA, " Nov. 8, 1939.

79. Ibid., Fr. 418365–418367, RWM, "Letter to Deutsche Revisions und Treuhandgesellschaft," Oct. 17, 1939.

80. Ibid., Roll 2677, Fr. E402604, Rüdt, "Telegram to AA," Sept. 23, 1939.

81. Ibid., Fr. E402626, Rüdt, "Telegram to AA," Oct. 27, 1939.

82. Ibid., Roll 2729, Fr. E418414, Rüdt, "Telegram to AA," Dec. 11, 1939. Also, he had to place orders in Italy.

83. NAUS, RG 59, 812.6363/6173, Pierre de Boal, "Conversation with Minister Suárez," Sept. 26, 1939.

84. PRO, FO 371, File 24215, A/3166/57/26, Consul General Rees, "Telegram to Foreign Office," May 4, 1940.

85. NAUS, RG 165, Gordon H. McCoy, Mil. Attaché, "G-2 Report No. 9216," Oct. 27, 1939. Other opinions were that his visit was a competitive move by Veracruzana's Japanese competitor.

86. Ibid.

87. AHSRE, Exp. III–1329–3, Villa Michel/Tokyo, "Memorandum to SRE," Feb. 10, 1940.

88. Ibid., Villa Michel/Tokyo, "Telegram No. 2 to SRE," Jan. 12, 1940.

89. Ibid., Villa Michel/Tokyo, "Memorandum to SRE," Feb. 10, 1940.

90. Ibid., Exp. 28–1–110, "Viaje de la Comisión Técnico Económica para el Fomento del Intercambio Comercial entre México y el Japón," 1940.

91. Ibid., Ernesto Hidalgo, "Memorandum."

92. Ibid., Pedro Arena, "Memorandum," June 11, 1940.

93. *The Times*, London, Oct. 25, 1940. A shipment of five thousand barrels of petroleum and mercury in the value of one million pesos was

canceled. It was expected that outstanding Japanese orders for twenty-five tons of molybdenum concentrates and five hundred tons of fluorspar would soon be canceled, too.

Chapter 6

1. See Alan Knight, "The Politics of Expropriation," in Jonathan C. Brown and Alan Knight, *Mexican Petroleum Industry*, 90–129.

2. NAUS, RG 59, 812.00/30559, Daniels, "Transmission of Resume of Conditions in Mexico during March 1938," Apr. 15, 1938, 2.

3. LOC, JDP, Box 647, Embassy File 1936–1941, "Notes on Interview with President Cárdenas March 4th and March 7th, 1938." The author of this memo is most likely Standard Oil manager Armstrong.

4. Meyer, *Mexico and the United States*, 167.

5. ARMLC, FJM, Vol. 182, Doc. 2, Lázaro Cárdenas, "Letter to Múgica," Mar. 10, 1938.

6. Its board was staffed with familiar names: Minister of Hacienda Eduardo Suárez, Secretary of Economy Buenrostro, and Ingenieur Enrique Ortiz. The council's general manager became a former undersecretary of Múgica's ministry, Vincente Herrera.

7. O'Malley, *Phantom Caravan*, 170.

8. LOC, JDP, Box 657, File Oil Expropriation, "Bobbie MacVeagh's Mexican Memoirs," March 1938.

9. Ibid., Box 657, Embassy File: Oil Expropriation 1938–1940, John H. Mac Veagh, "Letter to Daniels," Mar. 12, 1946.

10. FDR, HMjr., Roll 31, Book 116, Frame 382–383, 389–390, Morgenthau, "2 Transcripts of telephone talks with Pittman," Mar. 24, 1938.

11. Ibid., Roll 31, Book 117, Morgenthau, "Telegram to Roosevelt," Mar. 25, 1938.

12. Ibid., HMjr., Book 117, Roll 31, Morgenthau, "Transcript Telephone Conversation with Wayne Taylor," Mar. 28, 1938.

13. Ibid.

14. FDR, HMjr., Morgenthau, "Telephone Conversation Transcripts with Wayne Taylor," Mar. 28, 1938, 334–62.

15. Ironically, Roosevelt put Morgenthau in charge of finding a way out of the quagmire.

16. Meyer, *Mexico and the United States*, 179.

17. PRO, FO 371, File 21464, A2205/10/26, Balfour, "Interdepartmental Memo," Mar. 24, 1938.

18. As an example, see ibid., A2472/10/26, Treasury, Board of Trade, Petroleum Department, Foreign Office, "Memo of Interdepartmental Meeting," Mar. 30, 1938.

19. *The Times*, London, Apr. 22, 1938.

20. PRO, FO 371, File 21468, A3295/10/26, O'Malley, "Telegram to London," Apr. 28, 1938; the draft of the telegram is found in ibid., File 21488, A3296/10/26, O'Malley, "Telegram to London," Apr. 26, 1938.

21. Ibid., File 21409, A4064/10/26, O'Malley, "Report to Balfour," May 10, 1938.

22. Ibid., File 21468, A3314/10/26, Balfour, "Letter to O'Malley," May 7, 1938.

23. Ibid., File 21469, A3663/10/26, Imperial Defense Committee, "Meeting Notes," May 9, 1938.

24. NAUS, RG 59, Box 4110, 712.14/121, U.S. Embassy, "Telegram No. 6650 to Secretary of State," May 12, 1938.

25. PRO, FO 371, File 21409, A3704/10/26, O'Malley, "Letter to London," May 11, 1938.

26. Lázaro Cárdenas, *Apuntes* (México: Universidad Nacional Autónoma de México, 1972), 394.

27. Still the Mexicans were careful to make sure that the British were not interested in any negotiated settlement. For that purpose, Mexican Minister of Hacienda Suárez was sent to O'Malley on the same day to see if any hint of a compromise with the British could be detected. Suárez returned from the talk without any new hope for a more cooperative British attitude in the near future. PRO, FO 371, File 21469, A3731/10/26, O'Malley, "Telegram to London," May 12, 1938.

28. At the end, the Danish minister in Mexico took over the representation of British interests.

29. AGN, Fo.LC., Exp. 432.2/253–9, Villa Michel, "Telegram to SRE," May 14, 1938.

30. PRO, FO 371, File 21472, A4932/10/26, O'Malley on Board of HMS Acquitania, "Report to London, June 24, 1938.

31. Powell, *Mexico and the Spanish Civil War*, 73.

32. AGN, Fo.LC., Microfilm, Cárdenas, "Letter to Roosevelt," Sept. 28, 1938.

33. Ibid., Roosevelt, "Letter to Cárdenas," Oct. 10, 1938.

34. In March 1939, when Hitler conquered the remaining parts of Czechoslovakia, Cárdenas protested again in the League of Nations and privately sent a letter to Roosevelt assuring him that the Mexican people backed him and his policy against the Axis countries every step of the way; see AGN, Fo.LC., Microfilm, Cárdenas, "Letter to Roosevelt," Apr. 16, 1939.

35. AHSRE, Exp. 39–10–3(I), Villaseñor, "Letter to Cárdenas," May 30, 1939.

36. AGN, Fo.LC., Exp. 432.2/253–9, Beteta, "Letter to Cárdenas," June 17, 1939. Also see SRE, Exp. 39–10–2(II), Nájera, "Letter to Cárdenas," June 15, 1939.

37. Ibid., Exp. 39–10–2(I), Nájera, "Memorandum for Cárdenas," June 3,

1939.

38. Ibid., Nájera, "Letter to Cárdenas," June 17, 1939.

39. Ibid., Nájera, "Memo to Cárdenas," June 15, 1939.

40. Ibid., Exp. 39–10–2(II), Cárdenas, "Letter to Nájera," Nov. 17, 1939.

41. Ibid.

42. Ibid., Nájera, "Letter to Cárdenas," Apr. 11, 1939. In April, Luis Quintanilla, from the Mexican embassy in Washington, had learned from Richberg during a luncheon that the companies' strategy was to filibuster. One week later, he told Ambassador Nájera that certain members of the oil companies were against any accord with the Mexicans; see ibid., Nájera, "Letter to Cárdenas," Apr. 27, 1939.

43. Ibid., Nájera, "Letter to Cárdenas," July 31, 1939.

44. Ibid., Nájera, "Letter to Cárdenas," Aug. 8, 1939.

45. Ibid., Nájera, "Letter to Cárdenas," July 31, 1939.

46. Ibid., Nájera, "Letter to Cárdenas," Aug. 1, 1939.

47. Ibid., Nájera, "Letter to Cárdenas," Aug. 23, 1939.

48. Ibid., Cárdenas, "Letter to Nájera," Aug. 23, 1939.

49. AGN, Fo.LC., Microfilm, Roosevelt, "Letter to Cárdenas," Aug. 31, 1939.

50. This remark was also aimed at the flow of oil to Germany through dealings with Davis. AHSRE, Exp. 39–10–2(II), Nájera, "Letter to Cárdenas," Oct. 19, 1939.

51. Ibid., Exp. 39–10–2, Castillo Nájera, "Letter to Cárdenas," Feb. 12, 1940.

52. AGN, Fo.LC., Exp. 550/39660, Eduardo Suárez, "Memorandum to Cárdenas," Mar. 8, 1940.

53. AHSRE, Exp. 39–10–2(III), Nájera, "Memo to Cárdenas," Apr. 23, 1940.

54. González, *Los Dias del Presidente Cárdenas*, 195f.

55. Ramona Falcón, *Revolución y Caciquismo. San Luis Potosi, 1910-1938* (México: El Colegio de México, 1984) and Dudley Ankerson, *Agrarian Warlord: Saturnino Cedillo and the Mexican Revolution in San Luis Potosi* (De Kalb: Northern Illinois University Press, 1985).

56. NAUS, T-120, Roll 3006, Fr. E484726-E484738, Northe, "Report to AA," May 31, 1938.

57. Ibid., Roll 1304, Fr. 487669, Freytag, "Secret Letter to AA," July 8, 1938. Also see OM-31-10, Confidencial, Cónsul de México en Guatemala, "Información sobre el Col. Ernesto von Merk", Mar. 26, 1937. The writer admits that it is absurd to claim that Merk introduced weapons to Mexico via Guatemala.

58. NAUS, T-120, Roll 1304, Fr. 487668, Northe, "Telegram to AA," May 30, 1938.

59. Ibid.

60. AGN, Fo.LC., Exp. 559–153/3, Ernesto von Merck, "Letter to Carlos

Domínguez," June 7, 1938.

61. NAUS, RG 165, Military Attaché Freehoff, "G-2 Report No. 3410-a," May 18, 1938.

62. PRO, A7284/491/26, British Chancery, Washington "Letter to American Department," Sept. 13, 1938.

63. NAUS, RG 59, 812.00/30645, Berle, "Memorandum of Conversation," Oct. 21, 1938.

64. United States, Stanford University, Hoover Institute, Gus Jones, "The Nazi Failure in Mexico," Unpublished Manuscript, 113.

65. Ibid., 281–83.

66. Pérez Montfort, "Hispanismo y Falange," 279.

67. NAUS, RG 165, U.S. Military Intelligence, "G-2 Report No. 9178," Sept. 22, 1939.

68. Ibid., 279.

69. Ibid., 280, n. 146. Pérez Montfort explains the administration's continued tolerance of Ibañez by pointing to his good contacts with Foreign Minister Hay, the fact that the Falange still operated within the law, and the more important threat that the Sinarquistas constituted at that time.

70. See the announcements in *NS Herold*, Mexico City, March 1936, 53.

71. *Mitteilungen der Deutschen Volksgemeinschaft in Mexico*, Mexico City (Mai 1938), 2–5, "Mexiko und Deutschland," Dec. 16, 1937.

72. Follow the development of these efforts in AHSRE, C-6-2-4 (1–5), Rüdt Diary 1939. Three obstacles remained before its successful creation. First, an older established group for the same purpose already existed within the German community: the Deutsch-Mexikanische Vereinigung. It was outside NSDAP control and it was enjoying respect in the Mexican scientific community. Mexican scholars were not eager to join the party-controlled group. Second, it was hard to find a respected Mexican or German individual who was willing to function as leader of the new organization under the control of party and legation. Third, German business had to be coerced into financing the new organization.

73. For example, see the magazine *Ejército Marina Aviación*, published by Faupel, in the holdings of the Ibero Amerika Institut, West Berlin.

74. For the importance of I. G. Farben for the Mexican chemical sector, see Schuler, "From Multinationalization to Expropriation: The German I. G. Farben Concern and the Creation of a Mexican Chemical Industry," *JbLA* 25 (Köln 1988), 303–20.

75. When the Mexican deputy minister of welfare planned to go to Germany, his trip was immediately announced to the I. G. Farben company.

76. After a long absence of Mexican journalists from Germany, the chief editor of *La Prensa* began to prepare for a trip to Germany. He received every possible support from Chamber of Commerce President Eversbusch.

77. AGN, Fo.LC., Exp. 704.1/124–1, Villaseñor, "Memo to Cardenas," Oct. 13, 1939.

78. Rüdt was mistaken when he wrote to Berlin that "after these six events the Liga has no more ammunition left. I don't believe it will be very important or influential in the future; particularly among influential Mexican intelligentia we still have many friends." NAUS, T-120, Roll 3006, Fr. E484727-E484730, Northe, "Report to AA," May 10, 1938.

79. Ibid., Roll 3006, Fr. E484781-E484783, Northe, "Note to Hay," Sept. 14, 1938.

80. Ibid., Fr. 484786–484787, Copy of poster.

81. AHSRE, C-6-2-4(1-5), Diary Rüdt, Dec. 14, 1938, 111.

82. On Nov. 16, 1938, the Jewish organization "Gesbir" organized a meeting to protest Germany atrocities against Jews. NAUS, T-120, Roll 3006, Fr. E484793-E484795, Rüdt, "Report to AA," Nov. 20, 1938.

83. Ibid.

84. Ibid., RG 165, Military Attaché McCoy, "G-2 Report No. 9158," Oct. 23, 1939.

85. Pérez Montfort, "Hispanismo y Falange," 279, and NAUS, RG 59, 812.00b/435, Gibson, "Memorandum to Secretary of State," Sept. 7, 1939.

86. AGN, Fo.LC., Exp. 704.1/124–1, Villaseñor, "Memo to Cárdenas," Oct. 13, 1939.

87. AHSRE, C-6-4-2, Diary Rüdt, Aug. 27, 1939, 34. He wrote: "I had to finish my spa early and return to Mexico without delay because of our oil negotiations and because of other reasons."

88. NAUS, RG 84, Box 1, File 1936–1940, Consul Monterrey, "Strictly Confidential Report to Secretary of State," n.d.

89. Herman, *Comintern in Mexico*, 137–40. Mexico's Communist party leader, Laborde, defended the Soviet occupation of Polish territory as an act "that saved the Polish people from the Nazis, but that also reclaimed lost Soviet territory."

90. For example, see NAUS, RG 59, 812.00/30809, Vice Consul K. Peyton, "Convention of the CTM in Chihuahua," Aug. 17, 1939.

91. Ibid., 812.00B/435, Daniels, "Discussion Protocol by Gibson about talk with Lic. Cuesta Soto/Gobernación," Sept. 7, 1939.

92. Ibid., 812.00/30840, Pierre Boal, "Report to Secretary of State," Oct. 2, 1939.

93. A copy of his allegations can be found in ibid., 812.00/30862, Oct. 13, 1939. Recently, William Chase and Dana Reed have gained access to Diego Rivera's FBI file and explored Rivera's activities more closely. A summary of their work was published in the Spanish magazine *Al Piñon*. An English version, "The Strange Case of Diego Rivera and the U.S. State Department," can be obtained by contacting them at the University of Pittsburgh.

94. NAUS, RG 59, 812.00B/446, U.S. Consul Blocker, "Report to Secretary of State," Dec. 14, 1939. This was later defeated and the publications of the Communist party of Mexico tried to walk a tightrope by emphasizing their adherence to Cárdenas's domestic politics.

95. Ibid., 862.20212/1867, "Report," Apr. 16, 1940; it appeared in *Ultimas Noticias* on the same day.

96. Herman attributes this purge to Laborde's refusal to lose all the gains that the Communist party had achieved under the Cárdenas administration, due to the upcoming execution of Trotsky. Herman also argues that the replacement of Vincente Lombardo Toledano by Fidel Velázquez was indirectly a result of the repercussions of the Hitler-Stalin pact. Herman, *Comintern in Mexico*, 143. Compare this with more recent discoveries by Barry Carr, in his *Marxism and Communism in Twentieth-Century Mexico*.

97. Herman, *Comintern in Mexico*, 143.

98. NAUS, RG 165, U.S. Military Attaché Mexico, "G-2 Report No. 9908," June 26, 1941. Also, see report from July 1, 1941.

99. Ibid., U.S. Military Attaché McCoy,"G-2 Secrete Report No. 9775," Apr. 1, 1941.

100. Ibid., T-120, Roll 143, Fr. 84763, Woermann, "Telegram to Stohrer, Madrid," Oct. 8, 1940.

101. Ibid., File 24218, A2679/2679/26, Marrett, "Letter No. 34 to Grubb," Mar. 12, 1940.

102. Ibid., File 26075, A 1123/1123/26, Rees, "Report on the Organization of Allied Publicity in Mexico," Jan. 17, 1941.

103. Ibid.

104. Ibid.

105. Ibid., File 24218, A2679/2679/26, Rees, "Letter to FO," Apr. 26, 1940.

106. Jones, "Nazi Failure in Mexico," 14.

107. NAUS, T-120, Roll 143, Fr. 84724, Rüdt, "Letter to Under Secretary of State Woermann," May 7, 1940.

108. They made inroads into *La Opinión* of Puebla, *El Regionál de Culiacán* of Culiacán, *Ecos de la Costa* of Colima, *El Heraldo Michoacana* of Morelia, and *El Diário del Sureste* of Mérida. See PRO, File 24218, A2679/2679/26, Marrett, "Letter No. 34 to Grubb," Apr. 30, 1940.

109. Ibid.

110. José Luis Ortiz Garza, *México en Guerra* (México: Planeta, 1989), 36–38.

Chapter 7

1. Edwin Lieuwen, *Mexican Militarism: The Political Rise and Fall of the Revolutionary Army* (Albuquerque: University of New Mexico Press, 1968); Roderic Ai Camp, *Generals in the Palacio: The Military in Modern Mexico* (New York: Oxford University Press, 1992); Alicia Hernández Chávez, *La Mecánica Cardenista* (México, D.F.: El Colegio de México, 1979); Jorge

Alberto Lozoya, *El Ejército Mexicano (1911–1965)* (México: El Colegio de México, 1970). James W. Wilkie, *The Mexican Revolution: Federal Expenditure and Social Change since 1910* (Berkeley: University of California Press, 1970), 106; David Ronfeldt, ed., *The Modern Mexican Military: A Reassessment* (San Diego: Center for U.S.–Mexican Studies, University of California, 1984, Monograph Series, No. 15), focuses primarily on theoretical issues concerning the role of the Mexican army in domestic politics.

2. Lieuwen, *Mexican Militarism*, 87–90.

3. Ibid., 93.

4. NAUS, RG 165, Marshburn, "G-2 Report No. 4871," Dec. 8, 1933.

5. Ibid.; in Tenextepango in Morelos, at the sight of an old hacienda, the government settled older officers of higher rank, including some division generals.

6. *El Nacionál*, Mar. 1, 1935, quoted in Hernández Chávez, *La Mecánica Cardenista*, 87. Other measures by Cárdenas included the reduction of the length of military service in 1936, speeding up the retirement of older revolutionary soldiers. Lieuwen, *Mexican Militarism*, 119.

7. Lieuwen, *Mexican Militarism*, 111.

8. Ibid., 93.

9. For a discussion of the Spanish/Mexican naval-construction cooperation, see NAUS, RG 59, Records of the Department of State Relating to Internal Affairs of Mexico 1930–1939, 812.348/291, 812.34/150 to 812.34/181, and 812.345/20–812.345/32.

10. NAUS, RG 165, Marshburn, "G-2 Report No. 5613," Oct. 5, 1934. He quotes a confidential report by Colonel Rubén García.

11. AHSRE, Exp. 25–7–20, Chief of Staff Azcárate, "Military Study," Jan. 1, 1934, 102.

12. NAUS, RG 165, Marshburn, "G-2 Report No. 5639," Oct. 16, 1934.

13. Mexican army circular, found in ibid., Marshburn, "G-2 Report No. 6351," Aug. 15, 1935. The reorganization of the Secretariat of National Defense was decreed on Dec. 10, 1937; see ibid., Freehoff, "G-2 Report No. 8208," Dec. 20, 1937.

14. Mexican army circular, found in ibid., Mil. Att. Marshburn, "G-2 Report No. 6351," Aug. 15, 1935.

15. Ibid.

16. Mexican Military Attaché to Washington Azcárate argued for a strong Mexican army since its new central objective was to deter or defeat an invasion from the northern neighbor; see AGN, Fo.LC., Exp. 523.60, Azcárate, "Informe No. 78 to Secretaría de Guerra y Marina," June 11, 1935.

17. Ibid.; the U.S. military attaché in Mexico City operated outside the control of the embassy. At his disposition was a small budget for espionage activities, which progressed without the ambassador's knowledge.

18. U.S. Secretary of War to Daniels," May 15, 1933, cited in Cronon, *Josephus Daniels*, 66.

19. NAUS, RG 59, 812.248/203, Marshburn, "G-2 Report No. 8220," July 2, 1935.

20. Powell has argued that Mexican efforts to purchase weapons in the United States at that time were mainly a scheme to supply the Spanish Republicans with arms. I suggest that the Mexican desire to purchase American weapons for domestic purposes was genuine. The sale of older weapons to the Spanish Republicans emerged later as a creative option that combined political sympathies with economic advantages. In that sense, Powell points out correctly that the Mexican "military assistance to the Spanish Republic . . . contributed to standardization and modernization of the country's weaponry. Powell, *Mexico and the Spanish Civil War,* 74.

21. Richard W. Leopold, *The Growth of American Foreign Policy* (New York: Alfred E. Knopf, 1962), 504–9.

22. NAUS, T-77, Fr. 5658791, Von Boetticher, "Report to OKW," Jan. 7, 1935. It is often overlooked that the French attachés in Washington cooperated closely with their British colleagues.

23. AHSRE, Exp. III–204–5, "Conveñio Visitas Barcos de Guerra entre México y Alemania," Dec. 15, 1932.

24. For a complete list of Mexican orders see ibid., Exp. OM-95-1, "M.A.N. Sales to Mexico 1900–1945."

25. NAUS, T-77, Roll 897, Fr. 5649030–5649042, Frh. v. Harsdorf, "Bericht Kommandant Karlsruhe," June 12, 1934. Volland places this visit mistakenly in April 1935.

26. Cited by Volland, *Das Dritte Reich und Mexico,* 56.

27. Ibid., Roll 803, Fr. 5535135–5535139, "Bericht über den Aufenthalt des Kreuzers Emden in La Paz Mexico," Mar. 9, 1936.

28. Ibid., Roll 904, Fr. 5658746, German Military Attaché to Washington, "Report to AA," Oct. 8, 1934.

29. Ibid., Fr. 5658789, "Vortragsnotiz: Bericht des Militär Attaches Washington vom 7.1.1935," Jan. 24, 1935. Von Boetticher was the first German military attaché to Washington and Mexico since 1915; see AHSRE, Exp. III–279–15, Mex. Enc.d. Neg., "Restricted Note to SRE," Jan. 14, 1933.

30. Ibid., C-6-2-4, Rüdt, Diary Entry, Jan. 12, 1937, 3.

31. Ibid., 4.

32. NAUS, T-120, Roll 3190, Fr. E527051–527060, Burandt, "Aufzeichung über meine gestrige Audienz beim Staatspräsidenten Lázaro Cárdenas," Jan. 1, 1937.

33. AHSRE, Exp. C-6-2-4, Diary Entry, July 1, 1938, 72.

34. NAUS, T-120, Fr. E491563-E491564, Beauftragter der Wirtschaftsgruppe Luftfahrt-Industrie Beier, "Report," Apr. 12, 1937.

35. Ibid., RG 59, 812.248/217, Marshburn, "G-2 Report No. unreadable," Jan. 9, 1936. At this time, rumors emerged in Mexico City that Mexico was thinking of purchasing fifty commercial planes in exchange for oil.

36. Ibid., 812.248/257, Dillon, "Naval Attaché's Report No. 55–38," Dec. 18, 1938.

37. Ibid., 812.248/259, Daniels, "Telegram to Secretary of State," Feb. 18, 1939. This source shows just one possible offer that Davis was supposed to have made.

38. Ibid., 812.248/262, "Memorandum of Conversation between Ambassador Nájera and Undersecretary Welles," Feb. 18, 1939. Later, the U.S. State Department claimed that the deal collapsed because of U.S. intervention. See ibid., 812.248/293, Naval Attaché Dillon, "Report to Secretary of State," Aug. 11, 1939. However, this source showed that Cárdenas himself was the central reason for the end of the German airplane deal. The German sources do not reveal whether this offer had any backing from German military circles. More likely, it was motivated by commercial interests of the German airline industry and the German Economic Ministry.

39. The Mexican government had bought the small Canadian Car and Foundry company from Azcárate and planned to enlarge it. Ibid., 812.248/258, Daniels, "Report to Secretary of State," Feb. 17, 1939.

40. Ibid., 812.244/249, Freehoff, "G-2 Report No. 8619," Sept. 9, 1938.

41. Ibid.

42. Ibid., 812.248/262, "Memorandum of Conversation between Ambassador Nájera and Undersecretary Welles," Feb. 18, 1939.

43. Ibid., 812.248/266, Daniels, "Report to Hull," Mar. 22, 1939.

44. Ibid., Naval Attaché Dillon, "Memorandum," Mar. 16, 1939.

45. Ibid., 812.248/293, Daniels, "Memorandum to Secretary of State," Aug. 11, 1939.

46. Ibid., Naval Attaché Dillon, "Report to Secretary of State," Aug. 11, 1939.

47. AHSRE, Exp. 39–10–2(II), Nájera, "Letter to Cárdenas," Oct. 17, 1939.

48. Ibid., Nájera, "Letter to Cárdenas," Oct. 19, 1939.

49. Ibid., Nájera, "Letter to Cárdenas," Jan. 10, 1940.

50. Cárdenas was convinced that the United States was able to protect its interest from her own bases without using Mexican territory. Ibid., Cárdenas, "Letter to Nájera," Oct. 28, 1939.

51. Ibid., Exp. 39–10–2(III), Nájera, "Letter to Cárdenas," June 4, 1940.

52. NAUS, RG 218, Box 5, MDC 4960, H.R. Stark, "Secret Memorandum for the Secretary of Navy," Aug. 31, 1940.

53. Ibid.

54. Ibid., Secretary of War Henry L. Stimson, Secretary of Navy Frank Nox, "Secret Letter to the Secretary of State," Oct. 24, 1940.

55. Conn and Fairchild argue that the Mexican government was unwilling to create political hurdles for itself or to assume financial obligations that might lead to budgetary pressure and thus remained unwilling to accept U.S. financial help. There exists no evidence for this position. To the contrary,

there is no indication that the United States actually offered them financial help. Rather, the United States continued to disregard Mexican requests. Conn and Fairchild, *The Framework of Hemisphere Defense*, (Washington: Office of the Chief of Military History, 1960), 353.

56. Cárdenas, *Apuntes*, 440.

57. AGN, FO.LC., Nájera, "Letter to Arq. Guillermo Zárraga," June 4, 1940.

58. Ibid.

59. Ibid.

60. Ibid., Exp. 550/46-8, "Memorandum Junta Celebrada 19 Junio 1940," June 19, 1940.

61. Ibid., "Memorandum Junta Celebrada 19 Junio 1940," June 19, 1940.

62. AHSRE, Exp. 39-10-2(IV), Nájera, "Letter to Cárdenas," June 11, 1940.

63. Ibid., (III), Nájera, "Letter to Cárdenas," June 12, 1940.

64. Ibid., Exp. 39-10-8, Cárdenas, "Letter to Nájera," June 1940.

65. Ibid., Exp. 39-10-2(IV), Cárdenas, "Letter to Nájera," June 16, 1940.

66. AHSRE, Exp. 39-10-2(IV), "Cooperación México y E.E.U.U. En Defensa del Hemisphero," July 19, 1940.

67. ARMLC, F0.LC., Caja 29, Carp. 1, Doc. 15, Nájera, "Letter to Cárdenas," Oct. 4, 1940.

68. Ibid., Caja 28, Carp.1, Doc. 22, Nájera, "Letter to Cárdenas," Oct. 3, 1940.

69. Ibid., Doc. 23, Cárdenas, "Letter to Nájera," Oct. 11, 1940.

70. NAUS, RG 59, 812.001/Avila Camacho/103, Daniels, "Memo: Conversation between Avila Camacho and Ambassador Daniels," Dec. 14, 1940.

Chapter 8

1. AGN, Fo.LC., Exp. 432.2./253-8, E. Calderón, Presidencia de la República, Comisión de Estudios, "Memorandum Sobre El Tratramiento Diplomático Y La Publicidád En El Caso Petrolero," May 18, 1938, 21.

2. Ibid., Exp. 545.3/236, Dr. Jesus Díaz Barriga, Presidencia de la República, Comisión de Estudios, July 26, 1938.

3. NAUS, RG 59, 812.00/30342, US Consul General, "Memo to Department of State," Mar. 13, 1936.

4. AHSRE, Exp.13-8-69, Informe VIII, "Informe al Sr. Luis Rodriguez para la presidencia," July 1936.

5. Ibid., L-E-588, Azcárate, "Telegram No. 18 to SRE," Apr. 26, 1939. This notice was also sent to the Ministry of Hacienda.

6. Ibid.

7. Ibid., Exp. 564.1/2016/leg 1, Dr. Jesus Díaz Barriga, "Memo: La Actual

Guerra Europea Y Su Influencia En La Economía Nacional," Dec. 16, 1939.

8. Ibid., Exp. 550/46–4, Rafael Sánchez Tapia, "Memorandum al Presidente Cárdenas," May 16, 1940.

9. Ibid., Exp. 31–1–5, Alfonso Guerra, Mexican General Consulate Hamburg, "Informes Comercial Num. 76, Reservado," May 1940, Tomo II.

10. Ibid., Exp. 564.1/2016/3, Sria. de Agricultura y Fomento, "Ponencia: Esbozo de Programa Para Neutralizar o Utilizar En Beneficio Del País Las Repercussiones De La Guerra Europea," Sept. 19, 1939.

11. Ibid., Exp. 513/2, Memorandum, "Junta Celebrado En El Palacio Nacional Con El Secretario General Del Syndicato De Trabajadores Ferrocarrileros d.l.Rep. Mexico," July 11, 1940.

12. Ibid., "Junta Celebrada Con El Elemento Ferrocarrillero En El Palacio Nacional," July 16, 1940.

13. See the discussion in the previous chapter.

14. AGN, Exp. 550/46–6, "Junta Celebrada en El Palacio Nacional, con Asistencia de los CC. Secretarios de Gobernación, Relaciones Exteriores, Defensa Nacional, Subsecretarios de Hacienda, Relaciones, Economia Nacional y Lic. Isidro Fabela," June 21, 1940.

15. Still excellent descriptions and analyses of events are found in Daniel Cosío Villegas, *La Sucesión Presidencial* (México: Joaquín Mortiz, 1975), and Albert L. Michaels, *The Mexican Election of 1940* (New York: Council on International Studies/Special Studies, SUNY–Buffalo, 1971).

16. NAUS, T-120, Roll 143, Fr. 84748–84749, Rüdt, "Telegram to AA," June 20, 1940.

17. Ibid., Roll 2729, Fr. E418596, Rüdt, "Telegram to AA," July 27, 1940.

18. Ibid., Roll 143, Fr.84756-84757, Rüdt, "Letter to AA," Aug. 29, 1940.

19. Ibid., Fr.84743–84744, Rüdt, "Telegram to AA," June 14, 1940.

20. Ibid., Fr. 84745, Rüdt, "Telegram to AA," June 15, 1940.

21. Andrew Almazán, "Report to the People," in *El Hombre Libre*, Mexico City, Jan. 25, 1941, and Feb. 2, 1941, collected in NAUS, RG 59, 812.00/31627–1/2.

22. An Almazán representative told the U.S. State Department that the move to Havana was coincidental, which remains very doubtful. See NAUS, RG 59, 812.00/31260, Bursley, "Memo to Duggan and Henderson," Aug. 1, 1940.

23. Ibid., 812.00/32044, J. A. Crane, "Confidential Memorandum," Aug. 7, 1940.

24. Alfonso Taracena, *La Revolución Disvirtuada* (México: Costa Amic, 1971), Tomo VIII, Año 1940, 127.

25. Ibid., 812.00/31276, Du Bois, "Telegram to DOS," Aug. 10, 1940.

26. Ibid.

27. Andrew Almazán, "Report to the People," in *El Hombre Libre*,

Mexico City, Jan. 25, 1941, and Feb. 2, 1941, collected in NAUS, RG 59, 812.00/31627–1/2.

28. Ibid., 812.00/31229–1/2, Bursley, "Letter to Welles," July 25, 1940.

29. During the Wilson administration, Creel had chaired the Committee on Public Information, which engaged in propaganda in Mexico. Throughout the 1920s, Creel continued to be active in efforts that tried to eliminate radical Mexican policies affecting foreign interests. He had worked as President Wilson's personal representative in the oil negotiations. See Robert Freeman Smith, *The United States and Revolutionary Nationalism in Mexico, 1916–1932* (Chicago and London: The University of Chicago Press, 1972), 144 and 180–84.

30. The source reads: "On Constantine's recent visit to the Embassy after relating conversations with leaders of the Almazán party with whom he seems to be on intimate terms, he gave me the following statement which he communicated with all appearance of having gained them from association with Almazán leaders:

1. He says ultimately the question of who will be the next President of Mexican will be laid on the doorstep of the United States."

NAUS, RG 59, 812.00/31274, Josephus Daniels, "Confidential Report to SoS," Aug. 3, 1940. Daniels questioned Constantine's reliability.

31. Ibid., 812.00/31368, J. E. Hoover, "Letter to Berle," Aug. 23, 1940.

32. Ibid., 812.00/31233, Bursley, "Memo to Duggan," July 18, 1940.

33. Ibid., 812.00/31281, Welles, "Telegram to Dawson, Panama," Aug. 14, 1940.

34. Ibid., U.S. Ambassador Dawson, Panama, "Telegram to Secretary of State," Aug. 14, 1940.

35. The United States granted him an immigrant visa. Ibid., 812.00/31262, U.S. Consul Coert du Bois, Havana, "Strictly Confidential Letter to Secretary of State," July 31, 1940.

36. Andrew Almazán, "Report to the People," in *El Hombre Libre*, Mexico City, Jan. 25, 1941, and Feb. 2, 1941, collected in NAUS, RG 59, 812.00/31627–1/2.

37. Ibid., 812.00/31297, Hedergard, "Telegram to Chapin," Aug. 19, 1940.

38. Ibid., 812.00/31327, Hull, "Telegram to Daniels," Aug. 26, 1940.

39. Ibid., 812.00/31416, Comeleven, "Telegram to DOS, Aug. 27, 1940.

40. The Ministry of Gobernación had assured local interests along the U.S.–Mexican border that it was prepared to make sure that the extreme right would have no chance to exploit the situation. NAUS, RG 59, 812.00/31104, U.S. Consul R. Wormuth, "Confidential Report to Department of State," June 17, 1940.

41. Ibid., 812.00/31296, Boal, "Telegram to SOS," Aug. 19, 1940.

42. Andrew Almazán, "Report to the People," in *El Hombre Libre*,

Mexico City, Jan. 25, 1941, and Feb. 2, 1941, collected in NAUS, RG 59, 812.00/31627–1/2.

43. They were Eduardo Neri, Gen. Francisco Cárdenas, ex-governor of Nuevo León, Gen. José Dorantes, the former commander of the garrison at Matamoros, and Col. Gabino Vizcarra, the Secretary of the Union of Veterans of Mexico. It was alleged that Callista labor leader Luis Morones was also present at the meeting. The FBI and local Mexican consuls observed the moves of these groups with great vigilance. Welles himself assured the Mexican ambassador, Castillo Nájera, that the group would remain under observation. AGN, Fo.LC., Exp. 571.3/1, Castillo Nájera, "Letter to Cárdenas," Sept. 21, 1940.

44. Ibid., 812.00/31456–1/2, J. E. Hoover, "Personal and Confidential Letter by Special Messenger to Berle," Sept. 11, 1940.

45. Later, on September 15, 1940, the Almazanistas ignored the official meeting of the Mexican Congress that confirmed Ávila Camacho as president-elect; see ibid., 812.00/31296, J. E. Hoover, "Personal and Confidential Memorandum to Adolf A. Berle," Aug. 9, 1940.

46. FDR, Personal Secretary File, Mexico: 1938, Box 44, 1939–1940, "Addendum to FDR Note to Cordell Hull," Sept. 19, 1940.

47. Ibid., RG 165, E. M. Almond, U.S. War Department, "G-2 Memo to Chief of Intelligence Branch No. 2657," Sept. 11, 1940.

48. Ibid., T-120, Roll 143, Fr. 84784–84785, Rüdt, "Secret Report to AA," Nov. 27, 1940.

49. AGN, Fo.LC., Exp. 432.2/253–16, Policia Judicial Federal Agente Num. 4, "Memorandum," Oct. 24, 1940.

50. AHSRE, Exp. 39–10–3 (I), "Informe Confidential A-88," Sept. 17, 1940. Also, see informe A-102 about cooperation between one manager of the PEMEX export division and Standard Oil.

51. NAUS, RG 59, Box 3957, 812.00/31426 1/2, "Memo," Oct. 2, 1940. Between 5/24/40 and 9/4/40, Flores and Cia transferred $416,923.86 in U.S. currency to Almazán. There exists the possibility that these transactions were related to Almazán's extensive business involvements. However, the timing of this large movement of capital makes it highly unlikely.

52. Andrew Almazán, "Report to the People," in *El Hombre Libre*, Mexico City, Jan. 25, 1941, and Feb. 2, 1941, collected in NAUS, RG 59, 812.00/31627–1/2.

53. Enrique Krauze, *Reformar Desde El Origen: Plutarco Elías Calles* (México: Fondo de la Cultura Económica, 1987), 144. Also, see AGN, Fo.LC., Exp. 544.1/34-33, Villaseñor, "Informe Confidencial to Cárdenas," Sept. 12, 1940.

54. NAUS, RG 59, Box 3958, 812.00/31457, "Confidential Memorandum," Sept. 12, 1940.

55. Ibid.

56. Ibid., T-120, Roll 143, Fr. 84755, Stohrer, Madrid, "Secret Telegram

to AA," Aug. 23, 1940.

57. Ibid., RG 59, Box 3960, 812.00/32033–1/5 ff. FBI Report, "Spanish Government Influence in the Mexican Presidential Election, 1940," 1941.

58. Ibid.

59. Ibid., T-120, Roll 143, Fr. 84760, Stohrer/Madrid, "Telegram to AA," Oct. 5, 1940.

60. Ibid., Roll 143, Fr. 84763, Woermann, "Telegram to Stohrer, Madrid," Oct. 8, 1940.

61. The Almazanistas already had established contact with the German legation in Mexico City in early 1940, as evidenced by at least one payment to German Press Attaché Dietrich. But this was a local connection designed to provide propaganda support for Almazán. See NAUS, RG 59, 862.20212/1932, J. E. Hoover, "Personal and Confidential Memo for the Attorney General of the U.S.," Jan. 11, 1941. The document shows that Almazán paid ten thousand pesos to Dietrich, allegedly to buy propaganda support for his campaign.

62. FDR, Office File 146, Mexico 1938–1940, F. D. R., "Memo to Sumner Welles," Oct. 2, 1940.

63. Ibid., Mexico 1938–1940, Sumner Welles, "Letter to Roosevelt," Oct. 4, 1940.

64. FDR, PPFile 2346, Creel George, EMW, "Memorandum," Oct.ober 8, 1940. The source does not say whether the Mexican issues were discussed.

65. FDR, Personal Secretary File, Mexico: 1938, Box 44, 1939–1940, Sumner Welles, "Letter to Marvin McIntyre," Oct. 29, 1940.

66. Andrew Almazán, "Report to the People," in *El Hombre Libre*, Mexico City, Jan. 25, 1941, and Feb. 2, 1941, collected in NAUS, RG 59, 812.00/31627–1/2.

67. Taracena, *La Revolución Desvirtuada*, Tomo VIII, Año 1940, 166.

68. NAUS, T-120, Roll 143, Fr. 84762, Transocean News Agency Report.

69. Ibid., RG 59, Box 3958, FBI Agent J. L. Fuller, "Field Report No. 64–186," Oct. 9, 1940.

70. Alexander M. Sarragoza, *The Monterrey Elite and the Mexican State, 1880–1940* (Austin: University of Texas Press, 1988).

71. Ibid., Box 3958, 812.00, FBI Memorandum, "Mexico—Political Situation," Oct. 3, 1940.

72. Taracena, *La Revolución Disvirtuada*, 160. This might also have been motivated by the fact that these refineries were vital for the fuel supply of the Mexican army. Almazanista interim president López had predicted that sabotage would occur after September 30; see NAUS, RG 165, Egon R. Tausch, "Military Attaché Reports No. 9341," Oct. 1, 1940.

73. Andrew Almazán, "Report to the People," in *El Hombre Libre*, Mexico City, Jan.u 25, 1941, and Feb.r 2, 1941, collected in NAUS, RG 59, 812.00/31627–1/2.

74. Taracena, *La Revolución Desvirtuada*, 198–203.

75. NAUS, RG 59, 812.00/31272, Gibson, "Memorandum," Aug. 1, 1940. Gibson noted in the memo: "The General stated that Lic. Lombardo Toledano would be dismissed immediately as the head of the CTM on the day that General Ávila Camacho will take the oath of office."

76. Ibid., 812.00/31279, Bursley, "Memo to Welles," Aug. 2, 1940.

77. Ibid., 812.00/31299–1/2, "Memorandum of Conversation between Welles and Alemán," Aug. 6, 1940.

78. Ibid., 812.00/31384, "Memo of Conversation between Mr. Duggan and Ambassador Castillo Nájera," Sept. 5, 1940.

79. Ibid., 812.00/31332, Daniels, "Report to SOS," Oct. 28, 1940.

80. Ibid., Daniels, "Report to SOS," Oct. 8, 1940.

81. Ibid., 812.00/11725, Enclosure 6, Ávila Camacho, "Letter to Welles," Nov. 5, 1940.

82. Mexican Ambassador Castillo Nájera and First Secretary of the Mexican Embassy in Washington Luis Quintanilla suggested this idea. The U.S. State Department responded enthusiastically; see ibid., RG 59, 812.001 Camacho, Manuel Ávila Camacho/21–1/2, Laurence Duggan, "Memo to Sumner Welles," Nov. 6, 1940. President Roosevelt followed his adviser's suggestion and ordered Wallace to cancel his planned vacation in Costa Rica and proceed to Mexico City instead. Ibid., 812.001 Camacho, Manuel A/24A, Hull, "Telegram to Daniels," Nov. 12, 1940.

83. Ibid., T-120, Roll 143, Fr. 84769–84770, "Rüdt to AA," Nov. 6, 1940.

84. Ibid., Fr. 84765, Rüdt, "Report to AA," Oct. 23, 1940.

85. Ibid., Fr. 84766–84767, Rüdt, "Report to Berlin," Oct. 28, 1940.

86. At that time, Pinzon had been in contact with Cárdenas and Ávila Camacho, exploring possibilities for the creation of a Latin American oil cartel; see ibid., Fr. 84777–84778, Rüdt, "Report to AA," Nov. 25, 1940.

87. Ibid., Fr. 84784–84785, Secret, Rüdt, "Telegram to AA," Nov. 27, 1940.

88. Ibid., Fr. 84768, Rüdt, "Report to AA," Oct. 30, 1940.

89. Rolland, *Vichy et la France Libre au Mexique*, 142. He bases his information on Pareyon Azpeitia, *Cárdenas Ante El Mundo* (Mexico: La Prensa, 1973), 127–28.

90. Gilberto Bosques, *Historia Oral De La Diplomacia Mexicana* (México: Secretaría de Relaciones Exteriores, 1988), 62–63.

91. Denis Rolland suggested that the foremost obstacle was the complicated and slow, bureaucratic way in which Mexican ministries processed the new refugees. This was certainly an issue, but the bureaucratic obstacles were secondary to the critical logistical challenge of getting the refugees out of France. See Rolland, *Vichy et la France Libre au Mexique*, 144.

92. NAUS, T-377, Fr. 274419, "Mexican Verbalnote to AA," June 24, 1940.

93. NAUS, T-120, Roll 377, Fr. 274414–274416, Azcárate, "Letter to Ribbentrop," Oct. 3, 1940.

94. Ibid., Fr. 274410–274419, Schmidt, "Aufzeichnung über die Unterredung zwischen dem Reichsaussenminister und dem Mexikanischen Gesandten Azcárate am 15 Oktober 1940," Oct. 15, 1940. The report reads: "Auf eine weitere Frage des RAM (Reichsaussenminister) erklärte er (Azcárate) sich namens der Mexikanischen Regierung auch bereit, der Deutschen Regierung die Auswahl der abzutransportierenden Flüchtlinge durch Vorlegen der Listen selbst zu überlassen. [In response to an additional question by the German Foreign Minister, he agreed, in the name of the Mexican government, to hand the lists to the German government, thereby leaving to them the selection of refugees who needed to be transported (my translation).]

95. Ibid., Roll 143, Fr. 84752, Heberlein, Madrid "Telegram to AA," June 28, 1940.

96. Rolland, *Vichy et la France Libre*, 145.

97. NAUS, T-120, Roll 143, Fr. 84764, Woermann, "Telegram to Rüdt," Oct. 18, 1940.

98. Ibid.

99. NAUS, RG 59, 812.001 Camacho, Manuel A./73A, Hull, Telegram to Wallace, Nov. 29, 1940. Betty Kirk, *Covering The Mexican Front: The Battle of Europe versus America* (Norman: The University of Oklahoma Press, 1942), 258.

100. Ibid., 256.

101. Jones, "Nazi Failure," 19. The Mexican was Major Alfonso Calve.

102. NAUS, RG 59, 812.001 Camacho, Manuel A./17, Daniels, "Report to SOS," Nov. 4, 1940.

103. Kirk, *Covering the Mexican Front*, 255.

104. NAUS, RG 59, 812.001 Camacho/116, Wallace, "Report to Hull," Dec. 16, 1940.

105. Ibid., 6.

106. Ibid.

107. Ibid., Box 3974, 812.001 Ávila Camacho, President Ávila Camacho, "Translation of Inauguration Speech," December 1940.

108. Ibid., Box 3975, President Ávila Camacho, "Translation of Speech", Dec. 9, 1941.

Selected Bibliography

Archives and Collections of Papers

Mexico.

Mexico, Mexico City, Archivo General de la Nación.
 Galeria 3, Presidentes: Fondo Lázaro Cárdenas.
 Galeria 5, Fondo Gobernación.
 Galeria 5, Fondo Lázaro Cárdenas: Microfilm Collection.

México, Michoacán, Centro de Estudios de la Revolución Mexicana
Lázaro Cárdenas.
 Fondo Francisco Mújica.
 Fondo Lázaro Cárdenas.

Mexico City, Archivo Histórico de la Secretaria de las Relaciónes
Exteriores.
 Record Collection Nivel General.
 Record Collection Nivel Official Mayor.
 Record Collection Nivel Subsecretaria.

United States.

National Archive, Washington, D.C.
 RG 59: Records of the Department of State Relating to Internal Affairs
  of Mexico, 1930–1944.
 RG 84: Records of the Foreign Service Posts of the Department of State,
  Mexico.
 RG 131: Records of the Office of Alien Property.
 RG 151: Records of the Office of the Bureau of Foreign and Domestic
  Commerce, Mexico.
 RG 169: Records of the Foreign Economic Administration.
 RG 165: Records of the War Department General and Special Staffs,
  Military Intelligence Mexico.
 RG 218: Records of the Joint Chief of Staffs, U.S.–Mexican Military
  Defense Commission.
 RG 226: Records of the Office of Strategic Services.

RG 229: Records of the Office of Inter-American Affairs.
RG 319: Records of the Army Staff.

National Archive Collections of Captured German Records.
T-71: Records of the Reich Ministry of Economics.
T-77: Records of Headquarters of the German Armed Forces High
    Command, Part I, II, III, VI.
T-81: Records of the National Socialist German Labor Party.
T-82: Records of Nazi Cultural and Research Institutions and Records
    Pertaining to Axis Relations and Interests in the Far East.
T-84: Miscellaneous German Records Collection Part II.
T-120: Records of the German Foreign Ministry.
T-253: Records of Private German Individuals.

Library of Congress, Washington, D.C.
Josephus Daniels Papers.
Harold Ickes Diaries.

The Franklin D. Roosevelt Library, Hyde Park, N.Y.
Franklin Delano Roosevelt Collection.
Official Files.
Personal Files.
Central Files.
President Secretary Files.
Map Room Papers.
FBI Collection.
Henry Morgenthau, Jr., Papers.
Correspondence.
Appointments.
Diary.
Henry R. Wallace Papers.
General Correspondence.
Hopkins Papers.
General Correspondence.
Subject Files.
Confidential Political File.
Office of Strategic Services.
Adolf A. Berle Papers.
State Department Correspondence.

Stanford University, Hoover Institute.

Great Britain.

Public Record Office, London.

Confidential Print:
FO 414 Confidential Print, America, North 1919–1947.
FO 420 America, South and Central 1920–1941.
FO 461 America 1942–1946.
Embassy Archives:
FO 203, 204, 205, 206, 207, 318, 696.
Foreign Office General Correspondence:
FO 50, 371, 898, 930.
Papers of the Prime Ministers:
PREM No. 1, 3, 4.
Cabinet Papers:
CAB 62, 63 War Cabinet Papers.
CAB 65 War Cabinet Minutes.
CAB 66 War Cabinet Memoranda (WP).
CAB 67 War Cabinet Memoranda (WP G).
CAB 77 War Cabinet Committee on Oil Policy.
Also consulted:
CAB 102, 115, 564, 373, Secret Green Files.

Germany.
Geheimes Preussisches Staatsarchiv, Berlin-Dahlem.
Dokumente des Ibero Amerika Instituts:
Rep. 218/No. 73, 212–214, 216–218.

Document Center, Berlin.
Personal Akte Rüdt von Collenberg.

Evangelisches Zentralarchiv, Berlin.
Akten Mexiko.

Staatsarchive, Documents of the War Criminal Trials, Nürnberg.
Microfilm Reproduktion:
NG 4420: Aussage Rüdt 17.12.1947.
984-PS: Schreiben OKM 29. 4.1940.

Koblenz, Bundesarchiv Koblenz.
Documents of the War Criminal Trial, Protokoll Fall VI:
Dokumenten Buch VII, Dok. No.56, 11.

Bayer AG Firmen Archiv, Leverkusen.
Firmen Archive Mexico:
Farbenfabriken Bayer, Order Mexiko-München.
Dr. Max Ilgner:
IG Konzern Bericht über meine Ibero Amerika Reise, Aug./Dez. 1936.
Bayer Meister Lucius.

Bericht über das Vermögen der IG Farbenindustrie AG in Süd und
    Mittelamerikanischen Ländern sowie Portugal.

Books

Almazán, Juan Andrew. *Memorias*. México: E. Quintana-Impresor, 1941.
Alvear Acevedo, Carlos. *Lázaro Cárdenas: El Hombre y el Mito*. México:
    Editorial Jus, 1961.
Ankerson, Dudley. *Agrarian Warlord*. DeKalb: University of Northern Illinois
    Press, 1984.
Asada, Sadao. *Japan and the World 1853–1952: A Bibliographic Guide to
    Japanese Scholarships in Foreign Relations*. New York: Columbia
    University Press, 1989.
Ashby, Joe. *Organized Labor and the Mexican Revolution under Cárdenas*.
    Chapel Hill: University of North Carolina Press, 1967.
Atkins, G. Pope. *Latin America in the International Political System*. Boul-
    der: Westview Press, 1989.
Baldridge. Donald Carl. *Mexican Petroleum and U.S.–Mexican Relations,
    1919-1923*. New York: Garland, 1987.
Benítez Fernando, Ki. *Lázaro Cárdenas y La Revolución Mexicana: El
    Cardenismo*. México: Fondo de Cultura Económica, 1978.
Bernstein, Marvin D. *The Mexican Mining Industry, 1890–1950*. New York:
    State University of New York Press, 1964.
Beteta, Ramon. "Economic Aspects of the Six Year Plan." In *The Economic
    and Social Program of Mexico*. Mexico: DAPP, 1935.
Blum, John Morton. *From the Morgenthau Diaries*. Boston: Houghton
    Mifflin Company, 1959.
Bolloten, Burnett. *The Spanish Revolution (The Left and the Struggle for
    Power during the Civil War)*. Chapel Hill: The University of North
    Carolina Press, 1979.
Bosques, Gilberto. *The National Revolutionary Party of Mexico and the Six
    Year Plan*. Mexico: Bureau of Foreign Information, 1937.
Brandenburg, Frank. *The Making of Modern Mexico*. Englewood Cliffs, N.J.:
    Prentice Hall, 1964.
Brown, Jonathan C. *Oil and Revolution in Mexico*. Berkeley: University of
    California Press, 1993.
Brown, Jonathan C., and Alan Knight, *The Mexican Petroleum Industry in
    the Twentieth Century*. Austin: University of Texas Press, 1992.
Caballero, Manuel. *Latin America and the Comintern, 1919–1943*. Cam-
    bridge and New York: Cambridge University Press, 1986.
Calvert, Peter. *The Mexican Revolution, 1910–1914: The Diplomacy of
    Anglo-American Conflict*. Cambridge: Cambridge University Press,
    1968.
Camp, Roderic Ai. *Mexican Political Biographies*. Tucson: University of
    Arizona Press, 1978.

Campbell, Hugh C. *La Derecha Radical en México, 1929–1949*. México: Sepsetentas, 1976.

Cárdenas, Enrique. *La Hacienda Pública y La Política Económica, 1929–1958*. México: Fondo de Cultura Económica, 1994.

Cárdenas, Lázaro. *Apuntes*. México: Universidad Nacional Autónoma de México, 1972.

Carr, Barry. *Marxism and Communism in Twentieth-Century Mexico*. Lincoln: University of Nebraska Press, 1992.

Chase, Allan. *Falange: El Ejército Secreto del Eje en America*. Traducción Felix Mantiel. La Habana: Edición Caribe, 1943.

Chassen de López, Francie R. *Lombardo Toledano y el Movimiento Obrero Mexicano (1917–1940)*. México: Editorial Extemporaneos, 1977.

Clendenen, Clarence C. *The United States and Pancho Villa: A Study in Unconventional Diplomacy*. Ithaca: Cornell University Press, 1961.

Contreras, Ariel. *México 1940: Industrialización y Crisis Política*. México: Siglo XXI Editores, 1977.

Córdova Arnaldo. *La Política de Masas del Cardenismo*. México: Ediciones Era, 1975.

Corzo Ramírez, Ricardo, José González Sierra, David A. Skeritt, Ana Laura Romero López.... *Nunca Un Desleal: Candido Aguilar, 1889–1960*. México: El Colegio de México, 1986.

Cosio Villegas, Daniel. *La Succesión Presidencial*. México: Cuadernos de Joaquín Mortiz, 1975.

———. *Historia Moderna de México: El Porfiriato: Vida Política Exterior*. México: Editorial Porrua, 1960–1963.

Cronon, Edmund David. *Josephus Daniels in Mexico*. Madison: University of Wisconsin Press, 1960.

Craig, Gordon A. *Force and Statecraft: Diplomatic Problems of Our Time*. Oxford: Oxford University Press, 1983.

Cypher, James M. *State and Capital in Mexico: Development Policy since 1940*. Boulder, Colo.: Westview Press, 1990.

Dallek, Robert. *Franklin D. Roosevelt and American Foreign Policy, 1932–1945*. New York: Oxford University Press, 1979.

Daniels, Josephus. *Shirt Sleeve Diplomat*. Chapel Hill: University of North Carolina Press, 1947.

Davis, Harold E., Wilson, Larman C. *Latin American Foreign Policies: An Analysis*. Baltimore, London: John Hopkins University Press, 1975.

de Garay, Gracia. *Gilberto Bosques: Historia Oral de la Diplomacia Mexicana*. México: Archivo Historico Diplomatico Mexicano, 1988.

de Jong, Louis. *Die Deutsche Fünfte Kolonne im Zweiten Weltkrieg*. Stuttgart: DVA, 1959.

Dulles, John W. F. *Ayer en Mexico*. México: Fondo de Cultura Económica, 1977.

———. *Yesterday in Mexico*. Austin: University of Texas Press, 1961.

Ebel, Arnold. *Das Dritte Reich und Argentinien*. Koln und Wien: Boehlau Verlag, 1971.

Everest, Allan Seymor. *Morgenthau, the New Deal and Silver: A Story of Pressure Politics*. New York: Da Capo Press, 1973.

Fabela, Isidro. *Belize: Defensa de los Derechos de México*. México: Editorial Mundo Libre, 1944.

———. *Las Doctrinas Monroe y Drago*. Mexico, 1957.

Farago, Ladislas. *The Game of the Foxes*. New York: David McKay Company, 1971.

Feller, H. Abraham. *The Mexican Claims Commissions, 1923–1934: A Study in the Law and Procedure of International Tribunals*. New York: Macmillan, 1935.

Fiebig-von Hase, Ragnhild. *Lateinamerika als Konfliktherd der deutsch-amerikanischen Beziehungen 1890–1903: Vom Beginn der Panamerikapolitik bis zur Venezuelakrise von 1902–1903*. Gottingen: Vandenhouk & Ruprecht, 1986.

Friedlaender, Saul. *Prelude to Downfall*. New York: Alfred E. Knopf, 1967.

Froeschle, H., ed. *Die Deutschen in Latein Amerika*. Tübingen, Basel: Horst Erdmann Verlag, 1979.

Frye, Alton. *Nazi Germany and the American Hemisphere, 1933–1941*. New Haven: Yale University Press, 1967.

Gaxiola, Francisco Javier. *Memorias*. México: Editorial Porrúa, 1975.

Gellman, Irwin F. *Good Neighbor Policy: United States Policies in Latin America, 1933–1945*. Baltimore and London: The John Hopkins University Press, 1979.

———. *Secret Affairs: Franklin Roosevelt, Cordell Hull, and Sumner Welles*. Baltimore and London: The John Hopkins University Press, 1995.

Gilly, Adolfo. *El Cardenismo, Una Utopía Mexicana*. México: Cal y Arena, 1994.

Gilderhus, Mark T. *Pan American Visions: Woodrow Wilson in the Western Hemisphere, 1913–1921*. Tucson: University of Arizona Press, 1986.

Glade, William P., and Charles W. Anderson. *The Political Economy of Mexico*. Madison: The University of Wisconsin Press, 1963. González, Luis. *Los Días del Presidente Cárdenas*. México: El Colegio de México, 1981.

Grieb, Kenneth J. *The United States and Huerta*. Lincoln: University of Nebraska Press, 1969.

Guerrant, Edward O. *Roosevelt's Good Neighbor Policy*. Albuquerque: The University of New Mexico Press, 1950.

Hall, Linda B. *Oil, Banks and Politics: The U.S. and Postrevolutionary Mexico, 1917–1924*. Austin: University of Texas Press, 1995.

Hay, Eduardo. *Discursos*. México D.F: Talleres Graficos de la Nación, 1940.

Herman, Donald L. *The Comintern in Mexico*. Washington, D.C.: Public Affairs Press, 1974.

Hérnandez Chávez, Alicia. *La Mecánica Cardenista*. México. D.F: El Colegio de México, 1979.

Hill, Leonidas E. *Die Weizaecker Papiere*. Frankfurt, Berlin, Wien: Propylaen Verlag, 1974.

Hilton, Stanley E. *Brazil and the Soviet Challenge*. Austin: University of Texas Press, 1991.

————. *Hitler's Secret War in South America, 1939–1945*. Baton Rouge and London: Louisiana State University Press, 1981.

————. *Brazil and the Great Powers*. Austin: University of Texas Press, 1975.

Hinsley, F. H., and C. A. G. Simkins. *British Intelligence in the Second World War*. 4 vols. New York: Cambridge University Press, 1990.

Hodgson, Godfrey. *The Colonel: The Life and Wars of Henry Stimson, 1867–1950*. New York: Alfred A. Knopf, 1990.

Hull, Cordell. *The Memoirs of Cordell Hull*. Volumes I and II. New York: The Macmillan Company, 1948.

Humphreys, R. A. *Latin America and the Second World War*. 2 vols. London: Athlone Press, 1981.

Ianni, Octavio. *El Estado Capitalista en la Epoca de Cárdenas*. México: Ediciones Era, 1977.

Ituriaga de la Fuente, José. *La Revolución Hacienda*. México: Secretaría de la Educación Publica, 1976.

Jacobson, Hans Adolf. *Nationalsozialistische Aussenpolitik (1933–1938)*. Frankfurt am Main, Berlin: Alfred Metzler Verlag, 1968.

Kamman, William A. *A Search for Stability: United States Diplomacy toward Nicaragua, 1925–1933*. Notre Dame: Notre Dame University Press, 1968.

Katz, Friedrich. *The Secret War in Mexico*. Chicago: University of Chicago Press, 1982.

Kent, George O. *A Catalog of Files and Microfilms of the German Foreign Ministry Archives, 1920–1945*. 3 vols. Stanford: Hoover Institute, Stanford University, 1962–1966.

King, Timothy. *Mexico: Industrialization and Trade Policies since 1940*. London, New York, Toronto: Oxford University Press, 1970.

Kirk, Betty. *Covering the Mexican Front: The Battle of Europe versus America*. Norman: The University of Oklahoma Press, 1942.

Kissinger, Henry. *Diplomacy*. New York: Simon and Schuster, 1994.

Knight, Alan. *U.S.–Mexican Relations 1910–1940: An Interpretation*. San Diego: Center for U.S.–Mexican Studies, University of California, San Diego, 1987.

Krauze, Enrique. *Reformar Desde El Origen: Plutarco Elías Calles*. México: Fondo de la Cultura Económica, 1987.

————. *General Misionero: Lázaro Cárdenas*. México: Fondo de Cultura Económica, 1987.

Krauze, Enrique, Jean Meyer, y Cayetano Reyes. *La Reconstrucción*

Económica. México: El Colegio de México, 1977.

LaBatz, Dan. *Edward L. Doheny: Petroleum, Power and Politics in the U.S. and Mexico*. New York: Praeger, 1991.

Lamborn, Alan C., and Stephen P Mumme. *Statecraft, Domestic Politics and Foreign Policy Making: The El Chamizal Dispute*. Boulder, Colo.: Westview Press, 1988.

Langer, William L, and S. Everett Gleason. *The Undeclared War*. New York: Harper and Brothers Publishers, 1953.

Leuchtenberg, William. *Franklin Roosevelt and the New Deal, 1932–1940*. New York: Harper and Row, 1963.

Lieuwen, Edwin. *Mexican Militarism: The Political Rise and Fall of the Revolutionary Army*. Albuquerque: University of New Mexico Press, 1968.

Loyola, Rafael. Cordinadór. *Entre La Guerra y La Estabilidád Política*. México,D.F.: Grijalbo, 1990.

Luquin, Eduardo. *La Política Internacional de la Revolución Constitucionalista*. México: Costa-Amic, 1957.

Manero, Antonio. *La Reforma Bancaria en México, 1865–1955*. México: Biblioteca del Justituto Nacional de Estudiod Históricos de la Revolución, 1958.

Maria Carreno, Alberto. *La Diplomacia Extraordinaria entre México y los Estado Unidos*. México: Editorial Jus, 1951.

McCann, Frank D. *The Brazilian–American Alliance*. Princeton, N.J.: Princeton Univeristy Press, 1975.

McKale, Donald M. *The Swastika outside Germany*. Kent, Ohio: Kent University Press, 1977.

Meyer, Lorenzo. *Los Grupos de Presión Extranjeros en el México Revolucionario, 1910–1940*. México D.F.: Secretaría de las Relaciónes Exteriores, 1973.

———. *Mexico and the United States in the Oil Controversy, 1917–1942*. Austin: The University of Texas Press, 1977.

———. *Su Majestád Británica*. México: El Colegio de México, 1992.

Michaels, Albert L. *The Mexican Election of 1940*. New York: Council on International Studies/Special Studies, SUNY-Buffalo, 1971.

Milward, Alan S. *War, Economy and Society, 1939–1945*. Berkeley and Los Angeles: University of California Press, 1977.

Mosk, Sanford A. *Industrial Revolution in Mexico*. Berkeley and Los Angeles: University of California Press, 1950.

Munro, Dana G. *Intervention and Dollar Diplomacy in the Carribean, 1900–1921*. Princeton, N.J.: Princeton University Press, 1964.

Munro, Dana G. *The United States and the Carribean Republics, 1921–1933*. Princeton, N.J.: Princeton University Press, 1974.

Nash, Gerald P. *The Great Depression and World War II: Organizing America, 1933–1945*. New York: St. Martin's Press, 1979.

Newton, Ronald C. *The Nazi Menace in Argentina, 1931–1947*. Stanford, Calif.: Stanford University Press, 1992.

Nicolson, Sir Harold. *Diplomacy*. Oxford: Oxford University Press, 1977.

O'Malley, Ilene V. *The Myth of the Revolution: Hero Cult and the Institutionalization of the Mexican State, 1920–1940*. New York: Greenwood Press, 1986.

O'Malley, Sir Owen. K.C.M.G. *The Phantom Caravan*. London: John Murray, Albemarle Street, 1954.

Ojeda, Mario. *Alcances y Límites de la Política Exterior de México*. México D.F.: El Colegio de México, 1976.

Ortiz Garza, José Luis. *México en Guerra*. México: Planeta, 1989.

Pan-American Union. *Foreign Trade Series: Mexico*. Washington, D.C.: Pan-American Union, 1939.

Pani, Alberto. *La Politica Hacendaria y la Revolucion*. México, D.F.: Editorial Cultura, 1926.

———. *Apuntes Autobiographicos*. México: Editorial Stylo, 1945.

Pike, Frederick B. *Hispanismo*. Notre Dame: Notre Dame University Press, 1971.

———. *FDR's Good Neighbor Policy: Sixty Years of Generally Gentle Chaos*. Austin: University of Texas Press, 1995.

Pogue, Forrest C. *George C. Marshall: Ordeal and Hope, 1939–1942*. New York: The Viking Press, 1965.

Pommerin, Reiner. *Das Dritte Reich und Lateinamerika: Die Deutsche Politik gegenüber Süd- und Mittelamerika, 1939–1942*. Düsseldorf: Droste Verlag, 1977.

Portes Gil, Emilio. *Autobiografía de la Revolución Mexicana*. México: Instituto Mexicano de Cultura, 1964.

———. *Quince Años de Política Mexicana*. México: Ediciones, 1954.

Powell, T. G. *Mexico and the Spanish Civil War*. Albuquerque: University of New Mexico Press, 1981.

Prewett, Virginia. *Reportage on Mexico*. New York: E. P. Dutton and Co., 1941.

Pyke, Joseph. *Economic Conditions in Mexico*. Department of Overseas Trade Report No. 642. London: H. M. Stationery's Office, 1936.

Quirk, Robert E. *An Affair of Honor: Woodrow Wilson and the Occupation of Vera Cruz*. Lexington: University of Kentucky Press, 1962.

Randall, Stephen J. *United States Foreign Oil, 1919–1948: For Profits and Security*. Kingston and Montreal: McGill-Queen's University Press, 1985.

Richardson, William. *Mexico through Russian Eyes, 1806–1940*. Pittsburgh: University of Pittsburgh Press, 1988.

Richmond, Douglas W. *Venustiano Carranza's Nationalist Struggle, 1893–1920*. Lincoln: University of Nebraska Press, 1978.

Riess, Curt. *Total Espionage*. New York: Putnam's Sons, 1941.

Rippy, Merrill. *Oil and the Mexican Revolution*. Leiden: E. J. Brill, 1972.

Rolland, Dennis. *Vichy et la France Libre au Mexique*. Paris: Harmattan, 1990.

Ronning, C. Neale and Vannuci, Albert P. *Ambassadors in Foreign Policy: The Influence of Individuals on U.S. Latin American Policy*. New York: Praeger, 1987.

Ross, Stanley R. *Fuentes de la Historia Contemporanea de México: Periodicos y Revistas*. 2 vols. México: El Colegio de México, 1965 y 1967.

Rout, Leslie, and John Bratzel. *The Shadow War: German Espionage and U.S. Counterespionage in Latin America during World War II*. Washington: Greenwood Press, 1986.

Ruiz Naufal, Victor M. *La Industria Petrolera en México: Una Crónica*. 2 vols. México: Editorial Porrua, 1988.

Sáenz, Aaron. *La Política Internacional de la Revolución: Estudios y Documentos*. México, D.F.: Fondo de Cultura Económica, 1961.

Santos, Gonzalo N. *Memorias*. México: Editorial Grijalbo, 1984.

Saragoza, Alexander M. *The Monterrey Elite and the Mexican State, 1880–1940*. Austin: University of Texas Press, 1988.

Schellenberg, Walter. *Aufzeichnungen*. Frankfurt: Limes, 1956.

Schoonover, Thomas David. *The U.S. in Central America, 1860–1911: Episodes of Social Imperialism and Imperial Rivalry in the World System*. Durham: Duke University Press, 1991.

Schwebe, Karl-Heinz, and Renate Hauschildt-Thiessen. *Führer durch die Quellen zur Geschichte Latein Amerikas in der Bundesrepublik Deutschland*. Bremen: dtv, 1972.

Sherman, John W. *The Mexican Right: The End of Revolutionary Reform, 1929–1940*. Westport, Conn.: Praeger, 1997.

Silva Herzog, Jesús. *Lázaro Cárdenas: Su Pensamiento Económico, Social y Politíco*. México: Editorial Nuestro Tiempo, 1975.

Simpson, Eyler N. *The Ejido: Mexico's Way Out*. Chapel Hill: University of North Carolina Press, 1937.

Sivachev, Nikolai V., and Nikola N. Yakovlev. *Russia and the United States*. Chicago and London: The University of Chicago Press, 1979.

Smith, Lois Elwyn. *Mexico and the Spanish Republicans*. Berkeley and Los Angeles: University of California Press, 1955.

Staatliche Archivverwaltung der DDR. *Ubersicht über die Quellen zur Geschichte Lateinamerikas in Archiven der DDR*. Potsdam: UNESCO Series, 1971.

Stimson, Henry L., and McGeorge Bundy. *On Active Service in Peace and War*. New York: Harper and Brothers, 1948.

Suárez, Eduardo. *Comentarios y Recuerdos*. México: Editorial Porrúa, 1977.

Taracena, Alfonso. *La Revolución Desvirtuada*. México: Costa Amic, 1971.

Thorp, Rosemary, ed. *Latin America in the 1930s: The Role of the Periphery in World Crisis*. London: MacMillan, 1984.

Tobler, Hans Werner. *Die Mexikanische Revolution*. Frankfurt: Suhrkamp Verlag, 1984.

Torres Ramírez, Blanca. *México En La Segunda Guerra Mundial*. México: El Colegio de México, 1979.

Townsend, William C. *Lázaro Cárdenas: Demócrata Mexicano*. México: Editorial Grijalbo, 1959.

Vázquez, Zoraida, and Lorenizo Meyer. *The United States and Mexico*. Chicago and London: The University of Chicago Press, 1985.

Vega, Josefa, y Pedro A. Vives. *Lázaro Cárdenas*. Madrid: Ediciones Quorum, 1987.

Vernon, Raymond. *The Dilemma of Mexico's Development*. Cambridge: Harvard University Press, 1965.

Villaseñor, Eduardo. *Memorias-Testimonio*. México: Fondo de Cultura Económica, 1974.

Volland, Klaus. *Das Dritte Reich und Mexico*. Frankfurt/Bern: Lang, 1976.

von Mentz, B., V. Radkau, D. Spenser, y R. Pérez Montfort. *Los Empresarios Alemanes: El Tercer Reich y La Oposición de Derecha a Cárdenas*. 2 vols. México: Centro de Investigaciones y Estudios Superiores en Antropología Social, Ediciones de la Casa Chata, 1988.

Watt, D. Cameron. *Succeeding John Bull: America in Britain's Place, 1900–1975*. Cambridge: Cambridge University Press, 1984.

Welles, Sumner. *Seven Major Decisions*. London: Hamish Hamilton, 1951.

West, Nigel. *British Secret Intelligence Service Operations, 1909–1945*. New York: Random House, 1983.

Weyl, Nathanial, and Sylvia Weyl. *The Reconquest of Mexico*. London: Oxford University Press, 1939.

Wilkie, James W. *The Mexican Revolution: Federal Expenditure and Social Change since 1910*. Berkeley and Los Angeles: The University of California Press, 1970.

Wilkie, James W. and Edna Monzon de. *México Visto en el Siglo XX*. México: Instituto Mexicano de Investigaciones Económicas, 1969.

Woods, Bryce. *The Making of the Good Neighbor Policy*. New York: Columbia University Press, 1961.

Zorilla, Luis G. *Historia de las Relaciones entre México y Los Estados Unidos, 1800–1958*. 2 vols. México: Editorial Porrúa, 1965.

———. *Relaciones de México con La Republica de Centro America y con Guatemala*. México: Editorial Porrua, 1984.

———. *Los Casos de México en el Arbitraje Internacional*. 2d ed. México: Editorial Porrua, 1981.

Articles

Altmann, Werner. "México: El Estado y la Unidad Nacional Cardenista."

Revue Historia São Paulo 115 (Jul/Dez 1983): 89–102.

Cothran, Dan A. "Budgetary Secrecy and Policy Strategy: Mexico under Cárdenas." *Mexican Studies* 2:1 (Winter 1986): 35–58.

Cott, Kennett, "Mexican Diplomacy and the Chinese Issue, 1876–1910." *Hispanic American Historical Review* 67:1 (February 1987): 63–85.

de la Vega-Leinert, Anne-Marie. "El Sinarquismo en México: Possibilidades de un Régimen Fascista en 1940." *Comercio Exterior* 26/9 (Septiembre 1976): 1077–78.

Frank, Waldo. "Cardenas of Mexico." *Foreign Affairs* 18 (December 1939): 91–102.

Gojmán de Backal, Alicia. "La Accion Revolucionaria Mexicanista y el Fascismo en México." *Jahrbuch für Geschichte von Staat Wirtschaft und Gesellschaft Lateinamerikas* 25 (1988): 291–302.

Halperin, Maurice. "Mexico Shifts Her Foreign Policy." *Foreign Affairs* 19 (October 1940): 207–21.

Hansen, Alvin. "Hemispheric Solidarity." *Foreign Affairs* 19 (October 1940): 12–21.

Harris, Charles E., III, and Louis R. Sadler. "The Plan of San Diego and the Mexican–United States War Crisis of 1916: A Reexamination." *Hispanic American Historical Review* 58:3 (August 1978): 381–408.

Herwig, Holger H. and Christon I. Archer. "Global Gambit: A German General Staff Assessment of Mexican Affairs, November 1913." *Mexican Studies* 1:2 (Summer 1985): 303–27.

Horn, James J. "U.S. Diplomacy and the "Specter of Bolshevism in Mexico (1924–1927)." *The Americas* 32:1 (July 1975): 40–41.

Hu-de Hart, Evelyn. "The Chinese of Baja California, 1910–1934." *Proceedings of the Pacific Coast Branch AHA* 12 (1985/1986): 9–30.

Katz, Friedrich. "Mexico und der Anschluss Österreichs." *Zeitschrift für Lateinamerika* 11 (1976): 113–20.

Knappe, John. "British Foreign Policy in the Carribean Basin, 1938–1945: Oil, Nationalism and Relations with the United States." *Journal of Latin American Studies* 19 (November 1987): 279–94.

Knight, Alan. "Cardenismo: Juggernaut or Jalopy?" *Journal of Latin American Studies* 26 (1994): 73–107.

LaFrance, David. "Germany, Revolutionary Nationalism and the Downfall of President Madero: the Covadonga Killings." *Mexican Studies* 2:1 (Winter 1986): 59–82.

Mares, David R. "Mexico's Foreign Policy as a Middle Power: The Nicaraguan Connection, 1884–1986." *Latin American Research Review* 23:3 (1988): 81–107.

McKercher, Brian. "Reaching for the Brass Ring: The Recent Historiography of Interwar American Foreign Relations." *Diplomatic History* (January 1992): 565–98.

Meyer, Lorenzo. "Los Límites de la Política Cardenista: La Presión Externa."

Revista de la Universidad Autónoma de México 25 (May 1971): 1–8.
———. "Mexico and the U.S.: The Historical Structure of their Conflict." *Journal of International Affairs*, 43:2 (Winter 1990): 251–71.

Michaels, Albert L. "Fascism and Sinarquismo: Popular Nationalism against the Mexican Revolution." *A Journal of Church and State* 8 (Spring 1966): 234–50.
———. "Lázaro Cárdenas y la Lucha por la Independencia Económica de México." *Historia Mexicana* 18:1 (1968): 56–78.
———. "The Crisis of Cardenismo." *Journal of Latin American Studies* (May 1970): 51–79.

Muñoz, Heraldo. "The Dominant Themes in the Study of Latin America's Foreign Relations." *World Affairs* 15:2 (Fall 1987): 129–46.

Ortiz Escamilla, Juan. "Visión Latinoamericanista del General Múgica." *Desdeldiez* (July 1985): 69–90.

Pérez Montfort, Ricardo. "El Hispanismo, Bandera Ideológica de la Derecha." *Revolución y Contrarevolución en México: IX Jornadas de Historia de Occidente*. Jiquilpán, Michoacán, México: Centro de Estudios de la Revolución Mexicana "Lázaro Cárdenas" (1986): 161–67.
———. "Los Camisas Doradas." *Sequencia* 4 (Enero/Abril 1986): 64–78.

Prewett, Virginia. "Nazi Trade Invades Mexico." *American Mercury* 52 (1941): 336–43.

Salisbury, Richard J. "Mexico and the U.S. and the 1926–1927 Nicaraguan Crisis." *Hispanic American Historical Review* 66:2 (May 1986): 319–39.

Salvucci, Richard J. "The Origins and Progress of U.S.-Mexican Trade 1825–1884: Hoc opus hic labor est." *Hispanic American Historical Review*, 71:4, (November 91): 697-736.

Schoonover, Thomas. "Germany in Central America: 1820s to 1929, An Overview." *Jahrbuch für Geschichte von Staat, Wirtschaft und Gesellschaft Lateinamerikas* 25 (1988): 33–59.

Schröder, Hans Jürgen. "Die Neue Deutsche Süedamerika Politik." *Jahrbuch für Geschichte von Staat, Wirtschaft und Gesellschaft Lateinamerikas* 6 (1969): 337–46.
———. "Die USA und die Nationalsozialistische Handelspolitik gegenüber Lateinamerika 1937/1938." *Jahrbuch für Geschichte von Staat, Wirtschaft und Gesellschaft Lateinamerikas* 7 (1970): 309–71.
———. "Hauptprobleme der Deutschen Lateinamerika Politik (1933–1941)." *Jahrbuch für Geschichte von Staat, Wirtschaft und Gesellschaft Lateinamerikas* 12 (1975): 408–33.
———. "Grenzen der Good Neighbor Policy." *Jahrbuch für Geschichte von Staat, Wirtschaft und Gesellschaft Lateinamerikas* 14 (1977): 378–85.

Schuler, Friedrich E. "From Multinationalization to Expropriation: The German I. G. Farben Concern and the Creation of a Mexican Chemical

Industry, 1936–1943." *Jahrbuch für Geschichte von Staat, Wirtschaft und Gesellschaft Lateinamerikas* 25 (1988): 303–20.

Scroggs, W. O. "Mexican Anxieties." *Foreign Affairs* 18 (January 1940): 266–79.

———. "Mexican Oil in World Politics." *Foreign Affairs* 17 (1938/39): 172–75.

Weinberg, Gerhard. "Hitler's Image of the United States." *American Historical Review* 69 (July 1964): 1006–21.

Newspapers and Magazines

Ejército Marina Aviación (Berlin), 1937. Ibero Amerikanisches Institut, Berlin.

El Hombre Libre (Mexico City), 1939–1941.

El Popular (Mexico City), 1936–1940.

Excélsior (Mexico City), 1936–1940.

"Mexican Oil to Berlin." *Business Week*, June 25, 1938, 38–40.

"Mexico in Revolution." *Fortune* (October 1938), 75–92.

Mitteilungen der Deutschen Volksgemeinschaft (Mexico City), 1935–1940. Ibero Amerikanisches Institut, Berlin.

Novedades (Mexico City), 1936–1940.

NS Herold (Mexico City), 1936–1940. Ibero Amerikanisches Institut, Berlin.

Nürnberger Zeitung (Nürnberg), 1935.

The Times (London), April 22, 1938.

Von Schnitzler, Georg. "Germany and the World Trade after the War." *Atlantic Monthly* (April 1940): 817–21.

Dissertations and Unpublished Manuscripts

Becker, Marjorie Ruth. "Lázaro Cárdenas and the Mexican Counterrevolution: The Struggle over Culture in Michoacán, 1934–1940." Ph.D. diss., Yale University, 1988.

Bickel, Heinrich. "Die Englischen Erdoelinteressen und der Wirtschaftsnationalismus der Rohstoffländer." Ph.D. diss., Universität Hamburg, 1941.

Brown, Lyle Clarence. "General Lázaro Cárdenas and Mexican Presidential Politics, 1933–1940: A Study in the Acquisition and Manipulation of Political Power." Ph.D. diss., University of Texas at Austin, 1964.

Campbell, Hugh Herald. "The Radical Right in Mexico 1929–1940." Ph.D. diss., University of California at Los Angeles, 1968.

Eversbusch, Wolfgang A. "Die Deutsche Mexiko Schiffahrt." Ph.D. diss., Universität von Berlin, 1941.

Ewing, Floyd F. "Carranza's Foreign Relations: An Experiment in Nationalism." Ph.D. diss., University of Texas at Austin, 1952.

King, Robin Ann. "Confrontation, Macroeconomic Management, and Private Sector Finance: Three Essays on Mexican External Debt and Debt Related Policy," Ph.D. diss., University of Texas at Austin, 1991.

Lehmann, Eduard. "Der Aussenhandel Mexikos in der Nachkriegszeit." Ph.D. diss., Universität zu Leipzig, 1927.

Lück, Karlheinz. "Die Entwicklung der Englischen, Deutschen und Nordamerikanischen Bankinteressen in Südamerika." Ph.D. diss., Universität Berlin, 1938.

McMullen, Jay. "Calles and the Diplomacy of Revolution: Mexican-American Relations, 1924–1928." Ph.D. diss., Georgetown University 1980.

Magnus, Arthur W. von. "Die Neue Phase der Monroe Doktrin Angesichts der Bedrohung Lateinamerikas durch die Totalitären Staaten (1933–1945)." Ph.D. diss., Freie Universität Berlin, 1956.

Morgan, Hugh. "The United States Press Coverage of Mexico during the Presidency of Lázaro Cárdenas." Southern Illinois University, 1984.

Paz Salinas, María Emilia. "The International Dimension of the Cárdenas Administration." Ph.D. diss., London School of Economics, 1987.

Pérez Montfort, Ricardo. "Hispanismo y Falange: Los Sueños Imperiales de la Derecha Española y México." Unpublished Manuscript, México, 1988.

Schuler, Friedrich E., "Cardenismo Revisited: The International Dimensions of the Post-Reform Cardenas Era 1937–1940," Ph.D. diss., University of Chicago, 1990.

Sengler, Rolf. "Das Auslandsdeutschtum in Ibero Amerika und der Weimarer Staat." Ph.D. diss., Universität zu Leipzig, 1932.

Sosa, Raquel. "Lucha Política e Intervencionismo Externo en el período de Lázaro Cárdenas." Tesis de doctorado, Facultad de Ciencias Políticas y Sociales, UNAM, 1991.

Stegmaier, Harry Ignatius, Jr. "From Confrontation to Cooperation: The United States and Mexico, 1938–1945." Ph.D. diss., University of Michigan, 1970.

White, David Anthony. "Mexico in World Affairs, 1928–1968." Ph.D. diss., University of California at Los Angeles, 1968.

Index

Mexico Between Hitler and Roosevelt

*Mexican Foreign Relations in the
Age of Lázaro Cárdenas*

Friedrich E. Schuler

This is the first book to analyze the link between Mexico's foreign and domestic relations in the 1930s. By studying the regime of President Lázaro Cárdenas (1934–1940), Professor Schuler substantially revises our understanding of how Cárdenas asserted Mexico's sovereignty and also consolidated one-party rule and state-directed capitalism.

Amid a deteriorating international climate and worldwide depression, a cadre of technocrats and ministers under Cárdenas consistently advanced domestic goals in their foreign policy initiatives, particularly the centralization of the economy and the industrialization of Mexico. Drawing on impressive research in Mexico, the United States, Germany, and Great Britain, Professor Schuler shows that Cárdenas was far less of a doctrinaire leftist at home and abroad than previously assumed, especially in his ongoing economic contacts with Nazi Germany before and after Mexico's expropriation of oil in March 1938.

"A groundbreaking work."—William H. Beezley, Texas Christian University

Friedrich E. Schuler is associate professor of history and director of the Center for the Study of U.S.-Mexican Relations at Portland State University.